Praise for the Books

"A thoroughly entertaining series debut, with enjoyable yet realistic characters and enough plot twists—and dead ends—to appeal from beginning to end."

—Booklist, starred review, on *Booked 4 Murder*

"Filled with clues that make you go 'Huh?' and a list of potential subjects that range from the charming to the witty to the intense. Readers root for Phee as she goes up against a killer who may not stop until Phee is taken out well before her time. Enjoy this laugh-out-loud funny mystery that will make you scream for the authors to get busy on the next one."

—Suspense Magazine on *Molded 4 Murder*

"Engaging characters and a stirring mystery kept me captivated from the first page to the last."

—Dollycas, Amazon Vine Voice, on *Divide and Concord*

"Well-crafted sleuth, enjoyable supporting characters. This is a series not to be missed."

—Cozy Cat Reviews on *Death, Dismay and Rosé*

"A sparkling addition to the Wine Trail Mystery series. A toast to protagonist Norrie and Two Witches Winery, where the characters shine and the mystery flows. This novel is a perfect blend of suspense and fun!"

—Carlene O'Neil, author of the Cypress Cove Mysteries, on *Chardonnayed to Rest*

Books by J. C. Eaton

The Wine Trail Mysteries

A Riesling to Die
Chardonnayed to Rest
Pinot Red or Dead?
Sauvigone for Good
Divide and Concord
Death, Dismay and Rosé
From Port to Rigor Morte
Mischief, Murder and Merlot

The Sophie Kimball Mysteries

Booked 4 Murder
Ditched 4 Murder
Staged 4 Murder
Botched 4 Murder
Molded 4 Murder
Dressed Up 4 Murder
Broadcast 4 Murder
Saddled Up 4 Murder
Grilled 4 Murder
Strike Out 4 Murder

The Marcie Rayner Mysteries

Murder in the Crooked Eye Brewery
Murder at the Mystery Castle
Murder at Classy Kitchens

The Charcuterie Shop Mysteries

Laid Out to Rest

Strike Out
4
Murder

J. C. Eaton

BEYOND THE PAGE
PUBLISHING

Strike Out 4 Murder
J. C. Eaton
Copyright © 2023 J. C. Eaton
Cover design and illustration by Dar Albert, Wicked Smart Designs

Beyond the Page Books
are published by
Beyond the Page Publishing
www.beyondthepagepub.com

ISBN: 978-1-960511-05-8

CHAPTER 1

Sun City West, Arizona

"Is that apple butter? Pass it my way!" Herb Garrett's voice could be heard at least four tables away at Bagels 'n More. He waited for someone to make a move but everyone around us was either busy stuffing food into their mouths or yakking. It was the usual cacophony of voices at the Saturday brunch at "gossip central," across the road from Sun City West, and I was certainly used to it. Not thrilled, but used to it.

I had been coerced that fall day into joining my mother, her book club ladies, her neighbor Herb, and his pinochle crew. Most of the time I managed to skip out on the weekly ritual since I worked every other Saturday morning. And on the days when I wasn't needed at Williams Investigations, I came up with great excuses. Usually involving laundry or cleaning. Unfortunately, today wasn't one of those days.

No one seemed to notice as I reached across the table, grabbed the tub of apple butter and handed it Herb.

"Thanks, cutie. Too bad your better half couldn't join us. I'm about to make an earth-shattering announcement."

Then, without waiting for me to respond, he clapped his hands, cleared his throat and straightened his back. I imagine he even tucked in his stomach, but it was hard to tell from where I sat.

"Listen up, everyone! I'm now an official member of the Sun City West Men's Softball Team."

All eyes were on Herb for a nanosecond before the women went back to talking and the men to eating. Undaunted, Herb tried again. "Didn't you hear me? I'll be on the ball field. Or the diamond, as we say in the game. The fall season has just started and even though I'll be with the newbies on the green team, eventually it will be league time for me."

Myrna Mittleson, who was seated next to Herb, took a sip of her coffee and cocked her head. A few loose brown curls fell above her right eye. "I didn't know softball *had* a fall season. I always thought they played in the spring."

"Of course they have a fall season," Wayne said. "It's not the major leagues. It's a retirement community. They play in every season as long as the men on the team are still vertical and breathing."

Myrna narrowed her eyes. "What about the women?"

"They have to have a pulse, too," Kenny added. "And they have their own team." He leaned forward and looked directly at Herb. "How come you didn't sign up for the coed team?"

1

Herb smeared the apple butter on his bagel and took a bite before he spoke. "I want to look up and see women ogling me from the stands, not throwing a slow pitch my way."

"More than likely they'll be taking bets to see how fast you can strike out," Kenny said. "And why all of a sudden did you decide to play a sport?"

The chatter at the table diminished as Herb stretched out his arms and spoke. "It wasn't exactly my idea. It was my cardiologist's. He said I needed to get in shape and lose some weight if I expected to make it through the next decade or two."

Shirley Johnson and Lucinda Espinoza both gasped at once, as if it had been orchestrated. But before either of them could utter a word, Louise Munson beat them to it. "Then why on earth did you order two bagels, scrambled eggs, and bacon?"

Herb shrugged. "The cardiologist said not to make dieting an obsession."

"An obsession?" Louise furrowed her brow. "In your case it's an over-thought."

At that instant, my aunt Ina's unmistakable voice permeated the restaurant as she thundered toward us. She was impossible to miss as she moved across the room in a blinding canary-yellow caftan with matching ribbons in her long braids. Impossible to miss, but still somewhat subtle for my eccentric aunt, who never left the 1970s.

"What did I miss? What did I miss? I told Louis I had to get here by ten but he kept futzing around with the garage door opener. It won't shut all the way. Finally he got it to work. Tell me, what's going on? Wait a sec, I need to wave the waitress over. I'm famished."

Maybe it was her outfit, or perhaps that guttural voice of hers, but no matter, my aunt caught the attention of the waitress with one wave of the hand. Seconds later, the woman took her order. Almost the exact same thing Herb had on his plate but with poached eggs instead of scrambled.

My aunt squeezed herself between Cecilia Flanagan, who pulled her black cardigan across her chest, and my mother, who reached for the coffeepot and poured a cup for my aunt. The staff at Bagels 'n More was used to my mother's entourage and always left extra cups and pots of coffee on the table.

"The only thing you missed," my mother said, "is that Herb fancies himself the next Babe Ruth."

My aunt eyed him. "Well, he's got the build for it, but can he bat a ball?"

"Forget my build." Herb took a gulp of coffee and propped his head on his elbow, leaning in my aunt's direction. "I'm getting in shape, which by the way is more than I can say for the rest of you."

At that point I thought Myrna and Bill would strangle him. "*You're getting in shape? I'll have you know that Bill and I are in excellent shape. We're on that bocce court all the time.*"

Yep. On that bocce court and at each other's throats.

Next, Louise chimed in. "Yeah, and for your information, I'm still doing cardio exercises on the library tower stairs. They reopened it once that murder was solved. And what about Cecilia? She's tapping her little heart out in the Rhythm Tappers."

Cecilia buttoned her cardigan right up to her neck and swallowed. "I wouldn't exactly say I'm dancing my heart out. More like trying to keep up with some of the younger members. What I wouldn't give to be fifty-five again and in the prime of my life. I miss the pinnacle of youth."

"You'll miss dessert if you don't order fast," my mother said. "They run out of apple cobbler on Saturday mornings. Ina had the foresight to order hers with the meal."

Cecilia nodded. "When the waitress brings Ina's order, I'll make sure to get dessert."

The kitchen staff must have been working at breakneck speed because my aunt's breakfast arrived a few minutes later. As she dug into her eggs and bacon, the conversation shifted from Herb's announcement to rumors of Whole Foods opening in the area and Curley's Bar adding a larger outdoor patio. Then, without warning, we were back to the dugout as Herb continued to vie for everyone's attention.

"I expect to see all of you in the stands this coming Friday. We're playing against Sun City."

Bill shot him a look. "The men's softball team always plays against Sun City."

"Yeah, but this time I'll be on third base."

My aunt swallowed a spoonful of her poached egg and eyeballed Herb. "Maybe with practice, you'll be able to play first or second base."

I rolled my eyes and tried not to shudder. While my aunt was a fine arts aficionado and an indispensable resource when it came to Italian and German opera, sports weren't in her repertoire. I remember once when my cousin Kirk was in the Pop Warner Football League, he told my aunt to watch him from the thirty-yard line. She promptly responded by asking, "And where exactly *is* that?"

I gave Herb one of those "Sorry about that" looks and said, "I'm sure you'll do great, but as you know, I'll be working." *Thank God.*

"Sure thing, cutie, but the rest of this crew doesn't have an excuse."

And then, like a hailstorm, the excuses rolled in—dentist appointment, church committee meeting, firing up the kiln at the clay club, and on and on. Finally Herb turned to my mother and sighed. "What about you,

Harriet? Don't tell me you've got a mah-jongg game, or worse yet another hair appointment?"

"What do you mean *another* hair appointment? I just had my hair done. If you'd stop yammering about softball or cramming bagels into your mouth, you'd see my new fall color—pastel pumpkin spice."

"Sounds more like a latte at Starbucks," Myrna said, "but it looks nice. Thankfully I still retain my natural color with a little help from Nice 'n Easy. Color 755 to be specific. Goes well with my curls. But your new color is very nice, Harriet. Very, very nice."

Nice was a safe word. I would have gone with words like *extreme*, *dramatic*, or even *shocking*. At first glance I wasn't sure if it was pinkish, orangey, or gold. I needed a long, hard look to realize it was a combination of all three. My mother's hair colors varied with the seasons, or her mood, and no one in our family could seem to remember her natural color. Not even my mother.

For me, the simple blonde highlights I added were enough. They gave my "dirty blonde" color an upbeat and perky look that I intended to keep well into the end of my forties.

"Can we stop talking about hair color and get back to softball? I'll get a game schedule out to all of you," Herb said. "If I have to huff and puff my guts on the ball field, the least you guys can do is come out and watch."

"I haven't been to a Sun City West ball game in years," Bill said. "Do they still have the concession stand?"

Herb nodded. "Yep. First thing I checked out. I mean, after I signed up. They've got hot dogs, brats, nachos, popcorn, and soda. No beer, though. Something about licensing issues."

"It's just as well," my mother said. "Last thing we need is a crowd of drunken ball fans getting into their golf carts."

Shirley, who was quieter than usual at the table, clasped her hands together and sighed. "Lordy, you can say that again. Once some of those people get in a golf cart, they zoom around as if it's an amusement park and not city streets. And forget turn signals. Yesterday I had to jam on my brakes when someone made a right-hand turn. Then, that horrible person had the gall to give me the finger when I honked my horn. The finger! Frankly, I'm still unnerved by it."

"You'll get over it," Wayne said. "People give me the finger all the time. I think it's the new greeting for the twenty-first century."

Shirley's dark skin seemed to lighten as she swallowed and turned her head to make eye contact with all of us. "It wasn't just the finger. The man yelled out, 'I know who you are so you better watch it.'"

"You should have called the posse," Cecilia said. "That man threatened you."

Shirley bit her lip. "I wanted to, but I thought it would make things worse."

Cecilia went on. "Did you get his license? See what kind of golf cart it was? Get a good description of the creep?"

"It was a beige golf cart. That's all I remember. Except for the finger. Lordy, I even had a nightmare about the finger. It was the size of a sledgehammer and coming right toward me."

As if the rocketing conversations weren't enough, my mother made sure I'd leave the brunch with indigestion. She looked directly at me and announced, "Maybe Phee can have Williams Investigations look into the matter."

"Chasing around Sun City West to look for random beige golf carts is hardly something Williams Investigations would tackle. Even on a slow day. A very, very slow day."

"Well then, perhaps you can do it, Phee, on one of those mornings when you take Streetman to the dog park."

I blanched. "What morning? And the only reason I've taken that neurotic chiweenie of yours to the dog park is when you needed me to pry information from Cindy Dolton."

"Aha! There's your answer. Maybe Cindy knows who that horrible man is. She knows everything else that's going around in Sun City West. And Streetman enjoys his time with you."

"He enjoys pouncing on unsuspecting dogs in the park with those amorous advances of his. Tell me, is he off of probation this month?"

My mother groaned. "As of last week."

"Goodness, Phee, you don't have to do that on my account," Shirley said. "I'll be fine. Chances are that man forgot all about the incident the minute he drove off."

Unfortunately, Shirley being fine wasn't the case and her sledge-hammer nightmare was only the beginning.

CHAPTER 2

I imagine having a daughter who worked for an investigative agency gave my mother some sort of peace of mind but I wasn't a detective. Granted, I was married to one, but that's as far as it went. I'm a bookkeeper/accountant from Mankato, Minnesota, and wound up in Sun City West through no fault of my own. Unless guilt can be considered a fault. I was guilted into flying out here a few years ago when my mother and her *Booked 4 Murder* book club ladies—Shirley, Lucinda, Cecilia, Louise, and Myrna—were adamant there was a book curse at large and that it was responsible for knocking off the other members of the club.

My mother insisted I check things out since, after all, I was employed by the Mankato Police Department. It was a civil service position, mind you, but that didn't matter as far as my mother was concerned. Dutiful daughter that I was, I acquiesced and found out what the real hubbub was all about. Then, the worst happened. My detective friend, Nate Williams, retired from Mankato's police force and talked me into taking a year's leave of absence to serve as the bookkeeper/accountant for the new detective firm he'd started in Glendale, Arizona, a stone's throw from my mother's quirky retirement community.

One thing led to another and before I knew it, I was working full-time for Williams Investigations. I sold my house near Sibley Park in Mankato and rented a marvelous casita in Vistancia, not far from the office—or my mother, for that matter. But that's not all. A year or so later, Detective Marshall Gregory, also from the Mankato Police Department, retired to partner with Nate, and when we reconnected, it was life-changing. Literally. We were married three months ago, having moved in together way before that. Frankly, if it wasn't for that idiotic book curse, I'd still be behind a desk in Mankato.

"Seriously?" Marshall asked when I told him about the golf cart. He had gotten home early, having tidied up a few loose ends at work. There was nothing pressing and nothing that couldn't wait until Monday morning. "Your mother wanted us to check out the owners of beige golf carts? That's a good one."

"Don't worry, she dropped the subject, although she still thought I should speak with Cindy Dolton to see if there's any scuttlebutt about an obnoxious man giving people the finger. Right now I'm off the hook about the dog park, but she really wants us to drop by her house tomorrow to look at her pottery contributions for the fall craft show."

Marshall shuddered. "I still can't get that vision of the Streetman platter out of my head."

"You'll have to make room for more. Apparently she made a few dog bowls with his likeness and some cat dishes with Essie's. She's keeping a few for herself but thought they'd be a big hit with the public."

Marshall grimaced. "What time tomorrow?"

"In the afternoon. Shirley will be dropping by as well and Myrna said she wanted to have a look-see too. Since Louise is now in the clay club, she's familiar with my mother's ceramics. Cecilia and Lucinda will be stuck at church. Something about polishing the pews." As soon as I said that, I burst out laughing. "Those pews have had so much polish they could probably blind someone."

"It's as good an excuse as any. Not a problem. We can swing by her house and then take the 303 back. Maybe even stop at Twisted Italian for an early dinner."

"Sounds great to me."

Unfortunately, our early dinner the following day never panned out, although we did get to see my mother's misshapen bowls and trays, complete with pet portraits, displayed on the kitchen counter.

"Which one is supposed to be the cat?" Myrna whispered to us as we leaned over the counter to take a better look.

I shrugged. "Maybe the smaller plates."

Suddenly the doorbell rang, followed by pounding on the front window. Streetman and Essie darted under the coffee table as Marshall raced to the door. My mother was inches behind him shouting, "Don't open it. It could be a maniac."

Just then we heard Shirley's voice. "Hurry up, Harriet! Open the door! Lordy, it's a dead body!"

A second later, the door flung open and my mother and Marshall stepped aside. Shirley gasped for air, clutched her chest and sputtered, "Ground . . . body . . . dead . . . horrible."

I was worried she'd hyperventilate so I flew into the kitchen, where my mother kept her reusable brown paper bags, and grabbed one. Meanwhile, Marshall ushered Shirley to the nearest chair, where she continued to gasp and sputter.

My mother opened the fridge, took out a bottled water and handed it to her. "Take a deep breath. Drink some water. Then hurry up and tell us what happened."

"Whose body?" Myrna asked. "Did you witness a car accident? They drive like hooligans on RH Johnson. Must have just happened because we didn't hear any sirens."

Shirley shook her head, opened the bottle of water, and took a giant gulp. "Not a car accident."

"What? What?" my mother kept asking.

7

Shirley appeared to be a bit more composed but that wasn't saying much. She took another gulp of water and then a deep breath. "I saw a dead man lying in a ditch by the golf course. The one right down the block from you."

"Are you sure it was a dead body?" Myrna asked. "Cecilia always sees dead bodies but they turn out to be fallen tree limbs, palm fronds, or river rocks."

"Not always," my mother added.

"Please," I said. "Let Shirley speak."

As if on cue, Shirley continued. "I had just made the right-hand turn off of RH Johnson when I drove by that roadway to the golf course. You know, the one with those little yellow flags on either side of it. I glanced over to make sure no one was about to charge into the road when I saw him. At first I thought it might be a pile of garbage, but garbage isn't strewn out like that. So I pulled over and, and . . . Lordy! I never should have pulled over and gotten out of the car."

"Lots of blood and guts?" Myrna asked.

Shirley shook her head. "A twisted-up man's body. It was dreadful. Absolutely dreadful. I drove here as fast as I could."

I turned to Marshall. "We probably should call the posse and maybe you and I should drive over there."

"We *all* should drive over there," my mother said. "They'll want Shirley on the scene and she needs us." Then to Shirley, "Don't you?"

"Yes, I suppose," she mumbled.

With that, my mother barked out orders like a five-star general. "Phee, call the posse. Marshall, you drive with Phee. I'll take Shirley and Myrna in my car. It's a good thing my sister and Louis have that opera fundraiser this afternoon. Ina would be such a distraction. And thank goodness Herb's at Walmart. Said something about having to buy a new bat since his old wooden one is outlawed or disallowed. Something like that."

I rolled my eyes as Marshall dialed the posse. Seconds later my mother gave Streetman and Essie treats, told them they were her precious fur-babies, at which point I thought I'd gag, and then ushered all of us out the door.

We were in our cars and down the block in record time. Shirley's description of the scene was about as accurate as could be, so Marshall had no trouble locating the spot and pulling over. My mother parked right behind him, and within minutes we were all standing between the yellow flags on either side of the golf course road.

"He's gone!" Shirley exclaimed. "Lordy, the man is gone. Up and gone. He was dead, I tell you. Absolutely stone-cold dead. How can a dead man get up and move?"

"Gott im Himmel," my mother said. "It's worse than Cecilia."

Shirley shook her head and paced back and forth between the flags. "The body was right there," she said and pointed. "I didn't hallucinate it. I saw it. *Him.* The dead man."

"You should have taken out your cell phone and snapped a picture of him," my mother said.

Before Shirley could utter a word, I grabbed my mother's arm and moved her a few feet away from Shirley. "Honestly. What were you going to tell her next? Take a selfie with a corpse? It's not the first thing that comes to mind when someone discovers a dead body."

At that moment, a Sun City West posse car drove up and two male posse volunteers stepped out. Marshall approached them before they walked all the way to the ditch. "I don't know how to say this, but there appears to be some mistake. Our friend was positive she saw a man lying in the ditch, but as you can see, there's no one here."

"But there was!" Shirley shouted from six or seven feet away. "I saw him. With my own eyes. And before you ask if I've been drinking or smoking that wacky weed, the answer is no. Plain and simple. I saw a dead man and now he's gone."

The posse volunteers looked at each other and motioned for Marshall and me to approach. When we were out of earshot, one of them half mouthed, half whispered, "Dementia? Drugs?"

I recoiled. "Absolutely not. Shirley Johnson is the epitome of healthy living. She's alert in mind and spirit and if she says she saw a dead body, then that's what she saw."

"Maybe she did see a body," the shorter of the two volunteers said. "And maybe, just maybe, *that* person had a little too much to drink and passed out before coming to and walking back home. We'll file a report and let it go. Can't call the sheriff's office to investigate something that's not there."

I was about to say something when Marshall gave my shoulder a slight squeeze.

"Sorry to trouble you. Thanks for responding so fast."

"No problem," the other volunteer said. With that, they got back in their car and drove off.

"What on earth was that about?" my mother all but screeched.

"They can't investigate a crime without evidence," Marshall replied. "But that doesn't mean *I* can't. Now, what do you say we take a closer look?"

Then, out of nowhere, Shirley's voice: "The undead. Lordy, it could be the undead."

CHAPTER 3

"On second thought," Marshall said, "why don't all of you head back to Harriet's house and Phee and I will poke around here a bit."

Shirley walked to a flat spot off to the left of the flags and looked down. "There's no other explanation. That man was dead as a doorknob when I saw him. Those glassy brown eyes staring into nowhere. Lordy, locking my door at night won't help when it comes to the undead."

"Last time I looked," Myrna said, "Dean Koontz, Stephen King, and Joe Hill were still in the fiction section of the library. No such thing as zombies or vampires."

"Vampires?" I didn't think my mother's voice could get any louder. "Who said anything about vampires?"

Marshall approached Shirley and put his arm around her shoulder. "It'll be okay. You've just had an unsettling experience."

"Unsettling? I saw a dead man who vanished into thin air. Face it, all those folktales and ghost stories had some truth to them."

I brushed past my mother and Myrna and stood directly in front of Shirley. "Maybe the posse was right. They've seen lots of weird stuff around here. Best thing you can do is go back to my mother's house and take it easy for a while. We'll be over there soon."

With a long sigh, Shirley agreed, and next thing I knew the three women got into my mom's car. I waved as she pulled away from the curb and headed home.

"The undead? Just when I think I've heard it all. And believe me, I've heard plenty from that book club, not to mention Herb's wacky crew."

Marshall laughed. "No kidding. But still, this is a bit unnerving. I mean, it's not like Shirley to imagine things."

"What about that ghost in the Stardust Theater a while back?"

"That was different. Shirley wasn't the only one with those sightings. Listen, what do you say we each take a side of this golf path and look around? Maybe someone dropped something. I don't see any golf carts and it's pretty quiet out there. The golfers must have moved on to other tees."

"Fine. I'll be on the right side. Yell if you spot anything."

For the next few minutes, Marshall and I scoured the area as if we were hunting for treasure. Other than sandy dirt, river rocks, and course grass that gradually morphed into a pristine green golf course, there was nothing unusual on the ground.

"Plan B," Marshall said.

"Huh?"

"There are two houses on opposite sides of this path, maybe the occupants of one or both houses saw something."

"I'm game."

We walked to the house on the right but stopped immediately when we noticed the weeds and pile of flyers wedged in the security door.

"Snowbirds," I said. "The place is vacant."

"Yeah, vacant and in need of a landscaping service."

"According to my mother, unless someone registers a complaint with the Rec Centers, no one does anything. It's not exactly a vigorous HOA according to her."

"Maybe that's a good thing. Come on, let's try the other house."

The house on the left was occupied but the owner, a man who was in his late seventies or maybe even early eighties, told us he didn't see or hear anything because he was otherwise occupied watching Netflix.

"Guess that was a bust," Marshall said when the man closed and double locked the door behind us. "Might as well go back to your mother's house and try to quell the hysteria."

As I opened the passenger side door, I heard a horn beep and jumped. Looking up, I realized it was Lucinda at the wheel of a nondescript older Buick. She pulled over and rolled down the passenger side window as I approached her car. "Cecilia will be right along. She's waiting for an opportune moment to sneak out some holy water."

"Um, I take it Shirley called you."

"No, your mother did. Said Shirley was too distraught. It's bad enough finding a corpse but having it up and disappear is another thing altogether."

"It might not have been a corpse," I said.

"I know. She told me. We call them *no-muertos* in Spanish."

"No, not that. A real person might have been temporarily knocked out, or inebriated."

"And all of sudden, they got up and walked or drove home? Come on, Phee, I think that's stretching it."

And the living dead isn't?

"Don't tell me you believe that nonsense?" Marshall shouted from the driver's side of the car.

"Oh, hi, Marshall! Nice to see you. And to answer your question, of course not! But maybe the body Shirley saw was a victim of foul play and whoever was responsible decided to move it someplace less conspicuous."

"Phee and I didn't find any evidence of an accident or foul play."

"I'm just saying, if someone turns up missing, this is where they were originally dumped. Oh, no. That could mean trouble for Shirley. Big trouble."

At that point Marshall exited the car and we both leaned into Lucinda's. "What do you mean?" he asked.

Lucinda looked around as if someone could have been in earshot. "Maybe whoever moved the corpse saw Shirley and figured *she* saw them. For all we know, poor Shirley could be next on the hit list."

Marshall and I all but tripped over each other's words. "What hit list?" he asked at the same time I told her, "Whatever you do, do *not* mention that to Shirley. She's already a nervous wreck."

"I won't have to once Cecilia gets there. If Shirley's nervous now, she'll need more than herbal tea and meditation to calm down."

No, those are the things I'll need.

"Um, let's talk about it once we get to my mom's house. No sense hanging around here."

"Okay. See you two in a few minutes."

With that, Lucinda stepped on the gas and took off down the block.

"Terrific," I said to Marshall. "Now all of a sudden it's a murder and Shirley is next. This is exactly how rumors get started around here."

"I know. I know. I liked it better when it was a zombie or vampire."

I gave him a nudge and we both broke up laughing.

When we walked inside my mother's house, Lucinda was already inside and seated next to Shirley in one of my mother's floral chairs. Streetman and Essie were visible under the coffee table as they stuck their heads and/or paws out from time to time.

Myrna stood by the counter and shook her head. "Got to admit, I don't get it. One minute there's a body and the next—poof—it's gone." Then she moseyed over to Shirley. "Are you positive it wasn't one of those Halloween decorations? Each year they become more lifelike."

"It was no Halloween manikin. And besides, that's at least six weeks away. This is September. People aren't even thinking about Halloween." Shirley wrung her hands together and looked down.

"I'm sure there's a logical answer," I said.

As if on cue, Marshall chimed in. "Phee's right. There's got to be a plausible, rational answer to whatever it was you saw by the golf path. *Rational* being the key word."

Suddenly the bell rang and Streetman took off for the master bedroom with Essie prancing behind him as if it was a game and not one of his neuroses. "Can you get that, Phee?" my mother asked. "I'm making lemonade in the kitchen."

I opened the door and Cecilia flew in, this time without her black cardigan draped over the usual buttoned-up white blouse. She held a small vial of water in the air and waved it around. "Where was the body, Shirley? We need to sprinkle the holy water around it right away. Just in case."

"In case what?" Myrna asked.

Cecilia shook her head a few times as if to indicate *don't go there.*

"Dead people don't get up and wander off. Something sinister is going on and I, for one, refuse to take any chances. Heaven knows what could be lurking behind the door."

And then, without missing a beat, the door swung open, because I'd neglected to lock it, and everyone gasped. That is, until Herb blew into the room and shouted to my mother, "Are you having a party, Harriet? I saw all the cars and figured it was some sort of get-together. If you tried to call me, my cell phone was on mute."

"It's not a party," I said. "More like a, a . . ."

"Funeral without the deceased?" Myrna blurted out.

I nodded. "Yeah. That."

CHAPTER 4

Herb took a step inside and closed the door behind him. "You lost me. What's going on?" Then he looked at Shirley, who was back in the floral chair with her head in her lap. "One of your relatives, Shirley? So sorry."

"Thank the good Lord my relatives are all alive and well," she said. "I saw a dead man by the golf course roadway and went to tell Harriet. When we got back, he was gone. Up and gone. Like the walking dead."

Herb widened his eyes and looked at each of us before he spoke. "Then he wasn't dead. Probably passed out. Won't be the first time."

Shirley sniffled a bit and wrung her hands. "Not with those glassy eyes. Oh, Lordy, it's like 'The Tell-Tale Heart' and right in my own neighborhood."

"It's not like you murdered the guy. And I'm not saying he was murdered." Then Herb walked toward my mother. "So, no party, huh?"

"Shh, can't you see how distraught Shirley is? Good grief. I probably should get us something to eat. I've got some frozen cabbage rolls somewhere in the freezer. I'll defrost those."

"No. Don't." The words flew out of me before I even realized I said them. "I mean, why go to all that trouble. Maybe we can get take-out or—"

Marshall didn't waste a precious second. He'd eaten my mother's cabbage rolls before and all but choked them down. An extended stay in the freezer wasn't going to improve them. "Pizza. I'll phone out for pizza. Grubhub delivers. Rays Pizza okay with everyone? I'll get cheese, pepperoni and veggie. That should do the trick."

A chorus of "good idea, sounds great and I'm chipping in" immediately followed as he pulled his cell phone from his pocket and proceeded to order online. The entire process took less than ninety seconds. "If you folks will excuse me, I need to place another call. Office business I need to take care of. I'll be right back."

"This can't wait," Cecilia said, clutching the vial of holy water. "Someone needs to drive over to where Shirley saw the body so I can sprinkle the ground."

"I'll go with you," Myrna said. "I know where it is. Besides, it'll take at least twenty minutes for the pizza to get here."

The two of them started for the door when Cecilia looked around and moved her palm to her mouth before releasing it to speak. "We need to call Louise and tell her what's going on. I know she'll want to comfort Shirley."

"Comfort Shirley?" Herb exclaimed. "She'll want to devour all the pizza like she did the last time. Have any of you ever watched her eat? And for your information, *I* have and it isn't pretty. She inhaled the food like a vacuum cleaner. Better tell Marshall to order another pie."

My mother gave Herb a look. "No need for another pie. Three large pizzas are more than enough. And like I said before, I can always open the freezer."

I tried not to shudder.

"We'll call Louise from the car," Myrna said. She and Cecilia made a beeline for the front door when I thought of something.

"Think we should let Aunt Ina know what's going on?" I asked.

My mother shook her head. "And take her away from an opera fundraiser? I'll give my sister a call tonight. Besides, there's nothing she can do about it."

Herb plunked himself on the couch and leaned back. "Maybe the guy had a seizure. I read somewhere people can have seizures and look as if they're dead. Next thing you know, they're up and headed out for a Zumba class."

"That corpse wasn't about to Zumba, cha-cha, or do the Macarena. And I doubt I'll get any sleep tonight thinking about what I saw." Shirley put both palms to her face and sighed. "I never should have gotten out of the car."

"You did the right thing," Lucinda said. "And don't worry about sleeping. I'll spend the night at your place. It'll be lots of fun. We can binge-watch sappy romance movies or cozy mysteries and make popcorn."

"Or," Herb said, "go back to where you saw the body and see if he shows up after dark."

"That's not funny!" my mother said. "That body is up and gone and that's all there is to it."

Certain that Shirley would be fine with Lucinda spending the night with her, and positive that the walking dead wouldn't be haunting anyone, Marshall and I went home following our impromptu pizza dinner.

"Maybe we'll get to the Twisted Italian another night," Marshall said as he clicked the garage door open. "I've got a full week including insurance fraud and possible infidelity. Nate's workload isn't much better."

"Speaking of workloads, what was it you had to call about when we were at my mom's?"

"Yeesh, I almost forgot. Not work. I called Bowman to see if he or Ranston had heard anything about someone going missing in Sun City West or that vicinity. I didn't want to say anything for fear of setting Shirley off, or worse yet, having Herb come up with a wackadoodle theory that would unnerve all of us."

"Good move. Any luck?"

"I called Bowman's cell since it was a Sunday afternoon. Remind me not to phone him on Sundays. It's spaghetti day at his place and apparently it involves quite a crowd. Lots of background noise. Go figure. I always pictured him as more of a loner. Anyway, he said he'd look into it and get back to me in the morning but that he and his partner hadn't received any alerts from the Maricopa County Sheriff's Office."

Deputies Bowman and Ranston were assigned to Sun City West, but like all MCSO deputies, they had jurisdiction in the rest of the county if needed. They'd probably been partnered up for years since, heavens knows, who'd want to work with them? True, they were capable and intelligent, but a month at a finishing school would have done a lot for their bedside manner. Bowman had the countenance of a grizzly bear and Ranston the looks and personality of a Sonoran desert toad. Still, they had a decent relationship with Williams Investigations and I wanted to keep it that way.

"I hate to say it, but maybe Herb was right. Maybe someone suffered a seizure but recovered and walked home. Could be they live in the area. We didn't see any cars parked on the street and no golf carts were in sight."

"It could have been anything. No sense speculating. If it turns out there's something to it, that rumor mill of your mother's will have news by daybreak."

"Daybreak. I'm holding you to it. Last thing I need is a call from my mother before the alarm goes off."

• • •

Thankfully, no unwanted calls came in before the alarm went off the next day. Marshall headed out the door a good hour before I did, giving me a few extra winks of sleep. He and Nate were asked to consult with an insurance company regarding possible fraud—claims of property loss when that property might not have existed in the first place.

When I got to work, only Augusta, our secretary, was in the office. Her tightly sprayed bouffant hairdo looked higher than usual and she was as chipper as could be as she loaded paper into the printer. "Won thirty-seven bucks last night at canasta," she said. "This is a start to a lucky week. Heard you folks chased after a vanishing corpse. Mr. Williams could hardly keep a straight face."

"We weren't exactly chasing," I said as I plunked a K-Cup into the Keurig. "Only following up on Shirley Johnson's possible corpse sighting by the golf course."

"So I heard. Usually it's that other woman in your mother's book club who thinks she's seen dead bodies. You know who I mean. The one who reminds me of a nun."

"Cecilia Flanagan. I'd bet money she *is* a retired nun. Or a lapsed nun.

Or whatever you call them, but my mother says no. Says Cecilia is devout and has very conservative taste in clothing."

"Oh, honey, that woman's taste in clothing is way past conservative."

We both laughed just as the phone rang. Augusta picked up and gave the usual, "Good morning, this is Williams Investigations . . ." After a few seconds, she handed me the receiver. "It's your mother. Maybe this will be *your* lucky week and they've spotted another corpse."

"Not funny."

I took the receiver and tried not to grimace. "Um, hi, Mom. What's up?"

Augusta cocked her head and held her breath, almost as if she expected trouble.

"No," I said to my mother. "I'm not about to drive over and watch Herb attempt to catch balls at third base when I get out of work today. I thought he didn't have a game until Friday."

I dangled the receiver a few inches from my ear and rolled my eyes. My mother's voice was so loud I didn't need to put the call on speaker-phone. Augusta could hear every word.

"Yes, yes, that's a wonderful idea. You, Shirley, and Lucinda can cheer Herb on as he practices tonight. At dusk, you said?" I paused to wait for her answer. "Yes, I know they have good lighting at the ball field. What?" Another pause while she spoke. "Look, no one opens a concession stand for practices. Not even in the major leagues. Bring snacks if you think you'll be hungry after dinner. Listen, I have to get back to work."

I tapped my foot and waited for my mother to finish her thought. Then I all but dropped the receiver on Augusta's desk before I spoke into it. "Return to the scene of the crime? *What* crime? Forget the golf course. If that body reappeared, I guarantee one of the golfers would have spotted it. Just go and cheer Herb on. I'll talk to you this week."

I returned the receiver to the cradle and shook my head. "Unbelievable. According to my mother, Shirley and Lucinda spent most of the night on Google looking up sightings of the undead. Seems Central America and Europe hold the record. Shirley's convinced this isn't over."

"I know. I caught most of that conversation. I'm surprised they didn't involve that aunt of yours."

"Give it time. Give it time."

CHAPTER 5

The remainder of the day was all business. I sequestered myself in my office to work on invoices while Augusta handled the myriad stuff that landed on her desk. A former secretary for a tool and manufacturing company in Wisconsin, Augusta could handle most anything. And that was *in* the office. She grew up on a dairy farm and wasn't totally unfamiliar with hunting, fishing, butter churning, and pioneer cooking. How she wound up in Arizona was anyone's guess. I suppose retirement, or semiretirement in her case, does that to you.

Nate and Marshall were in and out with client meetings, so other than a quick "How's it going?" we barely spoke. Marshall did mention that he had heard from Bowman and the only missing people in Maricopa County were two elderly women from Chandler and Gilbert respectively, and an eight-year-old boy who had been taken by his noncustodial father in Avondale. No elderly men with glassy brown eyes were on the radar.

Marshall had paperwork to finish up but said he'd be home before seven thirty. Since we were having chilled soup and chicken salad for dinner, it would take very little prep and I figured I'd have it ready by then. At a little past five, Augusta and I left the office.

"Don't burn the midnight oil, Mr. Williams," she said. "You, too, Mr. Gregory."

She locked the door behind us, and as we stepped out of the office, we still felt the summer heat. Granted, it was warm, but ninety-eight was a far cry lower than the string of a hundred and tens that made for an insufferable summer.

"Have a good night, Augusta. See you in the morning." I walked to my car and within minutes was on my way home for a quick dip in the pool and then dinner with Marshall. I had hoped for a quiet restaurant meal last night but cozy home meals were even better. We could eat in comfortable sloppy clothes and stretch out as soon as we were done. Unfortunately, none of that happened.

At least I managed to get in a short swim with my friend Lyndy before everything went downhill. I texted her the second I got home and we met up at Vistancia's community pool at a little past six.

"You look frazzled," she said, brushing her dark wavy curls from her face. "Everything okay?"

"Sure, if you don't mind corpse hunting and possible zombie scenarios."

"Huh?"

When I told her about Shirley's discovery and paranormal explanation,

18

I thought Lyndy would bust a gut. She splashed her face and moved to the side of the pool. "And here I thought Shirley was one of the more rational ladies in that book club."

"She's rational, all right, but superstitious as all get-up-and-go. Cecilia isn't much better. Maybe Herb Garrett's newfound passion playing softball will take their minds off of it."

"Your mom's neighbor? The one who sucks in his stomach whenever we see him?"

"Yep, the very one. He's now on the Sun City West Men's Softball Team and insists we all come and watch him play. Thankfully I have a full-time job."

Lyndy chuckled. "It'll be a distraction, that's for sure. Can he really play ball or is it more for show?"

"I have no idea but Shirley, Lucinda, and my mother will be watching him practice tonight after dusk. I'm sure I'll get the full lowdown this week. Apparently the ball field is open to all of the players who want to sharpen their skills. Herb's going with Bill Sanders from his pinochle crew. Bill agreed to pitch balls so Herb can practice hitting them."

"Sounds like a real fun time."

"Nah, the fun time will be when the guys go over to Curley's for a beer and the women find an excuse to eat pie at the Homey Hut."

We splashed around for another half hour or so before we went our separate ways. I was fortunate to have met Lyndy when I first moved here. A young widow in her early forties, she came out West to start over, preferably in a place where she didn't have to shovel snow. Working for a medical billing company gave her the security she needed and decent work hours. Like me, Lyndy considered swimming right up there with eating and breathing.

I grabbed my towel, slipped into my Crocs and went home to change and start on the chicken salad. True to his word, Marshall pulled in around seven thirty and I gave myself a gold star for having the salad and cold cucumber soup ready to eat.

"Two words I don't want to hear until tomorrow," he said as he gave me a sweet kiss on the cheek and went into the bedroom to swap his shirt and slacks for an old T-shirt and shorts.

"*Streetman* and *Essie*? *Dead* and *body*?" I laughed. How about *undead* and *golem*?"

"None of the above but I'll add them to my list. I was thinking more in terms of *insurance fraud*. Nate and I are now up to our elbows in it. I'll bore you with the details after dinner, but first you can tell me about your day."

"Not much to tell you unless you consider invoicing an exciting topic.

Actually, it was a great day. No drama. No pulse-racing. Just a productive workday."

"I take it there was no news from your mother." By now we were at the table spooning cold soup into our mouths, pausing only to augment it with the chicken salad.

I shook my head. "Only an invite that I promptly turned down. Herb's practicing his batting at the ball field tonight. My mother, Shirley, and Lucinda will be watching. It's an open night for anyone to practice. Herb talked Bill Sanders into pitching. Next thing you know, he'll talk Bill into signing up. You know what those guys are like. They always drag each other into whatever they're doing."

"And then some. Say, this soup is really good. Is it a new recip—"

The landline rang at that very instant. "Let the answering machine get it," I said. "We can hear whoever it is and call back."

No mistake about it. We heard the caller—my mother. Frantic voice and all. "Phee! Marshall! I'm behind the ball field on RH Johnson. There was an attempt on Shirley's life. The paramedics are on their way."

Marshall jumped out of his seat and got on the line before she hung up. "What happened, Harriet?" Then he looked at me. "I'm putting it on speakerphone."

My mother rambled but at least it was coherent. "Shirley's passed out on the ground. Hit in the head with a softball. Not Herb's. He can't bat that far. She's just coming to. Lucinda's with her. Herb and Bill don't know. They're muddling around the baseball diamond. As soon as they hear the sirens, they'll be over here. You know what a yenta Herb is."

Again Marshall asked, "Do you know how it happened? Sounds like an accident. Look, never mind. Phee and I are on our way. Hang tight."

Without wasting a second, I put the dishes in the sink, wiped the table and grabbed my bag. Marshall snatched his wallet and cell phone from the counter, shoved them into his pocket and off we went. Worrying about our attire was the least of our concerns.

My hair was only slightly damp from my earlier swim and I was positive no one would notice when we pulled up to the Kuentz Recreation Center on RH Johnson Boulevard, where the ball field was located. Off to the rear of the center's pool and adjacent to the fenced-off outfield were three official vehicles—an ambulance, a Sun City West fire truck and a sheriff's posse car.

"This doesn't look good," Marshall said when he turned off the engine.

"They always send an ambulance and a fire truck. The posse car goes without say. Come on, looks like there's a small crowd between the pool and the ball field. How on earth Shirley wound up over there is anyone's guess."

Other than my mother and Lucinda, the small crowd turned out to be Herb, Bill, two bicyclists who spotted the emergency vehicles, an older couple walking a gray poodle, and three women on their way to a crafting club meeting. Marshall and I rushed toward the scene and were relieved to see Shirley in an upright position on the ground. Two EMTs were fast at work taking her blood pressure and applying an ice pack to the back of her head. A few feet away a lone softball rested on the dirt path.

The second my mother spied us, she charged over. "They want to take Shirley to the hospital to check for a concussion."

I nodded. "That's not a bad idea."

"It is if you hate doctors."

I did a mental eye roll and tried not to raise my voice. "Chances are she won't even see a doctor for more than five minutes. The technicians and medical assistants will be doing all the work. A concussion, or worse yet, brain swelling, would be disastrous."

"Did you hear that, Shirley?" my mother yelled. "That bump on your head could mean brain swelling. You need to go with the EMTs. Lucinda and I will meet you at the ER." Then she rushed back to where Shirley was still situated and said, "Tell Phee and Marshall everything you tried to tell me before you got too garbled. Better do it now before they cart you off."

Shirley looked as if she'd been tossed from a boat at high seas sans the wet clothes. The EMT who took her blood pressure widened his eyes at my mother's statement. Then he spoke to Shirley. "We'll give you a minute. Looks like the posse volunteers are ready for a statement as well."

Sure enough, the male and female posse volunteers approached Shirley. The man took out a pad and cleared his throat. "Can you describe what took place Miss, Miss . . . ?"

"Johnson. Shirley Johnson. I still have my faculties. Do you want to know who the president of the United States is? They always ask that."

The volunteer shook his head. "Not necessary. Just tell us in a few short words what happened."

"Oh, Lordy, no one will believe me. Might as well make a phone call to my nephews and send me to *the home*."

I bent down and took Shirley's hand. It felt ice cold even in the ninety-degree heat. "It can't be that bad. Tell us."

Shirley motioned for me to lean forward and whispered in my ear, "I saw another dead body."

CHAPTER 6

S hirley pointed to a spot a few yards from where we all stood. "It was right over there. I didn't conjure it up. In fact, I did what your mother told me I should have done with the first body—take a picture of it. I half covered my eyes because—Lordy—who wants to get up close and personal with a dead body? Then I crept toward it and reached into my pocket for my cell phone. That's the last thing I remember other than the pain that came out of nowhere."

"Were you able to snap a picture?" my mother asked.

I shot her a look and cringed. "I don't think she even got the phone out of her pocket."

Shirley felt the outside of her pants and gulped. "Maybe I did because the phone's not in my pocket anymore."

"Step back, everyone!" the male posse volunteer shouted. "We need to look for a cell phone. And by *we*, I mean my partner and me. We can't have people trampling all over the place."

"I'll have a look-see, too," Marshall said as the crowd stepped back and gave them some room. "Thank goodness there's plenty of lighting from the pool area."

Meanwhile the EMTs lifted Shirley onto a gurney and hoisted her into the ambulance. "If I die," she said, "don't let those nephews of mine ransack my house. My will is in the refrigerator inside an old milk carton."

Lucinda shook her head. "You're not going to die. It's probably a nasty old bump on the head, that's all."

"Or a concussion," Herb added.

I wanted to kick him in the shin but I stood too far away. Just then, Marshall called out, "Found it! The glass is scratched but it appears to be working." He picked up the phone and raced to the ambulance with me on his heels.

"If you tell me your password," he said to Shirley, "I can check to see if you took a photo."

Shirley motioned for him to approach. Her voice was exceptionally low but audible enough for Marshall to reply, "Got it." In less than ten seconds he pulled up her photo icon but the last photo was one of Streetman dressed like a gourd. "Sorry," he said. "Whoever hit you in the head did it before you had a chance to snap a photo."

My mother inched her way to the ambulance and told Shirley she'd "hang on to the phone for her," citing instances of phone theft in the ER. The drivers buckled Shirley in the gurney and within seconds took off for the hospital.

"Shirley's probably beside herself." I took Marshall's arm and bit my lip. "Probably even questioning her own sanity at this point."

"I don't think her sanity is the issue right now. Give me a sec."

He walked to where the posse volunteers stood and said, "Can you keep everyone away from that area straight ahead? It appears as those are drag marks on the ground. I noticed it when I looked for the cell phone. Could be Miss Johnson did indeed spot something."

With that, the posse volunteers motioned for everyone to step away or go about their business. The only one who did exactly as told was the gray poodle, compelling its owners to retrieve a doggie bag and clean up. The others stood around speculating about what had happened.

"Before anyone picks up that softball," Marshall told the posse volunteers, "you may want to place a call to the MCSO deputies. They can have a forensic team dust for prints on the ball and see what else they can ascertain from the scene."

"You don't think it was a random accident?" the female volunteer asked.

Marshall shook his head. "I'm a licensed detective with Williams Investigations and no, I don't."

"So Shirley's not nutsy-coo-coo after all," Bill exclaimed. He elbowed Herb and the two of them exchanged glances. "Lucky for you that you can't bat a ball more than four yards."

"I was warming up. I'll be hitting that sucker out of the ballpark in no time."

Marshall approached my mother and Lucinda and told them he and I would be sticking around to chat with the MCSO deputies once they arrived.

"Tell me everything you find out," my mother said. "Lucinda and I are going to the ER. Lucky for Shirley that Lucinda drove them here. We don't have to deal with Shirley's car."

Yep, first lucky break all day.

My mother and Lucinda started for their cars when my mother suddenly turned around and walked back to us. "You know how long it takes in those ERs. Would you mind terribly going over to the house to let Streetman out?"

"Wasn't he out right before you left? It hasn't been *that* long."

"He doesn't know that. Dogs can't tell time."

"If he can't tell time then he won't know how long you've been gone. Oh, never mind. Sure. We'll let him out."

"You can't just let him out and leave. You need to reward him and spend a little time with him and Essie. Besides, he's really warming up to you."

Warming up? He should be more than warmed up by now.

Marshall tried not to laugh. "Go on, hon. I'll be right here waiting on those deputies."

"Sure, you get the easy job."

In all fairness, Streetman and Essie were extremely well-behaved. Having an arsenal of treats didn't hurt. By the time I got back to the area where Shirley had her unfortunate encounter with a rogue softball, the lookie-loos and gray poodle were gone. And so were the posse volunteers. Only Marshall and Deputy Bowman were there along with a forensic tech.

"Did you find anything? I mean, other than the softball?" I asked them.

Bowman scratched the back of his head. "The drag marks are fresh. Something large was in this area, but for all we know it could've been a sack of potatoes. The path leads to the backside of the pool and the Stardust Theater. Oh, and don't let me forget all those craft rooms for who-knows-what."

By now I stood a few feet from Marshall and Deputy Bowman. I imagined Bowman's partner, Deputy Ranston, was otherwise occupied with county business. "Hmm, if Shirley *did* see a body, maybe someone saw her from a distance and acted fast. Then they got over here and made sure the body was dragged to the back of the building and loaded into a car trunk, or hatchback. Or maybe even a van."

"We mulled over that theory, too, hon. But it's speculation at this point. And the softball that hit Shirley . . . at least we believe it was a softball because nothing else was on the ground near her, is on its way to the county lab. They'll see if they can pull any prints but the tech wasn't too optimistic. Whoever threw it might have been wearing a baseball glove."

"No one was on the field except Herb and Bill. Speaking of which, where'd they disappear to?"

"Back to Herb's house, I think. He asked us to call him and let him know about Shirley." Marshall gazed at the ball field and then the rec complex. "About that softball . . . someone with a good arm could have thrown it from a distance. The parking extends all around the field, the pool, and even the lot across the street. Too bad none of the curiosity seekers saw anything when we asked them."

I watched as Bowman bent down beside the drag marks and shouted to the tech, "No sense wasting your time over here. Might as well get that softball to the lab and call it a night. I'm on my way to the hospital to get a statement from the victim."

"That's the last thing Shirley needs," I mouthed to Marshall while Bowman conversed with the forensic guy.

"Hey," Marshall said. "Miss Johnson's probably spooked as it is. How about if I get her statement for you? She knows us and will be more inclined to include every miniscule detail."

I was glad Marshall had a solid working relationship with those deputies. No surprise. Williams Investigations had been called to consult on so many cases that I lost count.

"Email me as soon as you're done," Bowman said. "I doubt she'll remember exactly which way she faced when she got knocked unconscious, but that might tell us the direction the ball came from. Meanwhile, I'm going to scope out the parking lot for anything suspicious. And I'll be checking their security cameras, too. Unfortunately, there are none in this vicinity, only the rear parking lot and the one in front of the theater."

I gave him a funny look to which he replied, "Ain't my first rodeo at a Sun City West Rec Center."

"Oh, brother," I muttered under my breath, hoping he didn't hear me.

Bowman wasted no time leaving the immediate scene. I walked a few steps and studied the drag marks. "Yeah, my vote is a potato sack, too."

Marshall laughed. "You've got to admit, isn't it kind of coincidental that a softball was used as the weapon? Most folks aren't walking around with softballs. It has to be someone in that club. But who? And more importantly, why?"

"I have a strange thought, but it's really out there."

"Go on."

"What if it was the same body? You know, the one Shirley originally saw yesterday?"

"You're right. It *is* 'out there.' Like a plot from an old Abbott and Costello or Pink Panther movie. Face it, what reason would someone have to move a corpse? If indeed it *was* a corpse Shirley spotted. On two occasions, no less."

"You don't believe her?" I asked.

"I believe that she believes she saw dead bodies, but maybe it's something else entirely."

"Like what?"

"I'm thinking something a bit more sinister. Maybe someone wanted to make Shirley think she's losing her mind."

"Gaslighting?"

"Uh-huh, just like that old movie."

CHAPTER 7

"How would that even be possible?" I asked. "Think about it. If Shirley's faculties are discredited, who would believe her? Look, I think Shirley saw something she shouldn't have when she spied the first body. And yes, I'm going with the assumption she *did* see a body. Whoever dumped it, saw her. All they had to do was follow her and figure out what she was up to. Then, when she joined your mother and Lucinda at the ball field the next day, her stalker, or in this case, stalkers, for lack of a better word, kept her in sight."

I tried to grasp what he was saying. "Then what?"

"The easy part. Whoever it was circled around the path where Shirley walked. They got ahead of her and stretched out on the ground, pretending to be dead. Meanwhile, their accomplice remained behind to lob that softball at Shirley. Not sure if they actually meant to sock her in the head as much as startle her long enough for the so-called body to disappear."

"Wow, that's actually making sense. Do you plan on sharing that theory with Bowman and Ranston?"

"Not yet. Not without evidence. Keep in mind, what we thought were drag marks could very well be the indentation from someone getting up from the sandy ground. Not an easy feat. Anyway, we'd better head over to the hospital and see what we can find out from Shirley."

The hospital was less than a mile from the ball field and thankfully Marshall found a decent parking spot not too far from the ER. In a matter of minutes we were in the ER's waiting room, where my mother was seated.

"Over here, Phee!" my mother called out. "Don't get too close to the coughing woman by the potted plant on that table. And steer clear of the man with that bloody elbow cut. You'd think someone would have seen him by now."

"Where's Lucinda?" I asked.

"They only let one person in with the patient and Lucinda went. She'll be out any minute and then I can go in. All I know is that they have Shirley scheduled for a CT scan. That could take hours."

Marshall gave her a nod. "I'll see if they'll let me speak with her. It may mean having me verify my intent with the sheriff's office for them. I'll be right back."

He walked to the reception desk in the rear of the room and I watched as the woman behind the glass window slid it open. I couldn't hear the conversation, but the next thing I knew she motioned for the security officer who stood against the doorway to the ER to approach.

"What's that all about?" my mother asked. Before I could respond, the security officer and Marshall walked through the doorway leading into the ER. Marshall turned his head and gave me a thumbs-up.

"Clearance. Marshall got clearance to go inside."

"I could see that."

"Deputy Bowman planned on taking a statement but Marshall convinced him it would be better for him to speak with Shirley. You know how flummoxed she gets around those deputies. Especially after that last incident when Ranston sat on her scissors."

"That wasn't Shirley's fault. Oh, look, here comes Lucinda. Maybe she knows something."

On a good day, Lucinda looks as if she blew in from a windstorm with her grayish blonde hair flying about her face, but tonight, it was much worse, almost as if someone had plastered a clown wig to her head.

"There you are, Harriet," she said. "And Phee. I just saw Marshall going inside with the security guard. I was going to send you in to see Shirley," she went on, "but they'll only send you out."

"How's she doing?" I motioned for Lucinda to take the seat next to mine.

"About as good as could be expected. They've got one of those fake ice compresses on her head but won't give her any pain pills until after the CT scan."

My mother leaned forward so she and Lucinda could face each other. "Did she remember anything else? See anything else? Smell anything else? Hear anything else?"

I poked my mother with my elbow. "You don't need to recite all the senses."

Lucinda shook her head. "No. All she said was that she felt dizzy and nauseated."

"She'll feel even more nauseated when they feed her that hospital food."

"Huh?" I muttered. "What did I miss? They didn't admit her, did they? They usually wait until test results are in."

"Honestly, Phee, I'm merely making a statement. How was my Streetman? And my Essie? Did they eat? Did he do his business? My poor little man must wonder where I am."

"Your little prince is fine and so is the cat. He went outside and I cleaned up. All's well with the world."

"For Harriet's pets, maybe," Lucinda said, "but not Shirley. I think someone has a target on her back."

I bit my lip. "Most likely it was random. An accident."

"An accident is when you forget the car is in reverse and you step on the gas like your aunt Ina did a few months ago. *That's* an accident. Throwing a softball is a deliberate act."

I hated to admit it, but my mother was right. However, the last thing I needed to do was to get the entire book club in a tizzy, let alone those pinochle cronies of Herb's. The word *overreact* is their mantra.

"Herb keeps phoning me," my mother said. "I told him I'd call him when I found out something, but you know how he is. He thinks pestering will get him quicker results. Can you imagine?"

Loud and clear.

Lucinda plopped herself down next to my mother. "I called everyone in the book club, including your sister Ina, to let them know what happened. I told them not to bother driving over here and that we'd call them back."

"Good idea," I said before my mother could speak. "Listen, it's going to take a while for Shirley's CT scan. When Marshall gets back after speaking with her, what do you say we grab a cup of coffee or something?"

I couldn't believe I'd just suggested going out for coffee. Usually I dodge those invites like incoming missiles. Still, it was a better alternative than hanging around an ER waiting room. A few minutes later Marshall returned to tell us he spoke with Shirley. She didn't recall seeing anything unusual on her walk from the ball field to the restroom, but when she thought about coming across that first body yesterday, she did recall something.

"What?" My mother nearly jumped out of her seat. "What did she remember?"

Marshall stood directly in front of my mother but made sure to make eye contact with all three of us. "A white van came screaming down the block. Whizzed past her but that's all she saw. She was too intent on what she spied on the ground by the golf course roadway."

"It was probably one of those white Amazon delivery trucks," Lucinda said. "I happen to like the shiny black ones better with the blue logo but those nondescript white ones with the black line on them seem to be everywhere."

My mother stretched her arms, nearly poking me in the face. "Forget the logos and black lines, Lucinda. It might not have been an Amazon truck. It could have been a rental vehicle that someone used to move a body. That happens in the movies all the time. They could have dumped the body on the golf course then made a right-hand turn on the next side street only to come plowing back to get the heck out of there. It makes perfect sense."

Yep. Perfect sense with no way to prove anything.

"According to the ER nurse," Marshall said, "It's going to be at least an hour and a half before the CT scan is completed. Then someone in radiology will need to read and interpret it before any decisions regarding Shirley's status are made."

"In other words, it's a good time to hit the Homey Hut for pie," my mother said. "In fact, your wife was thinking the same thing."

"Coffee," I said. "Coffee. I made no mention of pie."

"Pie goes without saying," Lucinda added.

Marshall laughed. "I don't know about Phee, but pie sounds pretty good right now. Another hour or so isn't going to make a difference tonight and I know how worried everyone is about Shirley. We'll meet you over there."

Then Lucinda uttered three chilling words—*the phone tree.* Next thing I knew she made one tap on her phone and I knew without a doubt the Homey Hut would need to move two tables together.

"You think Shirley's going to be all right, don't you?" I asked him when we got into our car.

"She was cognizant of everything going on around her but struggling with the pain in the back of her head. I'm surprised she remembered about that white van. Even people without head injuries can't always pull up details."

"Think that van had any significance? I mean, as far as that body sighting was concerned?" I was careful to say *sighting* since there was no tangible evidence of a body. But things were about to change. Too bad we didn't know it at the time.

CHAPTER 8

"Even the smallest detail can have significance," Marshall said as he pulled out of the parking space and turned right on Granite Valley Drive en route to the Homey Hut. "Frankly, I'm surprised Shirley remembered it at all. Maybe that's a good sign."

"The van or Shirley?"

"Both."

My mom and Lucinda arrived at the Homey Hut the same time we did. "Well?" I asked. "Did you spread the word about Shirley like manure in a horse pasture?"

"We can't keep the book club in the dark. Don't know who'll be able to make it here tonight but I'll have them move two tables together just in case." No sooner did she say that when Herb and Bill walked in.

"That was quick," my mother said to them. "What did you do? Hammer the gas on Grand?"

Bill shook his head. "Nope. Chugged our beers when we got Myrna's call and left Curley's. It's less than a half mile from here. Kevin and Kenny got the word but can't make it but Wayne's on his way."

"Is Myrna coming?"

Bill shrugged. "I didn't ask her. I only took the message."

Just then, a wave of purple and green clashed with the rustic yellow and red tablecloths as my aunt Ina made her appearance. Uncle Louis was a few feet behind her and looked as if he'd just awakened from a long sleep. "Cecilia said concussion and brain swelling," my aunt said. "We're right across the road in Grand so we got here as soon as we could."

Grand referred to Sun City Grand, where my aunt and uncle lived. It was a newer Del Webb community and similar to my mother's. My aunt had fallen in love with a house there and no amount of persuading was going to make her change her mind and move to Sun City West. Something about a cascading waterfall backyard and mountain views that were good for the soul. The pocketbook, too, I imagined.

"We don't know if Shirley has a concussion or brain swelling," I said. "Good grief. That phone tree of yours is worse than that old telephone game we played as kids. We'll know once they're done with the CT scan."

"No sense imagining the worst." My mother, along with a waitress and Marshall, shoved the tables together. Seconds later we were seated.

"Look!" Lucinda pointed. "Here comes Wayne. And isn't that Myrna at the entrance?"

Wayne immediately walked to where Herb was seated and shook his shoulder. "What'd you do? Hit her with a stray ball? And all of us thought

Myrna was pretty bad at bocce."

"Hey," Myrna snapped. "I'm right here if you don't mind and my bocce skills have improved if you haven't noticed."

Wayne flinched. "Only kidding. What's the scoop with Shirley?"

Marshall filled everyone in with the details as we looked over the dessert menu and made our selections.

"I thought Cecilia was coming," I said.

My aunt reached for a handful of sugar packets and piled them up in front of her. "She'll be along. She was finishing up her dinner when she got the call."

"What about Louise?" I asked.

"She had a root canal and is on pain meds. Can't go anywhere."

No sooner did my aunt offer up the explanation to Cecilia and Louise's status when Cecilia showed up at our tables dressed in her usual white and black. She had something clutched in her hand and for a minute I thought it might be rosary beads but it turned out to be her car keys. "As soon as we're done here, I'm going straight over to the hospital. This is horrible. Who would do such a thing to Shirley?"

My uncle Louis, who's normally pretty quiet compared to the rest of us, leaned forward and put his hand under his chin. "Does she owe anyone any money? Is someone trying to collect on one of their markers?"

"Louis, honestly." My aunt put her hand behind his balding head and stroked it. "Not everyone is a gambler. Especially Shirley."

"Just a thought." By now the waitress had served the coffees and my uncle added creamer to his.

For the next thirty minutes, in between bites of pie, dishes of ice cream, and too many coffee refills to mention, my aunt and uncle, along with my mother and her friends, offered up more theories regarding the vanishing corpses and the out-and-out attempt on Shirley's life.

Then Myrna cleared her throat and motioned for everyone to lean forward. "I have the most brilliant idea. Why don't Harriet and I mention the disappearing bodies on our next *Booked 4 Murder* broadcast on KSCW? We can discreetly slip it in by mentioning mysteries with disappearing bodies like *The Lady Vanishes*. Was that a book or Alfred Hitchcock?"

"Alfred Hitchcock," Bill said. "It was on Turner Classic last night."

I rolled my eyes and watched as Myrna turned to my mother. "It's our regular show this week, Harriet, isn't it? We don't do the fishing thing with Paul until next week, right?"

I struggled to get the words out of my mouth. "Not a good idea. It'll incite a panic." *Or worse, whatever that might be.*

My mother and Myrna had a weekly radio show for the purpose of discussing mysteries but half the time they were so off topic the audience

31

didn't know what to expect. Worse yet was the debacle with Paul Schmidt. Paul had his own radio show, *Lake Fishing with Paul*, or something like that. One morning they got their schedules mixed up and both were on the air at the same time. Disaster would be an understatement. However, the community seemed to like it, and next thing my mother and Myrna knew they also had a shared show with Paul. Guess that old adage *will wonders never cease* held true in their case.

"Phee's right," Marshall said. "The less everyone knows at this point, the better. Face it, there are no actual bodies, and until the deputies complete their investigation regarding Shirley's incident, all you'd wind up doing is creating a maelstrom."

"Oh, I suppose so," Myrna said. "But let's keep it on the back burner, shall we?" She gave my mother a look and a wink. Not a good sign.

Cecilia clasped her hands together and cleared her throat while Wayne, Bill, and Herb continued stuffing one spoonful of pie after another into their mouths. "Shirley's not going to be up for cooking or preparing meals. What do you say we each bring over casseroles, salads, and ready-made meals to her house? She's got that big relic of a freezer, doesn't she? Almost makes Harriet's look small."

"Wonderful idea," my aunt said. "Louis and I will see what AJ's has in its prepared meal section."

I tried not to laugh. My aunt hadn't cooked a meal since the Clinton administration and wasn't about to start any time soon.

Cecilia offered to organize the meals and the men offered to chip in. True, they were adept at grilling meat but that's about as far as it went. The sojourn at the Homey Hut drew to a close with a decision made. Marshall and I would drive back to the hospital followed by Lucinda and my mother. We promised to keep everyone in the loop, rather than create a crowd scene in the ER. Cecilia and Myrna reluctantly agreed and decided Myrna would call Louise.

All of a sudden, the ear-piercing ringtone on Herb's phone went off. "Why is that ringtone so jarring?" Myrna asked.

"So I can hear it," Herb replied. "Excuse me, got to take this call. It's Lyman from the men's softball league." Herb pushed his chair back and moved to the nearest wall while the conversation about who would be calling whom continued.

Within seconds, Herb raised a fist in the air and shouted, "Whoopi! Talk about luck!" He all but collided with Bill as he returned to the table and sat. "You won't believe this but that was Lyman from the league."

Bill readjusted his chair. "We know. You told us that already."

"Fine. Fine. I got great news! Buster LaRoo emailed Lyman and told him he had to be in Baltimore for the week. Maybe longer. Family business. This means I get to take Buster's place and play third base on the blue team. *The blue team.* A genuine league team. Not newbies. Well, what are all of you going to say?"

Cecilia wiped the sides of her lips. "Someone's actually named Buster? That can't be his given name, can it?"

I thought Herb would split a gut. "Never mind the guy's name," he said. "I'm now on the blue team. The game is this Wednesday. Bright and early at nine a.m. I'm going to be there at the crack of dawn to warm up but you guys can show up in time for the first pitch."

A series of groans followed. Then my uncle spoke. "Buster LaRoo, you said?"

Herb furrowed his brow and cocked his head. "Ugh, don't tell me you're stuck on the guy's name, too?"

"Not the name, the guy who goes by it. Real name is Millard LaRoo. And I'll wager that family business in Baltimore has nothing to do with kin."

"How do you know him, dear?" my aunt asked.

"He runs a backdoor gambling operation in the valley. Small stuff mainly, like college football and basketball games."

"So a bookie," Marshall said.

My uncle turned the palm of his hand up and down. "A bookie with more connections than a politician."

My aunt grabbed Louis's wrist. "Don't tell me you've placed bets with that man."

"Don't be silly. Since when have I ever placed bets in small-time operations? No worries, my sweet." Then he gave her a peck on the cheek, which all of us tried to ignore.

Herb pushed his chair back and stretched. "I don't care what he does as long as it's in Baltimore and I get to play on the blue team. Remember, everyone, nine o'clock sharp on Wednesday. I hope to see some of you in the stands."

"Maybe Shirley will feel better by then," Wayne said.

"Shirley!" my mother all but shouted. "We've forgotten all about poor Shirley what with Herb's baseball announcement and Louis's gambling recollections. We need to get over to the hospital right away. They should know what's going on with her by now."

My head felt as if I'd just gotten off a roller coaster when we left the restaurant and Marshall's wasn't much better. He gave my shoulder a pat and sighed. "No wonder you try to avoid those Saturday brunches. It's like a never-ending stream of consciousness, complete with an extra helping of pie."

"And indigestion."

CHAPTER 9

When the four of us returned to the ER, only two people were in the waiting room and neither of them appeared to be patients. Marshall approached the reception desk for the second time that night and was told to have a seat and wait, loud enough for all of us to hear.

A few minutes later, a patient advocate dressed in Cecilia Flanagan fashion with a dark skirt and white blouse called his name. My mother rushed over to the poor woman before Marshall could even stand.

"Oh, no," my mother said. Her hand flew to her chest in a gesture that my aunt Ina had perfected over the years. "Has something horrible happened to Shirley? Is that why they sent you?"

The woman shook her head. "I'm not allowed to speak about the patient's condition, only to inform you that she requested to speak with Harriet Plunkett, Lucinda Espinoza, and the Gregorys as soon as they arrived."

It was the first time I'd heard my name as part of a collective—the Gregorys—and I had to admit it made me giddy for a forty-something bride.

"Normally," the patient advocate went on, "we only allow one person per visit but in this case two of you may go in."

My mother started for the door like a bull moose, then suddenly stopped. "I think maybe Phee and Marshall should go in. Shirley might have remembered more about the incident and Marshall has those deputies on speed dial."

"We'll be right back," I said, wasting no time to walk into the hospital corridor before my mother had a change of heart.

"I wonder what's going on," I whispered to Marshall as we followed the woman. There were three smaller corridors off of the main one and they were all part of the emergency room setup.

The advocate pointed to room C12, Orange Wing, and said, "Miss Johnson is resting comfortably." With that, she turned and walked away. Marshall knocked, then opened the door to the room. Shirley looked a far cry better than I expected, although her dark skin tone appeared more lackluster and the usual rosiness in her cheeks was gone.

"Lordy, what a night. Are Harriet and Lucinda here?"

"In the waiting room," I said. "Is everything all right? I mean, with your CT scan and all?"

Shirley nodded. "No visible signs of brain damage and no discernible concussion but they said sometimes concussions don't show up and you have to go by the symptoms. I'm still dizzy but not as bad as before and the nausea is better."

Marshall moved closer to Shirley's bed, but before he could speak, my mother walked in. "Shh, I had to sneak in. Lucinda's holding down the fort in the waiting room. I had to pretend I got lost before someone directed me to your room."

"I can't believe you did that," I said. "You'll get all of us in trouble."

My mother ignored my comment and reached for Shirley's hand. "It's stone-cold."

Shirley nodded. "I'm positive they keep the temperature at fifty degrees in here. Something about slowing down germs, but if you ask me, they want to make sure the bodies of the people who pass on don't deteriorate before they can get them to the morgue."

I tried not to laugh but her comment made sense in a macabre sort of way.

"Are they going to admit you?" Marshall asked.

Shirley looked around as if the place was bugged. "That's the thing. They want to keep me here for observation but not officially admit me. I can't let them do that. Medicare doesn't pay a hospital when they keep you for observation, only when they admit you. The cost will be outrageous. Since I live alone, they'll only release me if someone stays with me for twenty-four hours."

"Aha," my mother said. "That's why they sent a patient advocate to the waiting room and not one of those aides. Don't worry, I can stay with you. I can bring Streetman and Essie to your house or Phee and Marshall can take them to their place."

I glanced at Marshall and he looked stricken. Fortunately Shirley saved us. "I can't inconvenience all of you," she said. "Do you think maybe Lucinda would be willing to sleep over?"

"Of course she would. Hold on a minute." My mother whipped out her phone and within minutes had her answer. "Not only is Lucinda going to stay but she's got the phone tree going so tomorrow morning someone else will be at your house. We're only calling the women because Herb and his cronies are useless in these situations." Then she announced, "It's probably a good thing that you get out of here. If someone hit you on the head on purpose, they'll try again. Especially in a hospital setting. They'll put on a pair of scrubs, pretend to be a nurse or aide, and next thing you know, they'll be injecting poison into your IV line."

Shirley looked at her IV line and recoiled. "I saw it, too, Harriet. On the Hallmark Channel. It was *The Gourmet Detective*. You know, the one where the restaurant owner is murdered. Oh, Lordy, why is someone trying to kill me?"

I gave my mother's ankle a slight kick. "Now see what you've done."

Marshall stepped in front of my mother and patted Shirley's arm. "I don't think anyone's trying to murder you and I'm sure you'll be safe in your house, especially with company. Deputies Bowman and Ranston are looking into the incident. I'm sure they'll figure out what happened."

"Marshall's right," I said. "Take it easy for a few days and try not to dwell on those bodies you saw."

Suddenly a shock wave hit *my* ankle. "Now look at who's upsetting her," my mother whispered.

"It's okay, Harriet. No matter what, I'll never get that vision of the dead body out of my mind. Maybe it's just as well I didn't get a close look at the second one. Tell Herb when you see him that I'm sorry I didn't get a chance to watch him at bat for more than a few minutes."

My mother looked at the clock on the wall. "You can tell him yourself on Wednesday. It's only a day away more or less. You should be fine by then, I imagine."

"Wednesday? Maybe that bump on the head messed up my memory but I was positive his game was on Friday."

"Oh, it was," my mother said. "But that was before someone named Buster LaRoo took off for Baltimore, leaving a league team in the lurch for a third baseman. Herb got a call from the manager while all of us were at the Homey Hut during your CT scan. I would've brought you back some pie but I didn't think you'd have much of an appetite."

Shirley widened her eyes. "I don't. Especially after hearing that name. Buster LaRoo. I had no idea he was still in Sun City West."

"You know him?" I asked.

She nodded. "I know *of* him and it's not pleasant."

At that moment, the door opened and the patient advocate stepped in. "I take it Miss Johnson will be spending the night with us," she said. "I just have a bit of paperwork that needs to be completed."

Shirley straightened herself in the bed and looked the woman square in the eye. "I most certainly will not. Please have my discharge papers ready. My good friends will be staying with me in my home and monitoring my condition. No sense my taking up a perfectly good bed when it may be needed for other patients. Not that I don't appreciate the offer."

Or the associated cost.

"Not a problem. The discharge nurse will be in here shortly with your instructions. Please be sure to call your PCP tomorrow and arrange for an appointment."

"PCP?" my mother asked when the advocate left the room. "Isn't that an illegal drug?"

"She means primary care physician," Marshall said and laughed.

"Good grief. I am so sick of all these initials. Just say so. Tell her to see her own doctor. I can't be deciphering initials all day long. I blame it on texting. No one can write a full word anymore that's longer than four letters."

With that, I took my mother by the arm and ushered her away from Shirley's bed. "We'll be in the waiting room, Shirley," I said. "Feel better."

"You and Marshall should go home. I'll be fine with your mother and Lucinda. You two have work tomorrow. And some deputies to nag. Tell them to get cracking."

"I think Shirley's feeling better," Marshall said when we got back to the ER. Like Shirley, my mother insisted we go home.

"Sure you'll be okay?" I asked.

"We'll be fine. I'll call you tomorrow."

I gave her a hug, thanked Lucinda for offering to stay with Shirley, and headed out the door with Marshall.

"Too bad that patient advocate interrupted Shirley," Marshall said. "I'm curious about what she knows regarding Buster LaRoo. Sounds ominous. Just as well the guy's in Baltimore, huh?"

"Well, two people are happy at least—Herb and Shirley."

"Make that three. At least we didn't get stuck with Streetman and the cat. Last time they stayed overnight they tore up two scatter rugs. And that was after the cat threw up a hairball."

I chuckled and gave his arm a squeeze. "You're wrong, make that four people who are happy!"

Chapter 10

"Still on your honeymoon, I presume," Augusta said when I walked into the office the following morning. She fluffed her bouffant hair and adjusted her tortoiseshell readers.

"Huh?"

"Mr. Gregory looked the same way when he came in—sleep-deprived. If you're wondering, he and Mr. Williams took off for Peoria. They're meeting up with the CEO of Lasher and Wellington Insurance."

"Lasher and Wellington? That's a huge Phoenix company. Marshall was going to tell me about the case but we got waylaid."

"That's an interesting term for it."

"Very funny. Our lack of sleep was a result of— Oh, never mind. It's a long story. Let me get a cup of coffee first."

"Don't tell me Shirley saw another dead body."

"Yup, only this time she got hit in the head with a softball just as she was about to snap a picture of it with her phone. Then *that* body disappeared."

"Is Shirley on any new medication?"

I shook my head. "No, and the softball was as real as could be. Our favorite deputies are having it checked for prints." At the word *deputies*, Augusta flinched. She, too, was more than familiar with Bowman and Ranston.

"You think she saw or heard something she shouldn't have?"

I shrugged. "Could be. Anyway, Lucinda spent the night with her so Marshall and I were spared babysitting my mother's menagerie."

"That happens when you don't grow up on a dairy farm like I did. You make up for it in later life by taking in all sorts of four-legged strays. Tell you right now, if I took in anything it would be a well-trained rottweiler. Can't be too careful these days."

"I'll keep that in mind. By the way, does the name Buster LaRoo ring a bell?"

Augusta shook her head. "No, should it?"

"I suppose not but Shirley was pretty cagey when we mentioned it to her at the hospital. Seems he's a league softball player in Sun City West who had to go to Baltimore, thus opening up a prime spot for Herb on the coveted blue team. Herb's got a game Wednesday morning and naturally wants my mother and her friends to go. Thank goodness I have a full-time job and intend to keep it that way. Starting right this minute with inputting some financial data that I've been putting off due to invoicing."

"Enjoy. Hey, deli for lunch or pizza?"

"Deli. I'm reserving pizza for dinner. From the way Marshall spoke about that case of theirs, it could be a late night."

As it turned out, it was a late night, but it had nothing to do with Marshall's insurance fraud case. When Nate and Marshall returned to the office in the afternoon, Marshall got a phone call from Deputy Bowman. No discernible prints were found on the softball but the forensic team did find something else while scouting out the area—golf cart tracks that led from the spot where Shirley thought she saw the body. And while the tracks were innocuous, since golf carts are driven everywhere in Sun City West, the crumpled note found on top of one of the grooves was not. It was handwritten on notebook paper and it detailed Shirley's schedule with chilling accuracy.

According to Bowman, the schedule read like a weekly planner and included a daily routine that consisted of club meetings, volunteer work, luncheons and church get-togethers. Marshall suggested it might have belonged to Shirley and fell from her pocket or even her bag when she got lobbed with that ball but Bowman put the kibosh to that.

"You're not going to believe this," Marshall said. "I'm going to need a cup of coffee to let it sink in." He stood in the outer office while Nate appeared out of nowhere, making a beeline for the Keurig. As he and I vied for the first cup, Augusta cleared her throat.

"Better let Marshall in line first, you two," she said from her desk, "or we'll never get the story."

Nate and I stood back but Marshall motioned us to go first. "On the side of the paper, in bold print, someone wrote, 'Best bet is to tail her as she leaves Liberty Field.'"

"Liberty Field?" Augusta asked.

I gulped. "That's the name of the baseball field where Herb's league plays. Oh my gosh. That means—"

"Yep, someone's got it in for Shirley." Marshall put his palms up before I could say another word. "Hold tight. Bowman's on it. They're making sure there's a deputy posted at her house. He and Ranston are on their way now to see Shirley."

I tightened my fists to the point where my knuckles turned white. "Shirley will be beside herself. Maybe we should call her first before those two bearers of ill tidings rap on her door and send her off the deep end."

Nate pointed to the phone on Augusta's desk. "You've got the skills for this, kiddo. Go for it."

What skills? I'm a bookkeeper/accountant, for crying out loud.

"I've got her number on my iPhone. It's easier. In fact, I've got all the book club ladies on it. Just in case. I'll turn up the volume so all of you can hear." I tapped the Call button and held my breath. "Shirley? How are you feeling?"

"Better. A milder headache and some body bruises. I didn't even know I had them. They're just setting in. My doctor prescribed some pain medication but I'm sticking with Tylenol. He was able to squeeze me in a little while ago."

"Uh-huh. Is Lucinda still staying with you?"

"Cecilia is for today and tonight. Louise will be over during the day, too, but she can't leave that darn bird of hers alone at night."

"Tell me about it!" Nate shouted. "Those African grey parrots are worse than two-year-olds. And they live forever. For-Ever!"

Marshall burst out laughing and turned away. While Louise had chosen to own an African grey, Nate got stuck with Mr. Fluffypants when his aunt in Sierra Vista had to move to assisted living. For weeks he'd come to work muttering about his lousy roommate.

"Is that Nate?" Shirley asked. "Is he with you?"

"Actually, we're all in the office and that's why I called. Deputies Bowman and Ranston are on their way over to speak with you."

"Did they find out who threw that softball?"

"Um, not exactly. But they did uncover some evidence that's well, um, er, a tad unnerving. First of all, the deputies are taking this seriously. In fact, they're going to have someone posted outside your door every night."

"Oh, Lordy! This can't be good. What evidence?"

I swallowed, hoping to stall for time. "It was a note on lined paper with your weekly schedule on it. Handwritten."

Shirley gasped. "Good heavens! I'm being stalked, aren't I? Some maniacal lunatic is stalking me. I don't write down my schedule on notepaper. It's on my calendar. How would anyone possibly know it but me?" Then she called out, "Cecilia, make sure the door is locked."

"All someone would need to know is what clubs you're in. That's public information for the Rec Centers along with meeting times and events. But, um, that's not all. When those deputies get to your house, tell them everything you think they should know."

"About what? What should they know?"

"There was something else written on that notepaper. It was off to the side. I didn't see it myself but Deputy Bowman spelled it out for Marshall."

"Spelled what?"

Again, I took a breath. This time longer. "It said to follow you as you left Liberty Field. Shirley, someone knew you were going to be there and waited for the opportune moment to strike."

"I'm a dead woman, aren't I? That body I saw was a decoy. It was me they were after." Then, to Cecilia, "Make sure the windows are closed, too."

Just then, I heard a shriek and yelled into the phone. "Shirley, are you okay? What's going on?"

"That was Cecilia. Those deputies just rang the doorbell. She screamed before she looked out the window."

The thumping in my chest slowed down and I rolled my eyes. "Good, let them in. We'll talk to you later. Don't worry. No one's going to get within ten feet of you. Try to relax."

"Tell that to Cecilia. I think she may need to change her undergarment."

CHAPTER 11

"Give it forty-five minutes and my mother's call will come in like clockwork. I figure that's about the time Bowman and Ranston wrap things up at Shirley's and the phone tree will be in full force."

"Got to admit," Nate said, "those deputies must really be concerned. Usually they don't respond with such expediency."

"You can say it, Mr. Williams," Augusta chirped up. "They'd be lolly-gagging around."

"Well, I'm not," I said. Then I looked at Marshall and could see the little crinkles above his nose that he always makes when he's troubled. I bit my lip and took a breath. "Bowman and Ranston are going to follow office protocol. You know, start with the most pressing info and go from there. But I have something different in mind."

"Hold on, Phee," Augusta said. "I might as well eat my afternoon snack while I listen to you. I made a batch of dehydrated turnips to go with my beef jerky. Got plenty to go around."

Nate stepped back, shook his head and muttered, "We're good."

"Okay, this is what I had in mind," I went on. "Shirley's in a zillion sewing clubs. That's where she spends most of her time when she's not with the book club ladies. Right now, everyone's getting ready for the fall craft show, and from what my mother told me, Shirley's making teddy bears and teapot cozies."

Marshall flashed a look at Nate. "Don't ask."

"Anyway," I continued, "I need her to give us the lowdown on all those club members. Maybe she doesn't realize it, but someone within her circle may have it in for her. It's going to take some time but I'm willing to pop over there tonight." Then I gave Marshall a smile. "That is, if you're willing to make, defrost, or conjure up a late dinner."

"If you mean take-out, name your restaurant. I've got a boatload of paperwork in my office and tonight's as good a night as any to tackle it."

"Splendid!" Nate gave Marshall one of those playful slaps on the shoulder. "I wasn't going to ruin your evening but I got a text from Sid Lasher at the insurance company. Seems they uncovered more sneaky business when we left their office."

Marshall chuckled. "Guess that means we won't be leaving ours any time soon."

"Well, I am," Augusta said. "At exactly five, I plan to put the *Closed* sign on the door and shut off my computer. Let me know if you still want the printer and Keurig left on. I've got a hot canasta night planned and itchy palms."

Nate took a step back. "Whoa. Wouldn't want to hold you up from a future windfall."

Augusta smiled and turned her attention once again to her computer screen. *Too bad I wasn't a betting person.* My mother's call came in as expected, but once I told her what I had in mind at Shirley's, she decided not to press things any further. "Keep me posted on whatever you find out," she said. "I'll nose around, too."

"If by nose around you mean send me to the dog park to pry information from their number-one gossip, forget it."

"You got off the hook with the man who gave Shirley the finger. Who knows what these other maniacs have in mind?"

"That's why the county has sheriff's deputies, detectives, and a forensics team."

"None of them have a vested interest like we do. I need to stay informed. People rely on my intelligence information."

Intelligence information? Is that the new euphemism for gossip-mongering?

When I arrived at Shirley's house, Cecilia had gone home for the night but Myrna had replaced her. They were expecting me since I called earlier to let Shirley know I'd be stopping by.

"Um, I don't want to alarm the two of you," I said when Myrna opened the door to let me in, "but there's a dark-colored car parked diagonal from the house and it looks like someone may be watching you. Maybe we should call the sheriff's office."

Shirley laughed. "You mean Starsky and Hutch? Take a closer look. It's Kenny and Kevin. Herb decided the pinochle crew should keep an eye on my house until that deputy arrives around nine."

"Wow, of all things."

Myrna waved at them from the door and closed it. "So far we've brought them donuts, sweet cider, and chocolate pretzels. I'd say it was a win-win."

Shirley motioned me to a comfy beige couch with two well-loved teddy bears sharing a cushion. Very little had changed since the last time I'd been to her house. The hand-sewn bears were all over the place and lots of cutesy tchotchkes were still on the bookshelves.

"At some point," she said, "I'll need to get out the Halloween decorations, but it's September so I'll let summer linger on a bit. Besides, my body's still sore and the last thing I feel like doing is dragging out Rubbermaid bins of holiday décor. Oh, dear, I should have asked you the minute you came in, can I get you anything to drink? Eat?"

"I'm fine. Marshall's working late and we'll have dinner when we get home. I don't want to keep you long but I was hoping we could go through the rosters of those sewing clubs you belong to. Is there anyone who might be carrying a grudge against you?"

"If it were the bocce club, they'd lob a ball at you," Myrna said. "No subtlety with that crew."

Shirley walked over to an old oak desk with a small dragonfly lamp on it. She opened a side drawer and pulled out a handful of binders. "This may take longer than you think but let's begin." Binder after binder, she read the names of the sewing clubs that she belonged to: Encore Needle & Craft, Creative Stitchers, and Rip 'n' Sew. I remembered attending a few of those meetings while trying to get the lowdown on the ex-girlfriend of the local radio station's program manager because I had succumbed to my mother's nagging.

As the evening wore on, we got nowhere. Unless of course I wanted to make a list of whose stitching was sloppy and whose was not. At a little past seven, Shirley closed the last binder. "Honestly, I can't think of anyone who would have it in for me. Not like that poor Geraldine Kremler from the Creative Stitchers." Then she turned to Myrna. "I told you about her, didn't I?"

Myrna shrugged. "Maybe."

"Anyway, it's a long story. Geraldine's now living with her son and his family somewhere in Nevada. She wrote the club about a year ago and said she liked her mother-in-law suite and enjoys being around the grandkids. If you ask me, what she liked was getting far away from Buster LaRoo."

"Buster LaRoo? The guy on the ball team who's now in Baltimore? The one Herb is replacing? *That* Buster LaRoo? You mentioned him at the hospital."

Hmm, maybe she'll fill in the blanks for me about that guy.

"If the team's lucky, Herb should replace him permanently. Oh, goodness. I promised myself I wouldn't go spouting off secondhand information and here I am doing exactly that."

"It's not as if you're gossiping, Shirley," Myrna said. She walked over to the kitchen counter and helped herself to a French cruller. "It's *secondhand* information. That means it came directly from someone and not passed around. There's a big difference."

I did a mental eye roll and stretched. It felt as if my body had adhered to the couch cushion. "What about Buster LaRoo and Geraldine?"

"The compressor on Geraldine's air-conditioning unit went out a few years ago. Three thousand dollars to replace. Who has that kind of money? True, she could have gone to her children but that was the last thing she wanted to do and she didn't have enough credit for a loan or available monies on her credit card. So, she borrowed it from Buster LaRoo. Apparently he ran a not-so-legit lending operation. Among other things.

They agreed on an interest rate but that lousy scoundrel kept raising the rate on Geraldine."

"That's as illegal as all get-up-and-go," I said. "She should have reported it to the authorities."

"And have everyone think she was duped? The woman had her pride, if nothing else."

"So what happened? She stuck it out and paid the bill?"

Shirley shook her head. "Not exactly. He offered to drop the remaining balance if she would agree to—"

"Ew! Don't tell me it's what I'm thinking. Ew!"

"Oh, Lordy, no! If you're thinking what I *think* you're thinking, it's no. Geraldine would have sold her car for the cash before she'd ever consent to, well, you know."

"Then what?"

Just then there was a knock on Shirley's door and Myrna went to answer it. "It's Kenny. He wants to know if you have any bottled water. He and Kevin are thirsty and they drank all the sweet cider."

"Goodness, yes. Tell him to come right in and help himself. Got lots of bottled water in the fridge. And more donuts on the counter."

Kenny wasted no time coming in. He gave me a quick wave and headed for the donuts. "All quiet on the Western Front," he said. "We'll hang out for another hour or so and then Wayne and Bill will show up."

"That's really not needed," Shirley said. "Appreciated, but not needed. All of you have your own lives. I'm fine. Myrna's staying tonight and that deputy should arrive around nine."

"It's no problem. None whatsoever. Boy, these donuts are good. Don't mind if I have another. Oh, I'd better bring one back for Kevin."

I glanced at the large clock over Shirley's sink and was surprised at how long I'd been at her house. As anxious as I was to find out more about Geraldine and Buster, the thought of Marshall standing over cold take-out food compelled me to get going.

"I really need to run," I said to Shirley. "If you can think of anyone at all who might be holding a grudge or even ruffled feathers over something minor, call me. Okay?"

"Sure thing, honey, but I doubt it's anyone in my social groups. Trouble is, I don't seem to know anyone else."

I opened the door, said good night to Myrna and Kenny and headed for my car. I waved to Kevin before getting in the door and then started the engine. If no one in Shirley's social circle had it in for her, it meant she must have seen or heard something that someone wanted to keep hidden. But at what price?

CHAPTER 12

"You've got a never-ending message on the landline," Marshall said when I got in the door.

"Let me guess. Were the words *dog park* mentioned?"

"Nope. You lucked out. Play it for yourself."

I clicked the button on the phone and held my breath as my mother repeated the same question over and over again. "What did you find out at Shirley's?"

I turned to Marshall. "Whatever I found out, which wasn't much, can wait. Come on, surprise me and tell me what you picked up for dinner."

"Hope you're in the mood for Taco Tuesday because I've got an assortment from Abuelos."

"Always!"

When we finished dinner and tidied up the kitchen, I braced myself for the return phone call I needed to make. My mother answered on the second ring. "Oh, good, Phee, you're home. So? What happened? Who's with Shirley now?"

When she was satisfied I'd given her the complete lowdown, she told me she and Louise would be at the ball field in the morning to cheer Herb on. Lucinda wanted to go but had some church flyers she needed to send.

"I can't ask Cecilia and Myrna," she said. "They're probably exhausted from staying over and guarding Shirley."

"Um, I don't think they're actually *guarding* her in the true sense of the word."

"You know what I mean. And your aunt is way too busy with Louis and all his nonsense so that means it's up to us. Anyway, I plan to put Streetman in the walking stroller so he can enjoy a day in the fresh air. People don't complain when the dog is in the stroller."

No wonder. It's hard to bite and snap through the mesh.

"Uh-huh. By the way, does the name Geraldine Kremler ring a bell?"

"I've heard Shirley mention it but not really, why? Does Shirley think she's the one who threw that softball?"

"Not unless she can land a pitch from Nevada where she's now living. Never mind. It's just that Geraldine was acquainted with Buster LaRoo. You know, the guy Herb's replacing."

"Everyone's acquainted with everyone in Sun City West. That's why it's so important to sift out the pertinent information from the local chatter to get a real sense of who might have it in for Shirley."

"Uh-huh, yeah. Listen, it's been a long day and tomorrow's work so have a good time watching Herb. Hope he doesn't strike out."

"You and the rest of the team, I'm sure."

• • •

Marshall had an early appointment with a new client in the morning and then he and Nate were off to deal with the insurance fraud case. I had a substantial workload myself with billing and account reconciliation so I didn't get a chance to chitchat with Augusta until a little past ten. She had unwrapped the package of Entenmann's donuts that Nate brought in and was about to offer one to me when the phone rang.

"Hold on, Phee, I need to take this call. Grab a donut yourself."

I never tired of the thick chocolate icing on the cakey dough that Entenmann's does so well but I didn't get the chance. Augusta held out the phone and announced, "It's your mother." Then she mouthed, "I'm putting it on speaker."

I rolled my eyes and grabbed the receiver. "What's up?"

"I'm at the ball field."

"Don't tell me Herb hit a home run?"

"No, a few minutes ago he hit the ball in the outfield and the other team caught it."

"And you're calling me at work to tell me Herb made an out?"

"Shh, let me finish. When the other guy caught the ball, he was right against the block wall and glanced back. That's when he saw it."

"Saw what?"

"A dead body. A man. The place is teeming with sheriff's deputies and they cordoned off the area. Listen—sirens. That means more deputies gawking around."

"I don't suppose you're able to bring the dog home, huh?"

"No, they want to question all of us. That's going to take forever. Some poor man probably had a heart attack during a walk. Then again, who walks behind the ball field? If he had walked behind the chain-link fenced area, he would have been spotted sooner. I don't suppose you could take an early lunch, drive over and bring my fur-baby home?"

I wanted to gag at the word *fur-baby* but restrained myself. "Give me an hour and I'll drive over. That savage of yours should be able to hang on a bit longer."

"Honestly, Phee. He's become quite the gentleman. Of course, when you get him home he'll need to go outside and— Oh my goodness. Another sheriff's car pulled in. Big yellow letters that read *MCSO Forensics Lab*. Maybe it wasn't a heart attack. I'm going to see if I can get closer to the dugout and see what Herb knows."

"Stay where you are. I'm sure you'll find out in good time. See you later."

I hung up before she could utter another word. But Augusta sure did. "Harrumph. Looks like someone else got knocked off in that delightful senior community. Better grab two donuts. It may be a while before you get to eat."

"Nah, all I plan on doing is dropping off the little darling and making sure he does his business outside before I leave. Then, it's straight back here."

"If you say so, but I have a hunch you'll get trapped like a fly on one of those sticky tapes."

"Ugh."

Talk about prophetic. Sometimes I wonder about Augusta. As it turned out, she was right. Not because of Streetman, thank goodness, but because the minute I arrived at Liberty Field, I knew I was in trouble. The KPHO van from channel 5 was there along with FOX's channel 10, ABC's channel 15, and NBC's channel 12.

There was no way I would be allowed into the stands where the crowd of league spectators thought they'd be spending a pleasant morning. I got as far as the edge of the parking lot with every intention of trying to cajole one of the sheriff's deputies into letting me retrieve my mother's dog when a gray-haired man from the posse approached me.

"Are you Sophie Kimball?"

I nodded.

"Good. Wait right here."

Seconds later my mother emerged with Streetman in his stroller.

"What's going on?"

"The poor dog isn't handling the crowd well. First, all those sirens. Then, the shouting. Everyone's anxious and he can sense it. Unfortunately he's developed a new habit of yowling. I think he learned it from the cat. It's quite unnerving."

I widened my eyes and didn't say a word as my mother continued. "Someone must have complained because the next thing I knew a posse volunteer asked if I could call someone to get the dog. Now aren't you glad you drove over here?"

Thrilled beyond words.

"I've got to get back to the stands. They're taking statements row by row. Don't forget to give my little man a treat and Essie as well. I'll call you when I get home."

No sooner did my mother say that when a piercing whistle all but blew my eardrums to smithereens. I turned and there was Louise Munson standing on the top bench and waving frantically at my mother and me.

"Harriet! Harriet! The scuttlebutt is the body belongs to Buster LaRoo."
Then, even louder, in case anyone in the Northern Hemisphere missed it—
"Buster LaRoo."

"Isn't that the man who's supposed to be in Baltimore?" I asked.

"Unless they've moved the Charm City a few yards past the outfield,
I'd say Buster LaRoo never made it there in the first place."

Then Louise yelled again. "The guy who caught Herb's fly ball said the
body looked like it had been dead for some time."

I looked at my mother. "How on earth would he know that? And better
still, how did Louise find out?"

My mother brushed a stray hair from her brow. "The Louise part is
easy. She can pick up gossip faster than a Hoover vacuum on full speed.
Not sure about the ballplayer. Maybe he got a really good look."

"He was yards away. *Yards* away. Please don't go spreading that rumor.
Let the deputies do their job."

"Speaking of which, I think the county sent in the militia. Looks like
Deputies Bowman and Ranston are getting out of that car over there. Look!
It *is* them. Quick, take Streetman and make a run for my house. No sense in
upsetting the dog any further."

Or the deputies.

CHAPTER 13

A queasy sensation in the pit of my stomach told me I should make another stop at the ball field before driving back to the office. In retrospect, I should have taken a Tums and the shortest route to Glendale.

If I had any thought that the crowd might have dissipated, I was mistaken. In fact, it had swollen to fill most of the parking lot. The new spectators, who appeared to be more interested in the crime scene than the score, had their own take on the situation. I couldn't believe my ears as I worked my way over to the area where my mother and Louise were detained.

"Got it straight from the horse's mouth—Someone got shot on the field!"

"It was a stabbing. Someone landed on second base when the baseman went berserk and stabbed him."

"I heard they detonated one of those pipe bombs."

Each new piece of gossip was worse than the one before. I tried not to listen, but given the volume of the speakers, it was impossible. Finally, I made it over to where my mother and Louise were seated but I couldn't get past the deputy who guarded the entrance.

Thankfully, my mother spied me and elbowed her way over to where I stood. "I called that cell phone of yours but it went to voicemail. So I called Augusta at the office but she wasn't much help."

"With what? I thought you and Louise had to give statements. What could possibly have happened in the twenty or so minutes I was gone? And by the way, your little fur-pile did one in your yard. You can thank me later for cleaning up."

My mother appeared more distracted than usual. "Shirley called. Those deputies are going over to her house. She got a call from the MCSO dispatch. You need to get there ASAP. A-S-A-P."

"You didn't tell her about the body, did you?"

"Of course I did. Why wouldn't I?"

I pressed my fingers to my temple and rubbed the skin in the hope of ameliorating the tension. "Okay, fine. Did she say why the deputies needed to see her?"

My mother shook her head. "They never do." Then she turned to Louise, who stood right behind her. "You don't remember any law enforcement people informing anyone on *NCIS* or *Law & Order*, do you?"

"I think once on *Magnum*," Louise said. "Or was it *Blue Bloods*?"

"This isn't a TV show. Oh, for heaven's sake. I'm on my way to Shirley's. I'll call you once I know something."

I'd gotten better at elbowing through the crowd and pulled out my phone the second I got in the car. With the office number on speed dial, Augusta answered immediately. "Caught in the fly trap, huh? I'm not surprised. Got a news flash on the computer. Something about needing crowd control in Sun City West. Guess the only foul was foul play."

"No, it was that pun of yours. Listen, I need to go over to Shirley's. All I know is that the deputies headed over there. It could be nothing with nothing or—"

"She's number two on a hit list?"

"You're worse than my mother. I'll call you when I find out something. Looks like I'll either be working overtime tonight or making up for it on a long Saturday."

"Want me to put in a good word with the boss?"

"Just hand him the box of Entenmanns when you see him."

When I arrived at Shirley's, Bowman and Ranston were at her front door but for some reason they kept backing up, and at one point I swore I saw Bowman put up both palms. I hurried over to the door and could hear Shirley say, "Down boy! Down!"

Then, I realized why the two deputies were hesitant to make a move. A giant dog stood on two hind legs with the front legs resting on the top frame of the door. It took me a second before I realized who it was—Thor! The harlequin Great Dane belonging to my mother's former neighbor, Gloria Wong.

The last time I had seen Thor was at my mother's house a few weeks ago. He had just gotten over being petrified of Streetman but cowered at the sight of Essie. I shouted to him as I brushed past the deputies. "Good boy, Thor. Good doggie." Then I leaned over his enormous frame and asked Shirley, "What's Thor doing at your house? I don't see Gloria's car."

"Cecilia had to go to the church to help Lucinda with the flyers and she insisted I have some protection in the house. Before I could stop her, she called Gloria, who offered Thor as my bodyguard. Truth is, it's the opposite way around. He's worse than that cowardly lion from *The Wizard of Oz*."

"Don't care what you say," Ranston grumbled, "get the cowardly lion out of the way. We need to have a word with you, Miss Johnson."

Shirley coaxed Thor away from the doorway and ushered us inside. "Can I offer any of you some lemonade?" she asked.

"We're fine," Bowman replied.

"Me, too," I said.

"Well, don't stand on ceremony, take a seat and tell me to what do I owe this pleasure?"

I rubbed Thor between the ears and took the nearest accent chair. "I'm here because my mother sent me." *Oh, good grief. I sound like I'm in kindergarten.* Then I motioned to the men. "And she sent me when she found out the deputies were headed here."

Thor settled on the floor between the couch, where Bowman and Ranston were seated, and my chair. "See," I said. "He's really a pussycat."

Bowman leaned over to take a closer look at the dog. "So I see. Unlike that terror of your mother's." He glanced at his partner and then turned to face Shirley, who had seated herself in a floral wingback recliner. "We don't want to take up much of your time, Miss Johnson, but I'm sure by now, given the rapid response time it takes to share information in this community, you're aware that the body of a deceased male was found behind Liberty Field."

"Yes, indeed. Oh, Lordy, the poor man was murdered, wasn't he? And you think I'm next. Was he hit in the head with a softball, too?"

"We're not at liberty to disclose any information of that sort until the coroner releases a statement based on completion of a postmortem exam. *That*, in addition to identifying the body and notifying next of kin."

"Harriet told me it was Buster LaRoo. She said someone identified him."

Ranston groaned with such force that Thor looked up. "If by someone you mean the ballplayer who discovered the body while leaning back to catch a fly ball, that's hardly a positive identification."

I smiled. "Positive or not, it's spreading all over the community like head lice. Listen, we all know that your office must have found something on the body that somehow connects to Shirley or you wouldn't be here." Then I looked at Shirley. "I seriously doubt you're on some sort of hit list."

"Miss Kimball, er, um, Gregory, is right," Bowman said to Shirley. "We did find a wallet with a man's identification but that is *not* considered a positive ID until all reports from the coroner have been completed."

"Well, did the photo look like the deceased?" I asked.

Bowman's and Ranston's eyes met for a split second before Ranston spoke. "The body was not, shall we say, in pristine condition."

How many dead bodies are?

I tried to keep my composure. "Okay. Sure. Look, those road yentas at the ball field are bandying Buster LaRoo's name all over the place. Is that the name on the ID in the wallet?"

"This is not public knowledge, Miss Kimball . . . Gregory. Understood?"

Shirley and I nodded our heads while Thor snored and made guttural sounds.

"The driver's license belongs to Millard LaRoo."

"Has to be Buster," Shirley said. "That shouldn't be too hard to find out but I don't understand why you're here unless I'm really in danger."

Deputy Bowman removed a plastic Ziploc bag with a business card in it. "Don't take it out of the bag," he ordered. "Recognize it, Miss Johnson? It was found on the victim."

Shirley held the bag up and I could see a yellow and pink business card with a teddy bear motif on it. She passed the bag to me and I looked closely. The lettering read *Shirley's Soulful Bears*. Beneath it, in a lovely font, were the words *Handmade teddy bears for children of all ages*. In small print was her name and email address.

"So what?" I said to Bowman.

"Look at the back of the card."

I turned the Ziploc bag over and read another message. A handwritten one that almost took my breath away. It said *It's bear hunting time*.

With shaky hands, I returned the bag to Deputy Bowman. "That doesn't really mean anything, does it? Maybe Buster, I mean *the victim until he's positively identified*, planned on purchasing one of Shirley's bears. You know how people are with the written language."

Shirley didn't say a word. Instead, she picked up what looked like a teddy bear's foot and proceeded to sew around the paw. Bowman pocketed the Ziploc bag and rubbed his chin. "Seemed like an odd business card for a middle-aged or senior citizen to be carrying on him. Since we've already violated protocol by releasing the name, we might as well proceed with something that's within our purview. We need to show you the photo of the deceased in case you might recognize him. That is, if you're not too squeamish, Miss Johnson."

Without wasting a second, Bowman took out his phone and handed it to Shirley.

"Oh, Lordy! Oh, heavens above! That's him! That's him!" Shirley gasped and continued to stare at the phone. "Those eyes. Those glassy brown eyes. That's him, all right!"

"You're familiar with the victim?" Deputy Ranston asked.

Shirley handed the phone to me and clasped her hands. "That's the body I saw on Sunday on the golf course path. That's the body that disappeared. The posse was called but when they got there the body was gone. Oh, Lordy! Would you look at that face! It wasn't as discolored and puffy but it was him, all right. It was the corpse I saw." She pressed her palms together and moved them to her chest. "Oh, thank the good Lord, I'm not going crazy after all." Then she sat silent for a moment before biting her lower lip. "I *am* going to be the next victim, aren't I? Someone must think I know who killed him."

Then, of all things, Ranston looked at Thor and then at Shirley. "Maybe you can talk your friend into letting this big guy stay with you for a while."

That's when Shirley lost it completely and began to sob.

CHAPTER 14

"Your sheriff's office posted a nighttime deputy at her house," I said to the deputies. "Can you pull some strings and make sure they keep him or her there until things are settled?" Then I thought of something. "That business card . . . the handwriting on the back . . . I think your office should get a sample of Buster's writing to see if it matches what's on the card. That shouldn't be too hard to do. His signature is on his driver's license, plus, I'm sure your office will have access to his house once the positive identification is made."

Bowman gave Ranston a nudge. "That's what happens when you work for an investigative agency and marry a detective." He let out a sigh and looked directly at me. "Believe it or not, we *are* trained and we know how to do our jobs."

"Good, because if the handwriting doesn't match Buster's, then it means someone else is in play and they could very well turn out to be Buster's killer." I watched as Shirley balled up a tissue and proceeded to squeeze it in her hand. "You *will* let Shirley know, won't you?"

"We will keep Miss Johnson apprised of anything that may involve her personal safety."

With that, the deputies stood in sync and moved closer to Shirley. "Remember, Miss Johnson," Bowman said, "keep your door and security door locked at all times. Make sure your garage door is down and the door from the garage to the house is locked at all times, even when you're home. The same for your windows, although I doubt that's an issue. Everyone's air-conditioning will most likely be on until November. Heck of a summer and fall, huh?"

Shirley nodded without saying a word. She walked them to the door with Thor at her heels. The second she pulled it open, Bowman and Ranston were greeted by Cecilia and Lucinda. They all but knocked the two deputies over in a frantic rush to get through the doorway.

"Shirley! Shirley! They found a dead body at the ball field! We rushed over here to tell you. It's all over the church! Someone called the deacon's wife. That's how we found out!" Lucinda shouted even though she stood a few feet from Shirley and me. "We brought the flyers with us so we can work on them here. Two cartons in the back of my car."

Meanwhile, Cecilia spun around and tapped Deputy Ranston's arm. "Shouldn't you and your partner be at the ball field? I thought Sun City West was your territory, so to speak."

It was a miracle Ranston didn't clench his teeth or his fists. Instead, he took a breath and spoke softly. "For your information, and everyone else's according to the gossip around here, we're following up on the disturbing ball field situation with Miss Johnson. That's exactly why we paid her a visit."

"Oh," was all Cecilia said before rushing inside. "We thought *we'd* be the first ones to tell you, Shirley. Did they mention it's Buster LaRoo? That's what Harriet said and she heard it from Myrna who spoke with the man who saw the body first."

Lucinda bent down and gave Thor a pat on the head before fixing her attention on Shirley. "Maybe you should ask Gloria if the dog can stay with you for a while. Harriet thinks Buster was murdered, and if it was with a softball to the head, that maniac may come looking for you."

In what could best be described as a fit of desperation, Bowman raised his arms in the air and bellowed, "No one knows if the man was hit in the head with a softball, a baseball, or a beach ball. That's why we have coroners. And medical examiners. And professionals who— Oh, never mind. Good day, ladies."

When the deputies left and their places on the couch were taken by Lucinda and Cecilia, Lucinda asked, "Were those deputies here to warn you? Was I right? About a lunatic?"

They don't pay Bowman and Ranston enough.

My workday was gradually getting eaten away. "Um, I need to return to the office. I'm sure Shirley will fill you in. And please don't listen to every piece of scuttlebutt my mother manages to dredge up. It's rumors, that's all."

"Rumors always have a bit of truth in them, and in Harriet's case, it's usually quite a bit," Lucinda said.

"Well, one thing isn't a rumor. The deputies were pretty clear about keeping your doors and windows locked. The garage, too." As I stood and made my way to the door, I heard Lucinda whisper to Cecilia, "I was right. There *is* a lunatic."

Shirley thanked me for stopping by and I reiterated once again that she shouldn't go overboard with worry, but who was I kidding?

Too bad the timing was off because I really wanted to know what heinous thing Buster wanted Geraldine to do in lieu of paying her three-thousand-dollar debt. And maybe the answer would bring everyone closer to a reason for his unfortunate demise. Too bad it had to wait for another day.

• • •

When I got back to the office, Augusta was anxious to give me the news. Or her interpretation of it, anyway.

"Those deputies called here less than twenty seconds ago. They need Mr. Williams or Mr. Gregory to call them about, and I quote, 'their availability in the near future.' 'Near future' my patootie! You know what that means. They can't find their way out of a potato sack even with one of them holding a flashlight. They need our office to assist theirs with the body that's not on base anymore."

"Hmm, that's odd. I just saw them at Shirley's house. They left a few minutes before I did and neither of them said anything to me. Wonder what could have transpired in the last half hour . . ."

"What couldn't have transpired? Now that you're back, tell me all the details and don't leave anything out."

"You were right after all. Trapped like a fly doesn't come close." I told her what had happened from the moment I arrived at Liberty Field to the second I left Shirley's place. The only thing I omitted was the detailed report of Streetman doing his business. The only one interested in that was my mother and I had already given her the full report.

Augusta relayed Bowman's message to Nate and Marshall when they returned in the early afternoon. They had barely gotten inside the office when she broke the news.

"It's the men's softball team, right?" Nate asked Augusta. "Bowman did say *men's*, didn't he?"

I stood between the Keurig and the copier waiting for some of my spreadsheets to print out. "What difference does that make?"

Marshall let out a belly laugh that preceded Nate's response. "I'm factoring in our time. Bowman and Ranston need to expedite the interviews. They'll need to speak with all of the ball team members—Sun City and Sun City West. Not to sound sexist, but the men will usually answer in one or two words. Sometimes even syllables. Unlike the women. And I guarantee none of them will take out photos of their grandchildren to show us, or worse yet, contact information for their single friends who are looking for companionship."

I shook my head and chuckled. "If that isn't sexist, I don't know what is."

"Sexist or not," Nate said, "it's the truth. Go ahead, Augusta, and get a time frame from one of those deputies." Then he looked at Marshall. "That is, if it's okay with you."

"I don't have a problem. I'll flash my wedding ring. Besides, we all know we're going to wind up dealing with that case whether or not we're called to consult. Harriet's book club ladies will never give us a minute of peace if they think there's a killer lurking around their neighborhood."

Augusta propped an elbow on her desk and leaned her head on it. "There's a killer, all right. Anyone can figure that out. If it was a heart attack, they would have loaded the body onto a gurney and called it a day, not brought in a slew of county deputies. When I call them back, Mr. Williams, do you want me to ask if the man was shot, stabbed, or otherwise?"

"On second thought, I'll call Bowman myself."

"Phee said that Shirley Johnson told Deputy Bowman it was the same body she saw on Sunday by the golf course on the access path. Dead bodies don't up and move themselves. I'd be asking about that, too."

Nate and Marshall exchanged looks and tried not to laugh. "Anything else you and Miss Marple want us to ask the deputies?"

"We're fine," I said, shooting Augusta a look. "And we have work to do." When the men weren't looking, I mouthed to Augusta, "We'll talk later."

As it turned out, the remainder of the day was busy with calls and appointments, making it impossible to have an extended chat with Augusta. Even lunch was rushed—a bagged deli lunch that I gobbled down in record time. By the time Marshall and I got home, we were both one step away from collapsing.

He put a casserole into the oven and pulled out two Cokes from the fridge. "Thank goodness we're making headway on that fraud case. Makes it easier to juggle interviews."

"Did Bowman give you a time frame for the interviews?"

"He's getting the team rosters and will email the info to our office in the morning. Then Augusta can set up the appointments for the posse station in Sun City West."

"Just interviews, right?"

Marshall winked. "For now."

I knew it would never be as simple as all that and somehow, my subconscious must have known it, too, because I woke up at a little past three—wide awake and antsy. I tiptoed out of the bedroom, retrieved my half-filled marble notebook from the desk drawer in the dining area and plunked myself at the kitchen table.

A half hour later, I had completed a murder chart for Millard (Buster) LaRoo.

CHAPTER 15

I drew a stick figure of Buster in the center of the page with spikes on one side indicating what I knew about him, which wasn't much. He played softball and ran a not-so-legit lending business according to Shirley, and he was also a bookie with a small-time gambling operation according to my uncle Louis. To add to the mix, Buster sought some sort of favor or payment from Geraldine, but again, I didn't know what.

I drew some other spikes to indicate possible suspects but it was pure speculation. I might as well have been writing a crime fiction story.

There was one more spike and it was for Shirley's business card. Again, I had no idea why it would have been in Buster's possession, let alone with a threatening note on the flip side. I thought about Shirley's reaction when Bowman gave her that disturbing news and, like it or not, I knew I had to do a little digging on my own. Preferably without my mother nosing in.

My primitive attempt at the murder chart did the trick and I was fast asleep within the hour. Unfortunately, that bright-eyed and spunky feeling I had at three in the morning was replaced by a dull headache and constant yawning at six.

"Tossed and turned, huh?" Marshall asked as he watched me put a K-Cup into the Keurig without a coffee mug underneath it. "Don't press Start yet." He handed me a cup and I rubbed my eyes. "Thanks. Good thing I'm not a surgeon."

"It's Buster LaRoo's death, isn't it? And whatever seems to be connecting it to Shirley."

"Uh-huh." I told him about my three a.m. awakening and my subsequent determination to insert myself into a possible murder investigation that's best left to the professionals.

"Listen, hon, as long as all you're doing is chatting with the usual crew in Sun City West, I don't see anything wrong with that. Heck, in the past year or so you've gotten more information from Cindy Dolton at the dog park than all of us put together."

"The dog park. Don't remind me. This time I thought I'd ask Uncle Louis if he could do a little prying and find out more about Buster. Betting and gambling are Louis's middle names."

"It's a good place to start. Of course, the league manager or one of the ballplayers could have had it in for Buster as well. We should get a better sense after interviewing them."

"And the fraud case?"

"Got your old buddy Rolo Barnes working the sidelines for us. He's now trying a vegan diet and mentioned something about contamination and needing a new food processor. No doubt an expensive one."

I rolled my eyes and cringed simultaneously. Rolo Barnes was the IT specialist when Marshall and I worked for the Mankato Police Department back in Minnesota. Rolo was a techie genius with a penchant for encryption, a skill set for tracking down offshore accounts, and an uncanny ability to eke out information that the FBI, CIA, and Homeland Security couldn't get near. He was also as weird as they come, especially when it came to being paid. Since he was always on some wackadoodle diet, he preferred to be compensated in kitchen gadgetry. *Expensive* kitchen gadgetry.

He resembled a black Jerry Garcia sans the guitar, and oddly enough had an entourage of females who, like Jerry, adored him. Without Rolo, Williams Investigations would have been hard-pressed to find someone who didn't mind lurking around the dark web to get what they needed. Thankfully he was on our side.

"Too bad he can't help us with vanishing bodies. That's still quite the enigma, huh?"

"For now," Marshall said. "Once we shore up the other details, the vanishing part may come easy. I mean, someone moved the body. Trouble is, we don't know who or why. And we have no idea if the person or persons who moved Buster to the new locale by the ball field is the same person who sent him to the afterlife."

"Aargh. I really need this cup of coffee. By the way, any idea when a preliminary postmortem will be available?"

"Bowman said today but it will take another two to three days for the preliminary tox screen. Then the actual report will be at least two weeks. Hopefully, one of our suspects will crack by then. That is, *if* we can narrow down the list to a viable suspect."

"Like I said, I really need this cup of coffee."

A couple of hours later, I called my uncle Louis during break time at work and he was more than willing to snoop around on my behalf. "I'm in between gigs," he said, "with a bar mitzvah coming up a week from Saturday and a marriage dissolution a week later."

"A what? A marriage dissolution?"

"Yeah. Fancy-schmancy way of saying divorce. It's amicable and the couple will be celebrating with friends in Fountain Hills. Hey, as long as they want a saxophone player, who cares?"

Betting the odds wasn't the only thing my uncle did. He played with countless bands on cruise ships before semi-retiring to Arizona, where he teamed up with other musicians for local gigs. I thanked him and he promised to get back to me one way or the other. "I'd hand the phone over to your aunt," he told me, "but she's having her nails done. Something about autumn hues. I just nod and say 'that's nice.'"

Three hours into the day and no word from my mother. It was odd that she hadn't called considering the visit those deputies made to Shirley's house, but then I remembered it was Thursday and she and Myrna had their *Booked 4 Murder* radio show on KSCW, the local Sun City West radio station. It must have dawned on Augusta as well because seconds later she rapped on my doorjamb.

"Hurry up. You've got break time left. Your mother's show is on and it's always a hoot. Who knows what they'll be saying next? We'll keep the break room door open in case someone walks in."

Please, Mom, don't mention Buster LaRoo no matter what.

I should have known better than to expect my mother and Myrna to stick to their loosely written script about cozy mysteries, but I never imagined they'd go off the rails with the discovery of Buster's body behind the outfield.

"Remember when that unscrupulous realtor turned up dead in the protagonist's backyard in V. M. Burns's novel *The Plot is Murder*?" my mother asked Myrna. "It's no different with that ballplayer they found yesterday behind the outfield at Liberty Field."

"You mean Buster LaRoo?"

"I don't think we should be saying his name on the air."

"Well, it's too late, Harriet, I already did."

I rolled my eyes and looked at Augusta.

"See what I mean," she said. "It's always a hoot."

"Shh, I hope they don't dig themselves into a deeper hole."

"Heard the man chewed tobacco like nobody's business," Myrna went on. "Louise overheard a few of the ballplayers yesterday and told me. Maybe that's what killed him."

"No one drops dead on the spot from chewing tobacco. They get a lung disease or something. No, my money says the man was murdered."

"I don't think you can say he was murdered on the air, Harriet. We don't know yet."

"Oh, come on, Myrna, they don't send out half a dozen sheriff's cars and a forensics crew if they think it was natural causes."

Then a miracle happened. They suddenly remembered they were supposed to be discussing cozy mysteries. And like that, the conversation flipped back to a body in the basement from one of Mary Feliz's books. I let out a sigh of relief while Augusta muttered, "Darn it all. It was just getting interesting."

The muscles in my neck loosened and I leaned back in the chair for another minute or so. That's when my mother announced, "You know, if

Buster *was* murdered, and for our listening audience I'm not saying he *was*, I'm saying *if* he was, he wasn't murdered behind the ball field. Our good friend Shirley saw the body first on Sunday by the golf course access road off of Limousine Drive."

"Is nothing sacred with those two?" I shouted. "They're likely to be arrested for interfering with a murder investigation."

Augusta chuckled. "Won't be the first time."

Thankfully, something else popped into my mother's head, and before I knew it, she and Myrna were back to mysteries, cozy or not.

"What was that cozy mystery where someone stole a corpse twice?" my mother asked. "It was Ellery Queen, but I can't remember the title."

"The Vanishing Corpse," Myrna replied. "But I'd say it was more of a detective novel than a cozy."

For the next minute or so, the two of them went on and on about the different types of mystery genres before their show ended and *Classic Tunes with Roy* came on the air.

"That wasn't such a disaster, now, was it?" Augusta asked.

"Only if anyone actually listened."

CHAPTER 16

Unfortunately, the radio show's listening audience turned out to be a substantial one given the number of "Likes" on their fan page. But worse yet, Ranston had it on his radio en route to the forensics lab and phoned me.

"This is a courtesy call, Miss Kimball Gregory. Please inform your mother to refrain from discussing active crime investigations on the air. I thought maybe you'd have more clout with her than our office does."

In what world?

"Uh, sure. I'll let her know. Any word on the preliminary autopsy that I can convey to our detectives?"

"Nice try, but no. It's only been a day. By the way, have one of them call our office when they're done with today's interviews, will you?"

"Sure." I rubbed my forehead when we ended the call and then left a message on my mother's answering machine. "You're lucky this is me and not Deputy Ranston. Stop talking about Buster's death on the air. I don't feel like bailing you or Myrna out."

I didn't hear back from her until much later in the day, but by that time the damage was done. "Too bad you didn't watch the noonday news, Phee. They mentioned our show on all four networks. All four!"

"What do you mean?" I shrieked. Augusta had just transferred the call to my office and heard the alarm in my voice. She stood by my office door and mouthed, "Speakerphone."

My mother's voice blared, "Of course, they haven't released the name of the deceased, but they did call it a suspicious death and we all know what that means—murder! Plus, we know who the victim is even if the media can't share that with the public. But the one thing they *did* mention was the *new development* courtesy of KSCW."

"Oh, no. Shirley's original sighting on Sunday?"

"Yes, that. All of the stations said they'd be pursuing the matter further."

"Call Shirley and tell her not to speak with anyone."

"I did. She was in the shower but I left a message with Lucinda. She's over there this afternoon. And Thor is staying with her, too. It worked out wonderfully. Gloria Wong and her daughter are taking a few days, maybe even a week, to visit relatives in California since Shirley agreed to babysit the dog. Or vice-versa. By the way, Shirley is doing much better. *Much* better."

"I guarantee she won't be if those reporters get ahold of her. Make sure she knows to keep mum."

The rest of the day moved along with no drama. Nate and Marshall returned to the office following their first bout of interviews with the softball teams. Unlike prior interviews, they didn't look as if they'd been beaten with hockey sticks.

"Get anywhere?" I asked when I heard them arrive.

"Yeah," Augusta chimed in. "What did you dig up?"

"Little tidbits here and there," Nate remarked, "but no aha revelations. Apparently Buster fancied himself quite the ballplayer right down to a nasty chewing tobacco habit. The manager had to bawl him out on more than one occasion for chewing the stuff while he was on the field. It's not allowed in the league."

I laughed. "We know. Myrna mentioned it on the air this morning during that book club radio show. She heard it from Louise, who overhead some of the players talking about it."

Nate groaned. "Yeah, but did Myrna know Buster blew up at Lyman over the tobacco?"

"Lyman?"

"Lyman Neal, the team manager."

"A motive for murder? Lyman's pride and all?"

Marshall shook his head. "I wouldn't rule anything out but it's a weak motive at that. We'll still press on tomorrow. Anyway, I need to see what Rolo's uncovered on that fraud case. If anyone wants me, you know where to find me."

He gave my shoulder a slight squeeze and walked to his office.

"Hey, before you go, Ranston called. He wants one of you to call him back. Oh, and he asked me if I would tell my mother to not discuss ongoing investigations on their radio show."

Nate winked before heading to his office. "Have fun with that."

"They're interviewing the team players but all the real action takes place at the concession stand," Augusta said. "Anyone who's been to a game knows that. Find out who was working the stand and you'll be the one with the home run."

"I don't mind picking up chitchat from my mother's circle of friends, but I really don't want to butt into Nate and Marshall's jobs."

"Since when? That pinochle crew's bound to know who was serving up the breakfast burritos."

"I suppose I can mention it when I talk with her again."

"See, you're one step ahead of the game already."

Augusta may have had confidence in my sleuthing abilities but I sure didn't. And while I relied on hearsay and scuttlebutt, Nate and Marshall were anxious for that preliminary autopsy report since they could use it for leverage during their interviews. Lamentably, the report took longer than usual due to an undisclosed anomaly.

It wasn't until Monday afternoon when they got the staggering news. By then, a series of events had already eclipsed their plan of action, starting on Sunday when Rolo located the IP address for the computer that housed the framework for the insurance fraud. The actual address was in a gated community in Gilbert, about an hour and a half from our office and within the purview of the Maricopa County Sheriff's Office.

Armed with information and young deputies chomping at the bit to make names for themselves, Nate and Marshall took off midday Sunday for Gilbert and wound up stuck there with the deputies until late Monday. When he called me Sunday afternoon to tell me he and Nate would be spending the night camped out at a Motel 6, I was sorry I hadn't insisted he take a go-bag with him.

"Walmart sells underwear and the hotel has everything else. I'll be fine, hon," he said. "So much for enjoying the rest of the weekend with you."

"I'll be fine. Don't worry about me. It's you and Nate I'm concerned about."

"It's insurance fraud, not domestic terrorists. The only scary thing is the paperwork that will go along with it."

With an entire evening to myself, I decided to follow Augusta's advice and do a bit of sleuthing on my own. A few days ago, my mother emailed me a copy of the softball league schedule that she, along with everyone else in her book club, received from Herb. I looked at the date, and sure enough, there was a game scheduled for seven p.m. The Sun City West red team against the Sun City Sidewinders.

Without wasting a minute, I called Lyndy and kept my fingers crossed she'd be free. "How do giant hot dogs with sauerkraut sound?" I asked her.

"You and Marshall are grilling?"

"Um, not exactly. Marshall's in Gilbert on a case and I'm heading over to the baseball field in Sun City West to snoop around the concession stand. The hot dogs are on me if you come."

"Uh-oh. It's that man's death, isn't it? The one whose body was found behind the outfield. It's been all over the news."

"Yeah. I should've told you sooner but I've been really preoccupied with it. Got a minute? I'll give you the CliffsNotes."

When I finished, Lyndy was more than happy to join me. "You know I live vicariously through your exploits."

"Great! I'll pick you up at six. That should give us plenty of time to sniff around the concession stand."

"I thought you were just going to ask the vendor questions."

"I was. I mean, I am. But I also want to get a good look at what's in that building. The concession stand is only part of it. Not that I'm looking for anything in particular, especially since we still don't know what the murder weapon was, but still, I want to see if anything jumps out at me. I figured you could be the distraction."

"You mean flirt with the guy?"

"Uh-huh. And if it's a woman, talk about the ballplayers or something."

"Oh, brother."

CHAPTER 17

A combination of LED and architectural solar area lights illuminated the ball field and the surrounding area with an intensity I hadn't expected. And although I hadn't planned on running into any of Herb's cronies, or the book club ladies, the lighting would give me a heads-up.

"My gosh," Lyndy said as we walked toward the park's entrance. "This place is packed. Must be Sunday night softball is really popular in these senior communities."

"Any venue that offers food and gossip is popular. Come on, the concession stand isn't crowded yet, let's see what we can find out."

A heavyset man with a ruddy complexion was behind the counter of the concession stand, a solid structure that looked like a cross between a small cottage and a food truck. Inside were two side-by-side refrigeration units, freezer and refrigerator, as well as a smaller freezer, and a four-burner stove with a large hooded grill. A dozen or so hot dogs were on the grill and I could see an uncovered Crock-Pot with sauerkraut and another one with chili. In addition, there were assorted bags of chips and all kinds of sodas and soft drinks.

On a small table adjacent to the stand were relishes, mustard, ketchup, onions, and napkins. What struck me immediately was how meticulous everything was. The working area of the concession stand was spotless and the food prep utensils were hung by size on the wall behind the grill. I couldn't even keep our kitchen that organized. Next to that was a longer work counter with photos of ballplayers and newspaper clippings above it, and off to the left was a door with a sign that read *Office, Employees Only*.

"What can I get you?" the man asked. He wore a starched white apron over a Diamondbacks T-shirt and khaki pants. A *spotless* white apron.

"We'll take two hot dogs with sauerkraut and two Cokes," I replied, handing him a twenty-dollar bill. "Heck of a thing about that ballplayer on Wednesday. Buster LaRoo. Did you know him?"

The tongs slipped from the man's hand as he went to retrieve one of the hot dogs. "Only by name. Didn't know him personally."

Lyndy, who stood next to me, kicked my ankle and motioned to the man's cell phone, which was a few feet away on the other side of the stand. "Would you mind terribly if I used your phone for a minute? My girlfriend left hers in the car and I forgot to charge the battery in mine. I need to check in with my babysitter."

Nothing like passing for a thirty-something when you're in your forties.

The man gave her a sideways glance and shrugged. "Hang on." He walked over to the phone, tapped it and handed it to her. As Lyndy turned away from us to place her phony call, I pointed to the Crock-Pot of chili. "I didn't realize you made chili dogs. We'll take another two of those, too."

"No problem." The man grabbed one of those cardboard food trays and put everything on it.

"Do I owe you more money?" I asked.

"Nope. In fact, you've got change coming." He handed me forty-three cents just as Lyndy returned the phone.

"Thanks," she said. "Have a nice night."

With an armload of food, I hustled to the nearest bench on the stands. The game had already started and one man was on first base. "Whoa! You're a natural. You're the one with the word *detective* written all over her. What did you find out? Was Buster's name on his contact list?"

"Name and two phone numbers. Home and cell. Not enough time to write them down, especially since I called your house pretending you were the babysitter."

"It doesn't matter. We know the guy lied. Now we need to figure out why and what his connection was with Buster. Too bad you didn't get a chance to find out *his* name."

"Who said I didn't? One fast in-and-out to Google with the location of the concession stand and *voilà*! There he was. The photo was dated, but whose isn't? His name is Karl Creedman unless that's a pseudonym. Meanwhile, we've got all this food in front of us. I say we eat first and sleuth later."

Back at our seats, having stuffed our faces with enough calories to warrant a year on a treadmill, we half-heartedly kept our eyes on the game. I glanced occasionally at the concession stand and noted a growing line of at least half a dozen folks. A rustling sound behind us made me turn my head. Two men in their forties or early fifties had just arrived at the ballpark.

"Looks like Willie's rounding third," one of them said. "The Side-winders need a win. Hey, any word on who's the new bookie in town? And I'd sure as hell like to know who they put in for Buster."

"Feathers still ruffled over that?"

"What feathers? My skin's as thick as leather."

I poked Lyndy, went to the Notes section of my iPhone and typed, "They're talking about Buster. Keep listening." She nodded and I deleted the note.

"He had a sweet deal, all right. Too bad it cost you."

"Like I said, I'll get over it."

"A shame your dad couldn't make it. He hates to miss a game."

"He hates to miss a bet but he had some business that couldn't wait."

I didn't want to be obvious about turning around again so I used a tactic I'd seen on a Hallmark movie. "Lyndy," I said in an extra loud voice, "take a photo of me, will you? My selfies always look awful."

She took my phone and clicked the shot but I knew she'd aimed it at the men seated behind us. "Thanks." With that, I slipped the phone into my bag and took a sip of my Coke.

I wasn't sure how long Lyndy wanted to hang out at the game but something told me if we stuck around long enough we might hear more telling information about Buster's not-so-defunct enterprise.

"This trash should really go in the container over there." I pointed to a spot by the concession stand. "Come on, let's stretch our legs."

Lyndy stood and the two of us ambled over to the garbage bins.

"I watched that same Hallmark movie, you know," she said. "Think they know Buster?"

"For sure. I'll float that photo around and see if my mother, Herb, or any of their cohorts recognize those men. Look, I know we both have to get to work tomorrow but what do you say we stick around a bit longer to see if we can pick up any more stray conversations from those guys?"

"I was about to mention the same thing. Good grief! I'm getting as bad as you are."

Our spot on the bench was still wide open and we scootched our way into the narrow space between that and the bench in front of it. The two men hadn't left their bench and didn't seem to pay any attention to our arrival.

"Holy cow!" one of them shouted. "Spudzee hit that ball right out of the park. The Sidewinders are rolling tonight for sure."

"Crap. I had money on this game."

"Keep your britches on. Half of the men we know had money on it, too."

"You didn't mention that to those sheriff's deputies on Wednesday, did you?"

"Give me a break. It's penny-ante stuff and the last thing any of us needs is to have them sniffing around. Five and ten bucks here and there isn't going to break the bank, unless of course—"

And then, out of nowhere, a deafening cheer from the crowd as the men on second and third came in for runs compliments of Spudzee. Whatever the guy behind us was about to say got swallowed up in the excitement of the three runs.

I gave Lyndy a nudge. "Might as well call it a night."

"My thought exactly."

We slipped out of our row and walked to my car. The cheering had quieted down, along with the line at the concession stand. We were a good four or five yards past the stand when a booming voice echoed in the space between the stand and the ball field. "Extra sauerkraut on that sucker and think about what I said the last time—you should have fried fish sandwiches."

The minute I heard the word *fish* I got the willies. "Shh, it's Paul Schmidt. From the *Lake Fishing with Paul Show* on KSCW, and worse yet, the combo show he does with my mother and Myrna. The airwaves will never be the same."

Lyndy spun her head around. "It's him, all right. Walk fast!"

But it was too late. Paul had already spotted us and bellowed out a greeting that no one could miss. "Phee Kimball! I thought that was you. Or are you going with Gregory as your last name now?"

"Both," I mumbled as Paul clomped his way over to us, munching on a heavily-laden hot dog.

He took a giant bite and wiped the mustard off with the backside of his hand. "Are you scouting out the competition for Herb? I heard about that stroke of good luck he had. Oops. Bad choice of words. Guess it wasn't what you'd call a stroke of luck for Buster, huh? He was quite the third baseman, that Buster. Any idea how he wound up kissing the ground? I figured your office would be all over it by now."

I shook my head. "I know as much as you do from the local media, and so far that's not much." Then I motioned to Lyndy. "You remember my friend Lyndy, don't you?"

Paul smiled. "Sure do. Remember, you can take me up on that offer to go trout fishing anytime."

Lyndy gulped. "Uh, thanks. I'll keep it in mind."

Paul took a step closer to us and pointed to the concession stand. "If I were conducting the investigation into the late Mr. LaRoo's death, that's where I'd start."

"The concession stand? Why? What do you know?" I could barely keep still.

And maybe Augusta isn't that far off.

"The action doesn't always revolve around hot dogs and nachos."

I widened my eyes. "Are you saying the owner was involved in something nefarious?"

"I'm saying I've heard my share of gossip around here."

"Aargh. We *all* have."

"Yeah, but did you hear Buster added another B to his repertoire?"

"Another B?" Lyndy asked.

Paul all but swallowed the rest of his hot dog. "Bookmaker, bettor, and blackmailer."

CHAPTER 18

"Think there's any validity to that?" I asked Lyndy once I started the engine and eased out of the parking space.

"Paul admitted it was gossip, but still, you know how that goes."

"My uncle Louis said more than one bookie met an untimely demise by inflating the margin on bets, but you heard those two men behind us. Buster was dealing in penny-ante stuff. Those were their exact words."

"For the bets, maybe, but what about blackmail?"

"I think it's back to the old-fashioned pen and pencil paper chase. Or in this case, social media. Now that we've got a name, I'm going to do a bit of prying into that concession stand owner—Karl Creedman. Marshall will be relieved. It's a desk job."

"Let me know what you find out about that photo I took, will you? I'm kind of getting into this makeshift investigation. Beats the dull life I have so far. When the high point of my week is watching a senior softball game, I know I'm in trouble."

I dropped her off in front of her house, which was only a block or so from the place Marshall and I were renting. "I'll be sure to share every mind-boggling detail."

"Good. Call me if you want to swim any night this week."

"Absolutely."

With Marshall spending the night in Gilbert and no dinner to prepare, I figured I'd make use of my free time and see what I could dredge up on Karl Creedman. I should have known better. Other than the few lotharios I'd run into in Sun City West, most of the men didn't gravitate toward Facebook, Twitter, Instagram, or, heaven forbid, Pinterest.

Frustrated, I tried a different approach. I googled his concession stand business and pulled up a few local articles about it. Ho-hum stuff at best but it was better than nothing. The concession stand had been around since the community opened it in the late seventies, but Karl had only owned it for a few years. He acquired it in a quick turnaround when the prior owner, a man in his late sixties, passed away suddenly.

The story lines centered on the food and best-selling items, as well as some structural improvements Karl had made. Again, as ho-hum as could be. I gave up and was about to do some channel surfing when my mother called. I hadn't spoken with her since Thursday, when she called our office with the news about her radio show. I crossed my fingers this wasn't a call to tell me she and Myrna had been taken off the air for unsubstantiated gossip.

"I thought I'd hear from you by now, Phee. It's been three days. Three days! Anything could have happened."

"Uh, *did* anything happen?"

"No, but something could have. The good news is that Thor is turning out to be quite the watchdog. Shirley's now staying on her own with Herb's crew driving by every now and then."

"What about the deputy the sheriff's office posted?"

"Shirley's house is now on their drive-by list. The grumpier of the two deputies gave her that news yesterday. Deputy Bowman, right? You know the one I mean. The big guy who looks like he needs a shave. He said they didn't believe she was in any imminent danger."

"Aargh. How did Shirley take the news?"

"Fine. She said Thor was better equipped to handle an intruder than, and I quote, 'The Ferris Bueller they had posted at my door.'"

"That's a relief."

"Tomorrow she's taking her car in to be serviced. Thor's going to spend an hour or so with Streetman and Essie. Too bad you have to work. You could enjoy watching their playtime."

Or poking my eyes out with a fork.

"Lyndy and I went to a men's softball game tonight at Liberty Field."

"Not one of Herb's games? I thought I had those posted on my fridge. And since when do you like softball?"

"Since I was following up on a hunch."

"And?"

"I was going to call you in the morning. I'm emailing you a photo Lyndy took of two men who sat behind us. Their conversation may have been related to Buster's death. Tell me if you recognize them and forward it to the book club ladies and Herb, will you? Maybe one of your friends will recognize them."

"Where's your husband and Nate? Why aren't they listening in on the ballpark conversations?"

"Because they're on another case that's now in Gilbert. And they're assisting the sheriff's office, not running things for the county."

"What about that conversation? What did those men say?"

"They alluded to gambling. Small-time stuff, I think. And before you say another word, I already have Uncle Louis looking into Buster's involvement for me. Oh, and lest I forget, we ran into Paul Schmidt at the game. Does that man ever think of anything but fish?"

"Bait. He spends a lot of time on the air talking about bait when we could be discussing murder mysteries. Bait! Still, our combined show seems to be a big hit."

"Listen, it's getting late. Let me know if anyone recognizes those men. Love you, Mom."

"Me, too."

Marshall phoned at a little before ten, apologizing for the late call. He and Nate, along with two sheriff's deputies and a Town of Gilbert police officer, homed in on the source of the insurance fraud, but making an arrest turned dicey when the three suspects pulled out guns.

The standoff would have escalated, according to Marshall, had it not been for a ploy he learned from watching my aunt Ina. With his best theatrical abilities and a wadded-up piece of double-sided sticky tape that was in his pocket, Marshall tossed the tape at one of the men and shouted, "Brown scorpion!" The man's reaction gave the deputies and the police officer enough time to move in and secure the weapons.

"It'll be on the late-night news, hon," he said. "When the officer phoned it in to dispatch, the call went out to the local TV stations."

"Oh my gosh. I'll get to see you on the news."

"Uh, no. You'll get to see Officer Rosenberg and deputies Abbasi and Gilmore. With any luck, I'll get to see the inside of my eyelids. Nate and I will be back in the office midmorning. We need to complete some paperwork at this end. Hope your night was quieter."

"Compared to yours, anything would be quieter. All's well. Get some sleep. I miss you."

"Miss you, too."

We said our usual lovey things but I refrained from clouding his head with the details from my evening's escapade with Lyndy. He'd find out soon enough, especially if my mother and her crew of road yentas could ID those men from that photo.

I was up and at work before Augusta arrived. A rare feat for me considering I even made a stop to get donuts at Dunkin'.

"Was there a break-in? Is that why you're here so early?" Augusta asked the second she opened the door and saw me.

"Very funny. I never get a good night's sleep when Marshall is out on a case."

"I know. Town of Gilbert. Mr. Williams called me last night. He was concerned I'd see the news and worry. I intend to send stock photos of Mr. Williams and Mr. Gregory to all the TV stations so they can use them when Williams Investigations breaks a case. Too bad they only showed the one police officer and those two deputies."

"My aunt Ina deserves the credit, you know."

"Huh?"

"It was one of her tactics that saved the day. Usually it's a mouse or rat on the floor. Remind me to thank her."

"You've got a strange family, Phee, but I suppose you already know that."

Augusta and I chatted briefly about the insurance fraud before I told her about my sleuthing around the concession stand with Lyndy and the rather telling conversation we overheard from the men seated behind us.

"You were right, Augusta, about checking out the concession stand. With me as the decoy, Lyndy was able to snatch the owner's cell phone and guess what? Buster LaRoo's name was in his contact list. And that was *after* the owner told us he really didn't know the guy. Suspicious, huh?"

Augusta pressed her fingertips into her hair and fluffed her bouffant. "Could be. What did you find out about the owner? Knowing you, those social media sites started buzzing the minute you got home from the game."

"Dead end. Karl Creedman, that's the guy's name, isn't on social media. Drat. If he was, I could have looked up friends of friends. Meanwhile, the only thing I found were a few newsclips about the concession stand."

"Maybe you'll have better luck with those gabbers if someone can identify them."

"Oh, they'll be identified, all right. My mother's worried sick about Shirley's safety and she's convinced whoever killed Buster isn't done yet. And I'm inclined to believe that as well. That softball was no accident. Shirley must have either seen something she doesn't remember clearly or has some information about who-knows-what that may matter to Buster's murderer."

"Whoa. All of this at the break of dawn. I honestly think you do your best thinking when you're sleep-deprived."

"Let's hope that holds true for my accounting ledgers."

CHAPTER 19

It was a little before ten when I stood, rolled my shoulders, and meandered to the outer office for a coffee refill and a much-needed break. Nate and Marshall still weren't back yet but I didn't expect them until much later, even though Marshall said midmorning. Completing paperwork, especially official city and county paperwork, is like removing glitter from a worktable. There's always more.

Augusta held out the box of donuts for me when the phone rang and she picked up. "It's for you," she said the second she heard the caller.

"Not my mother," I mouthed.

"No, it's Shirley and you better take this call. She sounds frantic."

I reached for the receiver instead of an iced donut with sprinkles, but before I could say hello, Shirley exclaimed, "I'm being tailed. Followed. Watched. Heavens above, Phee, I didn't know who else to call."

"Where are you? Can you pull over to a safe place?"

"I *am* in a safe place. I'm at the Buick dealer's in Peoria."

"I don't understand."

"I brought the car in to be serviced, and when they were finished, the mechanic asked me why I had a GPS tracker underneath the rear bumper, especially since I have that old Garmin hooked up in front. He thought perhaps someone had talked me into it since he'd come across seniors who had been taken advantage of, although he did question the placement of it."

"Oh, no."

"That's not all. He said it was a Qbit brand device, usually sold on Amazon. Micro-sized with a battery that only lasts three days, so if I planned to use it to track a trip, it would be for short trips before it had to be recharged. And why it was underneath the car, he had no idea. I could barely catch my breath when he told me. I said I didn't put it there and told him to take it off and give it to me. He's doing that right now."

Ugh. And probably without gloves.

"Shirley, you need to call those deputies right away and tell them. Don't touch the thing. Maybe they can still pull prints."

"Lordy, someone *is* stalking me. Maybe they plan to make another attempt on my life. I should own a gun, shouldn't I? A nice big gun with two barrels."

"Um, I wouldn't go that far. Not to scare you further but that tracker may not be the only device. Ask the deputies to check out your house for surveillance mechanisms. If they can't do it, I'll ask Marshall to go over there after work. Right now, he and Nate are finishing up on a case in Gilbert. Call me back once you speak with Bowman or Ranston. If they don't follow you home, I'll do that on my lunch break."

"I don't want to put you out."

"After all the time *you* spend making doggie and kitty outfits for my mother's pets? It's no problem. None whatsoever. Let me know what the deputies say."

"I heard that, Phee," Augusta said. "Shirley's voice was so loud there was no need for speakerphone. If those deputies want my two cents, it's plain and clear—they need to get off their duffs and solve that murder or plan on pitching a tent on Shirley's patio."

"Funny, but we don't actually know if it *was* a murder. True, the TV and radio stations are calling it a suspicious death, but the lab is taking its dear sweet time with the preliminary autopsy report. That thing should have been completed days ago."

I should have bitten my tongue because that old adage from Aesop's Fables, be careful what you wish for, certainly applied in this case, causing Nate, Marshall, and the sheriff's office to spin their tails off before the day was out.

Shirley called me back a few minutes later to inform me that a uniformed deputy would secure the GPS device from the Buick dealer and follow Shirley to my mother's house in order for Shirley to get Thor and return to her own place.

"Did he mention whether or not anyone would be over to scrutinize your place for unwanted listening devices?" I asked.

"No, he didn't, and in the panicked state I was in, I forgot to find out."

"Don't worry. I'll make some calls. One way or another we'll check it out."

I kept my fingers crossed Bowman and Ranston would do their jobs so Nate and Marshall wouldn't have to trek over to Shirley's after the exhausting standoff they endured in Gilbert. Augusta and I figured the guys would be tired when they got to the office, but we didn't expect them to look as if they'd spent a week at boot camp.

"My eyes are glazed over," Marshall said when he flung the office door open at a little past three. "I'll take my coffee intravenously."

Nate leaned against the four-drawer file cabinet by Augusta's desk and sighed. "If I have to look at another incident report form, I may keel over."

"I thought the police filled those out, Mr. Williams," Augusta said.

"Apparently some nincompoop came up with forms for consultants and cooperating agencies as well. Lucky us. We fit the category." He walked to the Keurig, grabbed the nearest K-Cup and put it in the slot. "At least that part's done for now. All we need to do is finalize things with the insurance company."

I gulped. "More paperwork?"

"And then some, but at least you can have fun invoicing them." Marshall gave me a quick kiss on my cheek. "Still no word on Buster's cause of death, huh? We expected Bowman or Ranston to text us. It's been five days."

"They may be tied up with an exterminating job at Shirley's house," Augusta said. "And I don't mean termites."

"What?" Nate took a giant gulp of his coffee even though it was straight from the machine and hot.

I explained about the GPS device and backtracked to include my own snooping around at last night's ball game. "I get the part about the betting and possible blackmail that Buster may have been involved in, but I can't figure how Shirley could possibly fit into the mix."

Marshall rubbed his chin, and like Nate, made himself a cup of coffee. "Did Bowman or Ranston tell Shirley they'd be at her house?"

I shook my head.

"Something tells me we'll wish we were back at that standoff," Nate said. "Checking for surveillance devices is a lengthy process and one that's best accomplished in teams."

Augusta sat up at her desk, almost as if she was at attention. "Pick the team with Mr. Gregory or you'll wind up with one of those ill-tempered deputies."

I tried not to laugh. "Maybe the sheriff's office will send in a crew of its own to assist them. This day has been long enough."

And then, like a spiteful retort to my comment, texts from Bowman buzzed on Nate's and Marshall's phones.

"This can't be good," Marshall mumbled as he read the screen.

Nate didn't say a word. At least not for a full thirty or forty seconds. Then he turned to Augusta. "What time does the evening news come on the air?"

"At five on all the major networks in the valley, but the channel five affiliate, channel three, has it on at four o'clock. Why?"

I tried to read the expression on Nate's face. It was a combination of fatigue and fear.

"At four, huh? That's only a half hour from now."

Augusta was persistent. "What's going on?"

"The coroner's office released the preliminary findings for Buster LaRoo's death," Marshall said. "He choked to death on chewing tobacco."

I narrowed my eyes at Nate and then Marshall. "Choked? That's an accident, not murder."

Marshall slipped his iPhone into his pants pocket. "It's murder when the chewing tobacco is laced with poison."

"Poison? What kind? Did they say what kind?" By now Augusta was

76

nearly out of her chair. "Remember that Tylenol poisoning in the early 1980s? It was in Chicago. I remember because my aunt Beula-Mae was there on a visit. The capsules were filled with potassium cyanide. Remind me not to eat anything from Chicago. What brand of chewing tobacco? Copenhagen? That's a pretty popular one. Skoal? That's popular, too."

Nate raised an eyebrow and sighed. "Right now, the sheriff's office believes this to be an isolated incident, not a threat to the nation's health and safety. But once channel three opens the lid on Pandora's box, who knows what kind of panic will follow."

I crinkled my nose and shook my head. "I doubt the women in my mother's book club will go off the rails. Maybe if the poison was found, say, in a brownie mix or in a bin of ice cream, they might be inclined to overreact, but not chewing tobacco. And none of Herb's buddies use that stuff either."

"Not the source," Nate said, "the reality. Someone in this community poisoned Buster, and until we can determine who that was, everyone will be walking on eggshells. If they can put it into chewing tobacco, who knows where else? Or who else?"

Augusta tapped her fingers on her desk. Each tap louder than the prior one. "I'd say the sheriff's office has two question marks now—the motive and the actual poison. We don't know why Buster was killed and we don't know what did him in."

"It's another text," Nate said. "Maybe Bowman will answer your second question."

CHAPTER 20

U nfortunately, he didn't. The second text was short but definitive: *Need your assist at the Johnson house. Six pm. Text only if a no-go.*

"Looks like we got our invitation to the ball." Nate rubbed the nape of his neck.

"Yep, got mine, too," Marshall said. "At least they didn't specify a dress code."

I looked at Marshall and winced. "Six o'clock doesn't give you a whole lot of time to unwind and have a relaxing dinner, even if it's something boring that we nuke."

"How about we order pizza and wings on the office budget?" Nate asked. "Lou Malnati's Pizzeria will deliver and they've got the best Chicago deep dish around." Then he shot a look at Augusta. "It's pizza, not Tylenol, and that was over forty years ago."

"I wasn't going to say anything, Mr. Williams. Not when it comes to dinner on the house. Besides, it's too busy in those kitchens to mess around with poisons."

Augusta was true to her word and ate three fully laden slices of the giant pizza that arrived forty-five minutes later.

"Don't expect me home until late," Marshall said when I walked into the outer office at a little past five. I gave him a quick kiss while he sorted through papers at the copier. Augusta had already turned off her computer and was headed toward the door. We were stuffed from eating the most spectacular pizza I'd had in years and I made a mental note to put Lou Malnati's on speed dial.

"After two days in Gilbert," Marshall went on, "I'm not sure if I'll head straight for bed or the shower when I finally make it home."

"The shower," Augusta blurted out. She was now at the office door with a hand on the knob. "Sweat can really do a number on bed linen. Better off showering first. And brushing your teeth. That pizza sauce has a way of hanging on."

I thought Marshall would double over. "Hygiene and personal care advice are always appreciated."

It was hard for me to not laugh. "Call me, okay? Especially if you find anything sketchy. If I don't answer, it means I'm at the pool."

"No worries. Catch you later."

"Think they'll find anything?" Augusta asked as we walked to our respective cars.

"Part of me is hoping they do and the other part is terrified. Poor Shirley. Imagine being spied on."

The landline was blinking when I got inside the house and I tapped the answer machine button.

"Call me, Phee. It's your mother." I rolled my eyes and kept listening. "Shirley just told me what's going on. You should have at least warned me a sheriff's deputy would be pulling up in front of my house. I didn't see Shirley's car on the other side of the driveway and thought something awful happened. Hold on a minute, Shirley's talking."—"Yes, the GPS *is* awful but I meant life-and-death awful. I need to finish this message for Phee."—"I'm back. Call me."

I kicked off my shoes, took a breath, and reached for one of my swimsuits hoping I could convince Lyndy to join me for a quick dip. No sense picking up the phone for a knee-jerk reaction to my mother's call. I figured I'd let it marinate for a few minutes. A few chlorinated minutes with an eighty-six-degree water temperature.

"Want to take a quick swim?" I asked Lyndy, thankful she answered my call on the second ring. "I need to decompress while my mind and body are still capable of doing that."

"Don't tell me something happened since last night's ballpark escapade."

"And then some. How fast can you get ready?"

"Really fast. I was about to throw on some jeans and a top but my bathing suit is in reach."

"Good. Ten minutes?"

"You got it."

No sooner did I end the call with Lyndy when the landline rang again. Call it a second sense but I knew it was my mother so I let the machine take the call and played it back.

"What kind of deranged person puts a tracking device on someone's car? I thought that was something they fabricated for *NCIS* and *FBI*. Shirley has to meet the deputies at her place and Streetman and I will follow her and Thor over there. Call me on my cell phone. We're picking up Arby's and bringing it to Shirley's. Streetman likes the roast beef."

Of course he does. It's always about that dog.

I cringed. The very thing the deputies and Williams Investigations needed—a Harriet Plunkett circus, complete with an Arby's dinner.

At the mention of food, I knew my mother wasn't that frantic and I decided to call her after my swim. By then, she and Shirley would be at Shirley's place and I'd get an accurate update.

Lyndy was already in the water in the deep end and motioned me over. Only two other people were in the pool and they were water walking in the shallow section.

In the crisp evening air, Lyndy's voice carried across the pool to where I stood. "What's going on? How much can happen in twenty-four hours?"

I eased into the water and swam to the deep end. "It's like those never-ending car commercials at Christmas. You think they're over and then the next one starts." I told her about the standoff, the poisoning, the GPS, and the incredible Lou Malnati's pizza. Not in any particular order.

"You're saying there's a whole crew at Shirley's house scouting around for nanny cams?"

"More or less. Did I mention my mother and Streetman are there, too?"

"Yikes, no. Hope the dog doesn't go berserk."

"You and the entire county sheriff's office. Honestly, I don't know what to make of it. It's like we said yesterday, Shirley must have some information only she doesn't realize it. You know, something she may have witnessed years ago that's now coming to light."

And then, out of nowhere, a lead I'd forgotten to pursue. "Geraldine," I announced.

"Huh? Who?"

"I completely forgot about her. A while back, Shirley mentioned a woman by the name of Geraldine Kremler. She was in the same Creative Stitchers club as Shirley and wound up borrowing money from Buster. From what Shirley said, Buster kept raising the payoff amount but told Geraldine he'd drop the whole loan if she would do something for him."

"Yuck! Ew! That's horrible."

"No, not what you're thinking, although that was my first thought, too, when Shirley mentioned it."

"Then what?"

"I don't know. Shirley never got a chance to tell me because we were interrupted at the time. Then the whole thing slipped my mind until now. Please don't tell me it's an aging thing or I'll splash water your way."

"Relax. Why do you think we have so many apps on our phones and packs of Post-it notes? No one can remember anything."

"I need to find out what deal Buster offered Geraldine. He may have offered the same deal to someone else and it backfired. Business dealings gone wrong are motives for murder. Hmm, if I can find a way to broach the subject with Shirley on the phone tonight, without having my mother listen to every single word, I will."

"Think they'll find anything at Shirley's house?"

I shrugged. "If they do, it might bring them closer to finding out what's going on, but the flipside is that Shirley will be a basket case."

"Hey, at least one mystery is solved—that insurance fraud case that drove your husband crazy."

"Got to hand it to Rolo . . . He may be way out there, but when it comes to cyberspace, no one's got him beat."

We finished our swim and I promised to keep Lyndy up to date with all the things that were unraveling right in front of me. When I got home and changed into comfy sweats, I picked up the phone to see how everything was progressing at Shirley's place. No sooner did I say hi when Shirley responded with, "I've been bugged. Bugged and tailed. Nate and Marshall are in the guest room and a crew of forensic detectives are all over the place. Between you and me they don't look old enough to shave."

"What about Bowman and Ranston? Where are they?"

"Watching the forensic crew."

"Tell me, what did they find?"

"When they looked under the bumper of my car, they said the GPS device was either not the first one, or it had been removed in order to put in a new battery. They were able to tell by the sticky residue marks that secure it to the car. There were three distinct ones."

I thought back for a moment and then spoke. "The batteries on those devices are usually good for three days tops in most models and I doubt whoever kept an eye on you paid a fortune for a device that could go ten days."

"Goodness, Phee. You really know your way around surveillance."

"Uh, not really. I repeat what I hear from Nate and Marshall. But getting back to the time line, it's quite possible someone saw you discover the original dumping spot for Buster's body and decided they needed to keep an eye on you. If there were three distinct residue marks, with the last one belonging to the GPS tracker that the deputies now have, that means the time line is approximately eight days. Battery change or new device. It wouldn't matter. What matters is that someone's been keeping tabs on you for the past eight days."

"The car is one thing, but good Lord, they found something in my kitchen. In a light socket. A light socket!"

I remembered Marshall telling me once about what he called *Surveillance 101*. He said most amateurs will put a device into a light socket thinking it's the perfect hiding spot, but it's the first place seasoned forensic teams and detectives look.

Before I could respond, Shirley went on. "What did they want? They didn't take anything. Nothing was moved. Now I'm sorry I used the Swiffer to pick up after Thor when he went outside. Maybe whoever came in had dust on his shoes but it's long gone. Detectives always look for dust and footprints in all the books we read. I'm out of luck."

"Um, not necessarily. Did you throw the Swiffer pad in the garbage?"

"Lordy, yes. It's in the kitchen trash bin. Do you think the dust will tell those deputies anything important?"

"Maybe." I'd seen episodes of *NCIS* where the forensic crew was able to determine what swamp the killer had occupied, but I wasn't that naïve to believe they could do the same in Sun City West.

"If they didn't steal anything, do you think they put poison in my food? I'm going to look at every single box in my pantry to make sure nothing was tampered with."

"Let the forensic crew do that. They've been trained. Just point out the Swiffer pad."

"Lordy, Phee, whoever did this listened in on me in my own house. *My own house.* Why?"

"I think they wanted to eavesdrop on whatever conversations you had on the phone. Years ago, when everyone had rotary phones, it was easy to put a device into the receiver, but now most of us have handheld phones that sit on a charger. You can't stick a listening device into one of those. Did the deputies tell you how they think the person or persons got inside your house?"

"Persons? You think there's more than one killer after me?"

"No, no, that's not what I meant."

But it was too late. Shirley already shouted for my mother to come to the phone.

CHAPTER 21

"I'll tell you how they got in the house," my mother said. "Now that you've scared Shirley."

"I think she was nervous already. And let's focus on it being *one* person who got into her house and not a ravaging horde."

"That forensic team scrutinized the doors and windows before they came inside. They saw that the back door had been jimmied by one of those pick-ax things."

I was about to clarify with *lock-picking tools* but decided against it. "Do you know how they made that determination?"

"He showed us the scratch marks on the lock. It was a dead-bolt lock and they were still able to get in. A dead-bolt lock. I thought those would prevent anyone from entering."

"Deter, but not prevent. That's why so many people have alarm systems."

"You sound just like your husband and Nate. In fact, Nate offered to install one of those Simply Safe systems in her house. I'll stick to the one I have. Plus, I have Streetman."

Oh, no. Please don't get started on the dog.

"Do you have any idea how long they're going to be?"

"It can't be that much longer. They've been here at least an hour and a half."

"Okay. Think Shirley's going to be all right tonight?" I asked.

"Deputy Ranston—that's the one with the big jowls, right?—said they would have a car posted in front of her house until her alarm system is installed. Plus, she has Thor."

"I'm sure the sheriff's office will track down whoever was responsible."

"You don't have to placate me, Phee. It's Shirley who's a mess, but yes, we'll tell her that. Meanwhile, keep nudging your boss and your husband to figure out who murdered Buster. I wasn't born under a rock. I know that man's death and Shirley's unfortunate possible concussion are not coincidental."

As much as I wanted to ask Shirley about Geraldine, I knew that wasn't the time. I told my mom I'd catch up with her tomorrow and to call me only if it was extremely urgent. Who was I kidding? In her world, expired cream cheese in the fridge was extremely urgent. I threw in a load of wash, tidied up the place and plopped down on the couch to watch mindless TV shows.

That lasted all of fifty minutes before I got antsy and pulled out my murder chart again. I had the uncanny feeling I had missed something, but what? I had no idea. Instead of torturing myself with a number of what-ifs, I jotted down the things I needed to do:

Have conversation with Shirley about Geraldine.
Ask Uncle Louis what he found out about Buster's gambling web.
Find out from Herb if any ballplayers got stiffed by Buster.

Then I thought of something else. No one mentioned Lyman Neal, the team manager. Buster had that blowout with him over the chewing tobacco and it was uncanny that Buster's chewing tobacco had been tainted. Revenge? Poetic justice? Of course, Bowman and Ranston hadn't disclosed the poison yet, but I banked on having that information pretty soon. And hopefully from the source.

The only stroke of good luck was that the TV stations hadn't yet released the news about the poisoned chewing tobacco, but that changed with the *News at Nine* on all four stations. It was immediately followed by yet another call from my mother.

"How much more of this can any of us take? Shirley is at her wits' end even *with* a sheriff's car smack dab-by her doorstop. And now some lunatic is going around poisoning everything we eat and drink."

"Whoa. Slow down. Calm down." I wasn't sure if my words were meant for my mother or me at that point. "There is no lunatic at large and no food products have been tampered with."

"Ha! Someone probably said the same thing with that Tylenol poisoning in nineteen eighty-two. Or maybe it was eighty-three. I can't be expected to remember all those dates."

Dear Lord, not that Tylenol poisoning again.

"As far as I know, it's an isolated incident. I-so-late-ed! That means it was planned and deliberate. Aimed for Buster LaRoo and no one else. You can rest assured everything you buy at Costco's and every supermarket in between will be fine."

"Since you seem to know so much about it, what kind of poison was it and why didn't you tell me when I spoke with you earlier?"

"You were a little preoccupied, and besides, I didn't have the details. You know as much as I do. And no, Nate and Marshall don't know what kind of poison it was either."

"As soon as you find out anything, let me know. I need time to digest all of this."

Digest or give me indigestion?

"Fine. Stop worrying."

When Marshall got home, he was whipped and I didn't add to it by relaying my mother's latest call. A quick shower and he was out like a light as soon as he got into bed. It wasn't until breakfast the following morning when we had a chance to talk and I told him about my mom's call. He chuckled and said he would have been surprised if she didn't call once she caught the late-night news.

Then I learned about Rolo's unsettling text message. Nate and Marshall had both received it while they were at Shirley's house last night. It was one word—*Klingons*. That was Rolo's way of saying that whatever case he was working on still had tentacles.

"I have this sinking feeling that Rolo may have found something else related to that insurance fraud. Ugh. Nothing is ever easy, huh?" Marshall took a bite out of a bran muffin and quickly washed it down with coffee.

Rolo's one-word text messages have been known to be the worst. In the past they've meant he's deep into the dark web or whatever web he's in and won't be able to provide more info for a few days. For Nate and Marshall, it means constantly checking for emails or alerts from Rolo.

"Guess that means you're on hold for a while," I said.

"On that case, yeah, but we've still got a load of interviews to finish. It may go easier knowing Buster's cause of death. When we left Shirley's house last night, Bowman said he'd fax over the toxicology screen on the poison. That should give us some additional ammunition with the interviews."

"Mind if I follow up with Uncle Louis on Buster's loan-sharking and gambling enterprises? Last thing I want to do is get in your way or Nate's."

"You won't be in our way, hon. We're just doing the interviews at this point and assisting as needed. This is Bowman and Ranston's baby. That is, until they wave the white flag in the air and we rush in."

"Good, because I wanted to ask Shirley about Geraldine Kremler."

"Who?"

"Oh my gosh. I never mentioned her, did I?"

Marshall shook his head.

"Okay, here's the abbreviated version—she borrowed money from Buster but he said he'd drop the loan if she was willing to do something for him." I held up my palm and added, "Stop right there. Not what you think."

Marshall chuckled. "All right then, what did he want?"

"That's the problem, I don't know. I got cut off the first time Shirley mentioned it and haven't found the right time to pursue it. Meanwhile, Geraldine is living happily ever after somewhere in Nevada with her family."

"Well, as long as you're doing some sideline sleuthing, wait until Shirley's hysteria passes and see what she says."

"Sounds like she was in pretty bad shape last night."

"Not as bad as Bowman and Ranston, who had to deal with your mother and Streetman."

"Oh, no. Now what?"

"For some reason, every time one of them went within a yard of the dog, he'd snap and growl at their feet."

"What about Thor?"

"Slept on the couch and snored."

"I'm beginning to like that Great Dane."

"He's certainly a formidable presence in the house. And to the untrained eye, he does look intimidating."

"Uncanny, isn't it? Streetman is adorable, and yet he can turn into a hyena in a nanosecond."

We both laughed as we cleared the dishes and I loaded them into the dishwasher. Minutes later we hustled to get washed, dressed and off to Williams Investigations in our separate cars, as usual. I kept my fingers crossed Bowman would come through with the tox report and made a mental note to call my uncle Louis after ten thirty, his usual wake-up time.

"A musician's sleep schedule has different circadian rhythms," my aunt Ina once said, but when asked about her own penchant for waking up at the crack of noon, her own reply was "beauty sleep."

CHAPTER 22

With a fresh K-Cup of McCafé in my hand, I called Uncle Louis during my break that morning to either find out what he had dredged up on Buster or light a fire under him so that he would dredge something up.

"Phee, you must have read my mind. I planned to call you today. Hold on a moment, will you? Your aunt's yelling from the other side of the house." Then, to my aunt, "No, it's not the opera committee, it's your niece. About that murder." A second later, he was back on the line. "What I'm about to tell you is what I managed to piece together from the usual cadre of small-time gamblers in these retirement communities. Don't take it as gospel, but I believe there's some truth to it."

"What? What did you find out?"

"Apparently Buster took a decent sum of money from the softball team to purchase new equipment. Told the team manager he had a good connection and could get a great deal with an under-the-table cash purchase."

"Uh-oh. I think I see where this is going."

"After weeks of Buster's stalling and no equipment to show for the money, the team manager learned that Buster had gambled away the money. All of it."

"Wow. That's a motive for murder if ever there was one. *That*, and an incident over chewing tobacco."

"I'm not familiar with the chewing tobacco, but pocketing a large amount of money is tantamount to theft. What do you know about the team manager?"

"Not a whole lot, I'm afraid."

"I'm no investigator, and most likely the county deputies have got this covered, but I'd give that team manager a good solid look, if you know what I mean."

"Loud and clear." *The question is, how?*

I thanked my uncle and he promised to let me know if any other information wafted his way. "I'd put your aunt on the phone but she's soaking in the tub. Some sort of new morning ritual for her pores. Don't ask."

I choked back a laugh. "No problem. Have a great day."

Biting my lower lip, I pondered my next move and acted quickly before relegating it to the back burner. Herb Garrett's phone number was on speed dial since he lived across the street from my mother and if I couldn't reach her and worried, I could always call him. Thankfully today's call didn't involve my mother. At least not directly.

Herb answered on the first ring and I could tell by his reaction he was surprised to hear my voice. Usually it was "Hi, cutie!" or some similar sexist greeting that I'd learned to ignore. I suppose the shock of getting a phone call from me out of the blue might have concerned him.

"Phee? Is Harriet all right? Last I heard she went over to Shirley's house while it was being searched by the deputies. Did something happen?"

"No, no. Everything's fine. I mean, she and Shirley are fine but Shirley's place was bugged for sure. And in a roundabout way, I'm trying to find out why. I think it may have something to do with Buster's death but I'm as clueless as the next guy."

"I'm not sure I can help you but I'll try."

"Great. What can you tell me about Buster's relationship with the other guys on the team?"

"I've only been on that team for one game and we never got to finish it. 'Course, I did attend some practices with the guys."

"Uh, that's good. Were you able to pick up any hearsay about Buster?"

"Oh, it was more than hearsay. More like written in stone."

"What?"

"Let's put it this way, if Buster wasn't such a keen third baseman, they would have axed him months ago for creating unrest on the team."

"How? What did he do?"

"He stiffed the guys when it came to paying off bets."

"The guys? More than one?"

"Oh, yeah."

"Hmm, I suppose Nate and Marshall will find out for themselves. They're helping the deputies interview the players."

"I know, but those players aren't about to tell someone what patsies they were when it came to placing bets with Buster."

"Can you keep your ears open, in case you hear anything particularly telling?"

"Sure thing."

"Um, listen. I have one more question. What about Lyman Neal? The team manager. And I already know about the dustup over the chewing tobacco. And that small matter over the equipment."

"Huh? What small matter over the equipment?"

I knew as soon as I let it slip out of my mouth that I shouldn't have. "Buster owed him some money."

"Harrumph. Who didn't he owe money to? Besides, Lyman doesn't strike me as the kind of guy who'd do something he'd regret. It might interfere with his social life. In case you didn't know, he's got quite the reputation for being a lady's man. It helps when you're only in your fifties.

The rest of us have to rely on our worldly knowledge as opposed to our prowess with dating sites or whatever they use nowadays."

"Yeah, things sure have changed. Used to be the bar scenes back in Mankato."

"Oh, don't get me wrong. Lyman's no stranger to the local sports bars on weekends. Even has a favorite seat at the Peoria Tailgators on Lake Pleasant Parkway. Heard that from more than one player. And in such a short time, too. Boy, do people talk around here."

And then some.

Suddenly, I had the most peculiar thought. Men, like Lyman, weren't about to open up to detectives and/or deputies during a murder investigation interview. But what about a more covert approach?

"Very interesting. Thanks for your help, Herb."

"Hey, whatever I can do. Too bad you're working full-time. We've got another game tomorrow. This time against the Sun City Rattlers. Ha! The only thing rattling are their teeth."

"Well, good luck."

I rubbed my chin as I hit the space bar to wake up the computer. An offbeat idea brewed in my mind and I wasn't sure if I was bold enough to pull it off. Especially since I wouldn't be the one up close and personal with Lyman. But I'd be in the vicinity for whatever that was worth.

Augusta nearly choked on her meatball sub when I told her my plan over lunch. We were in the break room and had just received word from Nate and Marshall that they were "plodding on with the interviews in Sun City West."

"I think I may have a way to extract information from the team manager without having him raise an eyebrow," I said.

"*Extract*'s an interesting word. Plan to give him any Novocain?"

"I'm serious. Those men aren't about to disclose anything that would make them look like fools, especially if they'd been taken in by Buster."

"All right. What did you have in mind?"

"It kind of depends on Lyndy. And her acting skills."

Augusta's eyes couldn't get any wider. "Now you've got my interest."

"Herb told me Lyman hangs out at Tailgators on the weekends and he's quite popular with women. All Lyndy needs to do is seat herself next to him, start up a conversation and get him to open up about Buster. She's cute and personable. I wouldn't go so far as to call her sexy, but a few beers under Lyman's belt wouldn't hurt."

"She better have damn good acting skills. And when did you plan on springing this little charade on her?"

"I thought I'd call her after work and see if she's willing. She's always been amenable to helping me out."

"Sure, in a library looking up stuff, or going door to door in broad daylight with a few questions, but cozying up to some guy at a bar? Like I said, her acting prowess better be Oscar-worthy."

"Forget *her* acting prowess. I need to work on mine. I'm the one who has to convince her!"

"And you think your husband is going to go along with this latest idea of yours?"

"After a day of interviewing tight-lipped senior ballplayers, he'll pay to give Lyndy acting lessons!"

CHAPTER 23

"You've got to be kidding me!" Lyndy exclaimed when I called her after work. It was a little before six and Marshall was still in Sun City West with those interviews. "I can barely carry on a conversation on a blind date, let alone pretend to be Mata Hari."

"You're not spying for the war effort, only trying to find out if Lyman was so angry with Buster that he spiked the guy's chewing tobacco with poison."

"I'd rather find out military secrets."

"Seriously, Lyndy, I can't do it. Everyone knows who I am and if they don't, my mother will distribute a vita. Besides, it's not as if you'd be totally on your own. I promise, I'll be seated at a nearby table, most likely with Marshall, and if he can't make it, I'll find someone else."

"I have absolutely no acting skills. None whatsoever."

"That won't be a problem. I know someone who does, and with a little bit of coaching, you'd be able to give the most seasoned spy a run for his or her money."

"Honestly, Phee, if it wasn't for the fact that poor Shirley is probably tearing the hair out of her head, I'd tell you to forget it."

"So you'll do it?"

"I suppose."

"Great. It needs to be this Friday."

"This Friday? That's only three days from now. Three days!"

"Relax. I need to make one more call to get you acting lessons."

"Someone in a theater group?"

"Better yet, my aunt Ina."

Suddenly, the line went dead. Or at least I thought it went dead. Seconds later, Lyndy spoke. "Your aunt Ina? Maybe I could just google acting tips on the internet."

"Trust me. It will be fine."

Who on earth was I kidding? *Trust me and it will be fine?* I sounded like a shady politician. Thankfully Lyndy didn't balk and I went on to my next phone call—Aunt Ina.

"Oh, my." My aunt's voice was more animated than usual when I explained the situation. "I'm simply flattered. Flattered that you consider my acting skills to be of such quality that you sought me out to assist with a murder investigation. When do I begin?"

"You don't have much time. The performance, for lack of a better word, is this Friday night at Tailgators in Peoria."

"Wonderful timing. Louis has a gig that night at Lake Pleasant. It's only a few miles from there. He can drop me off and you can take me home. And, fortunately for your friend, my modern mystics group had to cancel their regular meeting that night because two of the women developed shingles."

"Uh, what about tomorrow night? Can you coach Lyndy that night, too?"

"Oh, dear. I'm afraid not. Louis and I have a Mediterranean cooking class at Grand Learning. He's gotten quite adept at sautéing mussels and clams."

"Okay. Thursday it is. I hope Lyndy's a quick learner."

With everything in place at my end, I had to be certain Lyman would be filling a chair at the bar on Friday. That meant a third phone call. I grabbed a Coke from the fridge and plunked myself on the couch.

"Hey, Herb, it's Phee again. I know we spoke a little while ago but I may have found a way to get Lyman to open up. Any chance you or someone from the team could make sure he shows up at Tailgators Friday evening? Say around eight?"

"I'll put a bug in his ear after tomorrow's game. Maybe even offer to buy him the first drink if we win. It doesn't take much to talk him or any of the other fellas into going to a sports bar. Hmm, now that I think of it, I'll spread the word with the pinochle crew. We could all use a change of venue from Curley's."

"Great. Thanks."

"Aren't you going to tell me what you have in mind? Not your husband giving him the third degree?"

"No, no. Nothing like that. Friendly chitchat, that's all."

"Works for me."

With three days before "showtime," I worried my mother would get wind of it and drag the book club ladies to the sports bar, where they'd whine and complain about the food. That prompted yet another phone call. This one brief and to the point.

"Whatever you do, Aunt Ina, don't tell my mother about Friday night."

"Don't be ridiculous. Between you and me, she's always been jealous of my acting skills. And yes, yes, I know she was in that production of *The Mousetrap*, but my skills are far more refined. Your clandestine operation is safe, dear."

Safe, maybe, but I still had one more conversation to go. This one with Marshall when he finally got home.

"If it means we can sit in a dark corner and eat juicy hamburgers with greasy fries and onion rings, then more power to Lyndy," he said. "Do you have any idea how hard it is to conduct an interview with those guys? Prying open a clam with my fingers would have been easier. Look, if

Lyndy can get Lyman to open up about Buster, even if it's minor information, it will be more than any of us are able to find out."

I gave him a long hug and an even longer kiss. "If nothing else, the bar food should put a smile on your face. We're having salads and yogurt for dinner tonight. Part of eating healthy."

• • •

Nothing earthshattering happened at Herb's game on Wednesday, according to my mother, who caught the last few innings before joining the ladies for an early dinner at the Homey Hut. She called Wednesday night to let me know Shirley had calmed down enough to eat a full-course meal and a slice of apple pie.

The deputies continued to check hourly on her house but there were no further signs of any intrusions. The same sense of serenity, temporary as it may have been, could not be said for Williams Investigations.

Rolo was adamant he had uncovered a key player in that insurance fraud but needed more time to sort things out. That meant he was navigating the dark web with extreme caution.

• • •

"Aargh," Nate grumbled Thursday morning as he carried his morning coffee into his office. "And just when we were ready to wrap things up." Marshall was off on another case. This time searching for a birth parent believed to be in the Tolleson area, not too far from us.

I approached the morning with heightened energy in preparation for my aunt's coaching session with Lyndy. We planned on meeting at Lyndy's house so that Marshall could relax at home without listening to my aunt's soliloquies and heaven knows what else. Then, the proverbial roof caved in. My aunt called at a little before eleven to tell me she couldn't make the coaching session because her sciatica acted up and she needed a long day with full body soaks.

I want a long day with full body soaks too, but that's not about to happen.

"Don't worry, Phee," she said. "I have a foolproof plan. I'll sit on the sidelines while Lyndy strikes up a conversation and I'll subtly direct her with facial and body movements. I've had tremendous experience with improvisation and pantomime."

Just what Lyndy needs—on-the-job training.

"Um, I'm not so sure—"

"It will be seamless. Have faith in your aunt."

"I, um, er . . ."

"You said you thought the team manager would arrive at eight. To be on the safe side, I'll have your uncle drop me off at seven. We can nurse a ginger ale or something while I go over the logistics with your friend."

The plan had all the earmarks of a disaster but I didn't have much choice. Not if I wanted to get information out of Lyman. I reluctantly agreed and took a deep breath before shooting off a text message to Lyndy.

At a little before two, I got her response—*You are SO going to owe me for this one.*

At least she didn't back out. Although in retrospect, it might have been the best move anyone of us could have made.

Augusta shook her head when I told her about the change in plans. "Improv, huh? That should be a doozy. I'd go for the sheer entertainment but my canasta group has a game on Friday."

"Don't worry. I'll give you the sordid details on Saturday. It's one of my half days."

Sordid details was right. Sordid *and* bizarre. I still twitch when I think of that evening. It was a Friday night for the books, that was for sure.

Since Tailgators was close to where Lyndy, Marshall, and I live in Vistancia, Lyndy drove herself there and was already seated at a corner table when Marshall and I walked in. It was a little before seven and the place was already teeming with patrons. Herb had mentioned that there'd be plenty of room at the bar since the after-work crowd usually dissipated around eight, paving the way for the more serious drinkers and sports aficionados.

"Is Lyman at the bar?" I asked Marshall. "You're the only one who knows what he looks like."

Marshall turned slightly and looked. "I don't see him. He's tall, in his fifties, salt-and-pepper hair but mostly pepper, and in good physical shape. No beard or mustache and no discernible tattoos. How's that for my attention to detail?"

"I'd give you an A. Come on, Lyndy's waving us over."

No sooner did we seat ourselves at the small rear table where Marshall and I would camp out for the remainder of this production, when a flash of color illuminated the entryway. Drat. I should have told my aunt not to be obvious, but maybe the outfit she had on was her idea of demure.

As far as her wardrobe was concerned, my aunt never left Woodstock. That night she arrived in a cascading teal and gold caftan with a paisley print that all but blinded anyone who caught a glimpse of it. Her long grayish brunette braids hung down her chest and were woven with teal and gold ribbons. If that wasn't shocking enough, she chose to wear enormous gold earrings that were comprised of various orbs and some sort of sea creatures. The earrings started at her lobes and ended at her shoulders.

"Quick!" I said to Marshall. "Usher her over here before she calls attention to herself."

He gave me a look and laughed. "I think it's a little too late for that."

CHAPTER 24

All eyes were on my aunt as she made her way to our table. She stretched out her arms like Moses parting the Red Sea. Heaven forbid any patrons got in her way.

"There you are!" she exclaimed. "If this place was any darker, it would be a movie theater."

Before I could say anything, she extended her hand to Lyndy. "You must be my new protégé. Ina Melinsky, Phee's aunt."

Lyndy looked shell-shocked. "Um, nice to meet you as well. I believe we may have crossed paths at other events."

My aunt nodded. "Quite possibly. Quite possibly. Hmm, we don't have much time so I'll try to be clear and succinct. Since we can't rehearse or role-play, you'll simply have to follow my offstage directions."

"Offstage directions?" Lyndy looked totally lost and Marshall widened his eyes.

"Yes," my aunt went on. "First, I'll demonstrate a few techniques for getting and holding a man's attention and then, when you're actually seated next to the suspect, all you need to do is look my way and I'll demonstrate the technique you need to copy."

If this doesn't have CATASTROPHE written all over it, it will.

"I'm not sure I can—"

"You'll be fine, dear. Let's begin with the hair toss. True, true, it's a hackneyed technique but it does get results. Watch me and pretend I have shoulder-length hair like you do."

My aunt leaned her head back as if she was about to swoon and then, with one hand, brushed the imaginary shoulder-length hair from the side of her face while offering a close-mouthed smile.

"Now, you try it."

Lyndy brushed away some hair as if she was swatting at a fly and forced a smile. Just then, the waitress came over to our table to take our drink orders. Ginger ale for my aunt, beer for Marshall, and white wines for Lyndy and me. When the waitress walked away, my aunt resumed the acting lessons.

"Try to make slower, more deliberate movements. Now, let's try the all-attentive nod."

"The *what*?" I asked.

"It's a nod that involves intense eye contact. Meant to connect the listener to the speaker."

Again, my aunt demonstrated and Lyndy did her best to mimic it.

"Wonderful," my aunt exclaimed. "Now for the lean-in. It's really self-explanatory. Simply lean closer to the speaker and feign interest."

"I guess I can do that," Lyndy said, "but I'm not sure about striking up a conversation."

"Ah, yes, the accidental bump or elbow. Usually the man initiates the conversation but I'm from a different generation. If he sits there like a log, stand as if you're about to leave and bump into him."

"He'll think I'm snookered."

"Tell him the floor's slippery. See what that does."

"I'm not comfortable with any of this," Lyndy said.

"Just glance my way and follow my lead."

"It's so dark in here I'll be squinting. Too bad you can't be seated closer. I know, I know. Too obvious."

Our waitress arrived with our drinks and I couldn't wait for that first sip of wine. "Be yourself," I told Lyndy.

"Be myself? I don't frequent bars on my own."

"Act casual then. If he asks, tell him you're meeting a girlfriend and she's running late."

"Okay, I suppose."

"You'll be fine," I said. "I love that V-neck black top with the jeans. Very chic."

"Let's hope Lyman doesn't give me the brush-off."

Then, the *pièce de resistance*. My aunt reached into a floral satchel that she had placed on the table and handed Lyndy a piece of paper. "In case Phee didn't get a chance to write down the questions you'll need to ask." Then she glanced at me. "I took the liberty of writing down interrogation questions. I'm not totally unfamiliar with police procedural mysteries."

Marshall nearly choked on his beer. Then, she turned back to Lyndy. "And don't worry, you won't have to memorize them in such sort time. Look at me and I'll mouth the words to you."

"Let me see that paper, Aunt Ina. Hmm, looks like you started with an introductory greeting."

"Of course I did. Lyndy can't very well walk over to the man and give him the third degree. She needs to warm up first. Maybe even another glass of wine."

"Sounds good to me." Lyndy sat up tall in her chair and scanned the room. "Where's our waitress?"

"All you need to do is master the greeting and take it from there," my aunt said. "Give it a read. With emotion. Sincere emotion."

I rolled my eyes and listened to Lyndy's voice. It wasn't exactly animated, but after all, it was just a practice run. "Hey, I recognize you. You're Lyman Neal, the softball manager in Sun City West. Can't remember where I saw your picture, though. Maybe in the *Independent* with the team. Gee, what an awful thing about Buster LaRoo."

"Now give that greeting a bit of pizazz," my aunt said.

Marshall shook his head. "No time for pizazz. That's Lyman now. Hurry up if you want to grab the stool next to him. Looks like you've got your pick. Three seats at the bar opened up."

Lyndy stood, wineglass in hand, but feet glued to the floor. "I'm terrified."

My aunt patted her on the elbow. "No need to worry. Keep one eye on me and you'll be fine."

Famous last words.

As Lyndy walked toward the bar, my aunt whispered, "Stand straight. Posture is everything."

I watched with anticipation as Lyndy moved closer to where Lyman was seated. I hadn't been that anxious watching anyone walk since my daughter Kalese, now in her twenties and teaching in St. Cloud, took her first steps.

"Take a breath, hon," Marshall said. "The eagle has landed."

"Landed, but what about laying an egg?"

The three of us watched intently. At first, no movement whatsoever on Lyndy's part, but finally it appeared as if she turned and said something to Lyman. Unfortunately, my aunt must not have noticed because she immediately elbowed me in an exaggerated gesture that only the Marx Brothers could have come up with.

"Forget the bump or the elbow," I groused. "We're past that. See for yourself."

My aunt swayed to the side of her chair and looked at the bar. "She needs to keep the conversation moving."

"Can you walk past there?" I asked Marshall. "Act like you're going to the men's room?"

My aunt grabbed Marshall's arm. "Hold off a minute. Lyndy's looking this way."

"This might go better if I took a seat at the bar," Marshall replied. "I'd be in close range but not right on top of them. Herb was right about the proverbial changing of the guard."

I nodded. "Good idea."

Marshall was able to plunk himself two seats away from Lyman and three from Lyndy. Meanwhile, my aunt kept brushing the imaginary hair from her face as if she had developed a twitch. "Finally!" she gasped. "Lyndy's giving her hair that come-hither flip."

"I wouldn't exactly call it *come-hither.* I think it just got in her way."

Then the worst thing imaginable happened and nothing in the world could have prepared us for it—Paul Schmidt meandered into the bar, spied the vacant seat next to Lyndy and took it. The words *train wreck* sprung to mind but it wasn't a train wreck. It was apocalyptic.

"You need to get over to the bar, Aunt Ina, and put your acting skills to the test. Take a good look. That's Paul Schmidt from my mother's horrific mystery and lake fishing show. Any second now he's going to snare Lyndy and start talking about trout. Or bait. Or anything that has to do with fins and grubs. We've got to salvage this mess before it's too late. Hurry up. Do something!"

My aunt wasted no time. She flitted her way to the bar like a firefly, brushing anyone and everyone aside who was in her way. I watched speechless as she hurried toward him but it was already too late. Paul had his arm on the back of Lyndy's bar chair and had taken out a stack of what I presumed to be photos of fish, lakes, and bait. I took a closer look and cringed. I was right. Although I couldn't see the photos from where I sat, I was certain it was the same stack he had shared with the book club ladies numerous times at Bagels 'n More.

Wonderful. A killer will never be caught because Paul Schmidt just has *to share his fishing photos with anyone he comes in contact with.*

CHAPTER 25

M y aunt glanced my way and I motioned for her to return to our table. Poor Lyndy, she was a fly in Paul's spider-web. Just then, I heard Marshall's voice. It all but boomed across the bar. "Paul! I thought that was you!"

Marshall got up from his seat near Lyman and hurried over to Paul. I wasn't sure if my husband's voice was loud due to the bar chatter or because he wanted me to know what he was up to. "Are those new photos of your latest catches? Let me have a look."

Before Paul could respond, Marshall wedged himself between Lyndy and Paul, feigning interest in whatever snapshots Paul had taken.

"Hopefully Marshall will keep Paul occupied long enough for Lyndy to get Lyman to open up," I said to my aunt.

She cocked her head toward the bar and then shook it. "I don't think so. He keeps shoving those photos in front of your friend." And then, without warning, Paul got up from his seat and raced out the door. I grabbed my phone and texted Marshall—*Did U insult him or what?*

Marshall pointed to the entranceway and texted back. *No, I complimented his latest catch and he flew out of here.*

Since Marshall and I weren't conversant with texting lingo, by the time I received his text, it was too late. Paul rushed back into the bar with a green five-gallon pail and set it on the floor between Marshall and Lyndy.

"Oh, holy crap!" I exclaimed to my aunt. "The photos weren't enough. He had to bring in the damn fish."

Next thing I knew, Lyndy shrieked, *"Ew!"* and as she stood, her drink fell directly into Lyman's lap. I closed my eyes and wished the night would end.

"This is a disaster," I said. "A complete and total disaster."

My aunt stood, walked a few steps toward the bar, and returned to our table. "Not as bad as you think. See for yourself. Lyndy handed him a cocktail napkin."

"A cocktail napkin? Heck of a lot of good that's going to do. Wait a sec. The bartender's handing Lyman a towel."

Meanwhile, Marshall did his best to keep Paul focused on the prize catch in the green pail.

"We've got to get Paul and his fish out of here," I said, "or Lyndy won't have a chance to get information out of Lyman."

My aunt adjusted one of her earrings. "Hmm, seems like the only one leaving is Lyman. "Wait! He's motioning for Lyndy. They're moving over to that table near the popcorn machine. I'll be darned. I knew my coaching skills were good, but this far surpasses anything I could have imagined."

"Do you have any talent in getting someone to disappear? If I'm not mistaken, Paul slapped a huge fish on the bar. Oh, no! Now he's holding it up and waving it around for everyone to see."

"At least Lyndy's no longer seated next to him. Maybe Marshall can get him to put the fish back in the bucket before—"

But it was too late. With fish in hand, Paul charged past the popcorn machine. I watched in horror as he then made his way to Lyndy's table. Marshall was at his heels but never got to the table because my aunt, in an effort to remedy the situation, thundered toward the men, caught her caftan on the edge of table and fell forward, knocking down a waitress with a full tray of drinks. And while my aunt quickly recovered, the same could not be said for the waitress.

I prayed for the ground to open up underneath me as I moved closer to them. *Dear Lord—Why doesn't this state have sinkholes?*

But that wasn't the worst. The worst came when Paul, with fish in hand, spun around at the sound of the crash and dropped the fish on the waitress's head. Its tail slipped down to the open cleavage of her silky blouse, causing her to bellow as if she was about to be devoured by a shark.

Wasting no time, Paul tried to snatch the fish from her blouse, creating what could best be described as "the debacle from hell."

"Get your hands out of there!" the twenty-something waitress screamed. Her long blonde hair got tangled in what I believed to be the fish's fin or maybe even its tail. I was only a few feet from her but it might as well have been a mile.

By now, patrons had left their tables and bar stools to assist, but Paul fought them off with one hand while trying to grab the fish with the other. I saw Lyndy and Lyman both stand, but with so many people crowding the area, they couldn't make a move.

"Stop!" The waitress fended Paul off with a broken beer bottle while trying to extricate the fish from her hair.

Paul was undaunted. "I'm trying to help. Don't squeeze that trout too hard or I won't be able to grill it."

"Grill it? Are you insane?" She tugged and pulled at the thing, all the while getting it more tangled in her hair.

"Lucky for you I always carry a filet knife with me," Paul said. "I'll snip off some of that hair of yours and—"

With a firm grasp on the broken bottle, the waitress glared at Paul. "Make one move with the knife and I'll slice your throat!" She managed to stand but the broken glass beneath her, coupled with the spilled drinks, made it impossible for anyone to get near her without slipping or falling. Still, Marshall made a valiant attempt and tried to usher Paul away.

"I can still salvage that trout," he bellowed, ignoring Marshall's coaxing.

"No one's salvaging anything," the distraught waitress screamed. "Get away from me, everyone!"

I watched, speechless, as she continued to wrangle the fish from her hair and her blouse. By now, the once-edible trout had become a slimy mess with its innards oozing from it. I tried not to look. Finally, with enough tugging, she freed the fish, tossed it in the air, and bolted to the kitchen.

Seconds later, two kitchen helpers and a waiter arrived with a mop and a garbage can.

"Waste of a good trout," Paul grumbled. "I better get the rest of my catch home before it gets destroyed."

I opened my mouth to speak, but before I could say a word, he stomped his way to his bar stool, snatched the green pail, put what looked like some dollar bills on the bar, and exited the place without further ado.

Marshall, meanwhile, helped my aunt return to our table lest she trip on the wet floor. "Well," she said. "This isn't going exactly as planned."

You think?

"It might be going better than we think." He held out a chair for me and then took his. "Seems to me Lyndy and Lyman are hitting it off. See for yourself. They're laughing and looking right at each other."

I looked over my shoulder. "Who wouldn't be laughing after that circus? Except maybe the waitress. I hope this isn't one of Paul's favorite haunts because he's going to be persona non grata before closing time."

My aunt adjusted herself in her seat. "Maybe I could discreetly mosey past their table on my way to the ladies' room and see how Lyndy's getting on. You know, pause a bit when I get near them and see what conversation I can pick up."

"Um, I think maybe we ought to leave things alone. We've had enough excitement for one night."

I never should have uttered those words, because the moment they left my lips, Herb and the four other men in his pinochle crew, Kevin, Kenny, Wayne, and Bill, came through the door and charged the vacated table adjacent to where Lyndy and Lyman were seated.

"Oh, look," my aunt said. "There's Herb and his friends. Did you know they were coming here as well?"

I knew, all right, because I was the one who asked Herb to put a bug in Lyman's ear in the first place, but it had slipped my mind once my aunt began her coaxing lessons with Lyndy. Then the Paul Schmidt melee. It was a wonder there was anything left in my mind at all.

"Hey, cutie!" Herb's familiar voice rang out. He was at our table in seconds. "Thought that was you. What are you folks doing hiding out in that dark corner? We can move a few chairs over and all sit together." Then to Marshall and my aunt, "What's going on? I've seen happier people at a funeral."

"This is supposed to be a covert operation," I whispered to Herb. "Lyndy's with Lyman if you haven't already noticed, and we're keeping our fingers crossed she can find out if he had it in for Buster."

"Oh, so *that's* the bit of chitchat you referred to a few days ago when you wanted me to talk Lyman into coming here. Turned out he didn't need convincing. Hey, what happened over there?" Herb pointed to the spot where the waitress dropped her tray. "Looks like a regular cleanup crew in action. Someone toss their cookies?"

"No," I replied. "It was a fish. And one of Paul's, to be more precise. And don't bother looking for him. He and his bucket of trout left already."

Herb chortled. "Darn it. We missed all the fun."

CHAPTER 26

Herb looked directly at Lyman's table and then back to me. "Don't you think he'll figure out it's a setup? He's not stupid."

"Shh. He doesn't know Lyndy. If we can all stay out of their way, she might be able to glean some information. Heck, nothing else worked."

"You think Lyman could be our boy? Doesn't strike me as a killer."

I sighed. "They never do."

Just then, Kenny shouted, "We're ordering two pitchers of beer for starters. Get your butt over here, Herb."

"Wait," I said. "Your table is right next to Lyman's. Whatever you do, don't discuss the murder. Your voices carry."

"I can't put a gag order on the guys. You know the pinochle crew. Anything can come out of their mouths."

"Then change the subject if that happens. And don't go prancing over to Lyman's table."

"I can't very well ignore the man. He's the team manager, for goodness sake."

"Give him a wave, lift a beer, and call it a night. Don't do anything that will mess it up for Lyndy."

Then Herb turned to Marshall and my aunt. "Are Louis and Harriet floating around somewhere?"

I froze. "No. My uncle is at a gig and don't you dare call my mother. That's all we need."

"Sheesh." Herb started for his table and then pivoted back. "If you find out anything juicy, tell me. I put the bug in Lyman's ear about coming here. It's the least you can do."

"If anyone finds out anything juicy, I guarantee it will be on the news before we get to spread it around."

"Don't worry," Marshall said. "We won't leave you out of the loop."

Can we leave him out in the cold?

Herb returned to his table and I thought perhaps the original plan would continue without incident. Little did I know I had entered the world of "ignorant bliss" because a minute later my aunt exclaimed, "I knew I forgot something—the eyelash batting."

"The *what*?" Marshall furrowed his brow and took a drink.

"Batting her eyelashes," my aunt replied. "It's an extremely effective means of flirting. Centuries old."

I shrugged. "Frankly, I wouldn't worry about it now because—"

I never finished my thought. My aunt immediately sat upright, leaned toward Lyndy's table and cleared her throat with such gusto that everyone's head in a ten-foot radius turned our way. That's when she demonstrated the move. She fluttered her lashes as if her eyes were strobe lights.

All of a sudden, Lyman stood and shouted, "Someone help that woman over there. I think she's having a stroke. Call nine-one-one." He flew toward us, bumping into the back of Marshall's chair.

My aunt turned her head from side to side and looked. "Who's having a stroke?"

"I thought you were," Lyman said. "The way your eyes were moving and all."

Compared to this embarrassment, Paul's dead fish is nothing.

My aunt was aghast. "I'm perfectly fine, thank you. I was only demonstrating a technique for . . ." And then she looked at Lyndy, who stood inches from Lyman. "A technique for getting something out of one's eye."

Lyman shifted his gaze from my aunt to me, and then to Marshall. "Say, aren't you one of those detectives the sheriff's office sent over to interview the Sun City West Men's Softball Team? I'm their manager."

Marshall raised his palms in mock surrender and chuckled. "Marshall Gregory, Williams Investigations. I take it you had the pleasure of being interviewed by one of the deputies and not our firm."

"Actually," he said, "I had the pleasure of being interviewed by the lovely lady standing next to me."

Lyndy gasped. "How did you know?"

Lyman smiled. "Most women I meet talk at length about themselves. You were the first one who professed an interest in men's softball and went so far as to pry into every detail regarding the equipment purchases Buster LaRoo was supposed to make. Only someone familiar with how that plays into an investigation would have asked that."

"I'm sorry, everyone," Lyndy said. "From now on I'm sticking to medical billing and late-night swims." Then she mouthed, "I really blew it" to me.

"It's not your fault," my aunt said. "I didn't have sufficient time to adequately coach you."

Lyman gave my aunt a sideways glance. "Are you a private investigator as well?"

It's a good thing I didn't have food or drink in my mouth or I would have choked to death.

"No," my aunt responded. "I'm a seasoned actress whose skills are sought from time to time by various agencies."

There weren't enough mental eye rolls I could muster but I gave it my best shot. "This is my aunt, Ina Melinsky, and I'm Phee, Marshall's wife. Lyndy's our friend."

"Look," Marshall said, "no sense having the both of you stand there, we've got empty seats at this table, sit down for a bit."

"Thanks." Lyman held a chair for Lyndy and then spoke. "I might as well bring our drinks over here and tell one of the waitstaff. I have a funny feeling we won't be seeing our original waitress."

"The blonde?"

He nodded. "Don't think she'll want to serve seafood for a while."

All of us burst out laughing as Lyman walked over to their table to grab the drinks.

"He's really nice," Lyndy whispered. "Really, really nice."

I whispered back. "Don't get too attached. He could be our killer."

Lyman handed Lyndy her wine and took a seat. "I have to say, this was a far cry better than that miserable experience I had with Deputy Ranston. Twitchy fellow, huh? And irritable, too."

"You caught him on a good day," I said. "Sadly, the investigation is stalled. The ballplayers are pretty tight-lipped so that's why we tried a different approach. And Lyndy offered to help. Honestly, the sheriff's office had no idea."

Leaning back in his seat, Lyman let out a slow breath. "Okay, what would you like to know?" He looked at Marshall. "I already explained that Buster gambled away team money that was supposed to be used for the purchase of new equipment. Why I ever trusted that guy is beyond me, but everyone can get duped once. It was no secret Buster was into all sorts of small-time nefarious operations but nothing that warranted his murder."

"Like what?" I asked.

Lyman shrugged. "Loan-sharking, bookmaking, that sort of thing. The deputy took copious notes. I thought maybe Buster had a beef with someone and it escalated, but according to the news that came on earlier this week, the guy had been poisoned. I'm no detective but poisoning someone takes planning. That means whoever did it thought it out."

Marshall and I nodded simultaneously as Lyman continued. "Not to put my guys down, but from what I've seen, no one on my team appeared to be that meticulous. Heck, some of them were downright lackadaisical when it came to playing the game. In their minds it was, 'Go up to bat, bat the ball, and run if it's a hit.' I kept telling them to have a plan when they came up to bat, but did they? Heck, they'd hit a seagull if it showed up before the ball. And nothing has changed."

Lyndy gave Lyman's arm a shake. "What about fans or spectators? Did Buster ever mention crazed fans or anything of the sort?"

"He was a good third baseman but not a reason to draw a crowd. Nah, if anyone *was* in the stands to watch Buster, it was to wait until the game was over in order to shake him down for money owed."

The five of us chatted awhile about Buster but the conversation gradually drifted off to other topics. At a little before ten, Lyman said he had to get going since he had a busy day ahead. Then he asked Lyndy if she'd speak privately with him. As Lyndy stood, I mouthed the same words I did earlier—"could be our killer"—but it was too late. She had that glazed gaga look on her face that meant one thing—she'd been taken in by him.

CHAPTER 27

"He asked me out," Lyndy said. She rushed back to our table as soon as Lyman had left Tailgators. "Tomorrow night. For dinner. He's going to pick me up at seven thirty and we're going to Twisted Italian on Happy Valley Road." Then she plunked herself back in her seat, put her elbows on the table and propped her head in the palms of her hands. *Yep, still the same star-gazed look on her face.*

"Honestly, I don't think he's a murderer. He's much too charming," she went on. "Funny, but we only spoke for a little bit but I was so comfortable around him. I'd get a bad vibe, wouldn't I? I mean, if the man spelled danger. Don't you think?"

Does the name Ted Bundy sound familiar? He was cute and charming.

"I'm sure you have nothing to worry about," my aunt said. "It's not as if he's going to pick you up and abduct you. He knows those deputies and Williams Investigations have their eyes on him."

"Boy, if that isn't unsettling, I don't know what is. This is the first real date I've accepted since I moved out here. Not that I haven't been asked but up until now I wasn't interested. Oh, brother. I better not be falling for a killer."

"I think you can relax," Marshall said. "His motive for doing away with Buster is as weak as they come, but he may have more insight into who might have had a genuine reason to send Buster to his final resting place. That's what I hoped we could find out. Unfortunately, things didn't go as planned."

Lyndy smiled. A great big Cheshire cat grin. "No, they went better."

"Tomorrow night, huh?" I reached for a handful of mini-pretzels that were on the table next to a small bowl of nuts. "You can still eke out information from him. Get him to open up about the ballplayers and any possible motives."

"Goodness, Phee," my aunt said. "She's not Agatha Raisin or Miss Marple. Now those two would have been able to get Lyman to slip up and mention the poison that was used to kill Buster."

"Oh my gosh. The poison! I'd forgotten all about it." I turned to Marshall. "When Bowman faxed that information to our office last Monday, did he specify the poison? Augusta didn't say."

Marshall groaned. "The preliminary tox screen was incomplete. All it said was suspicion of plant-based poison. That could have been anything. Bowman said we'd have the complete report tomorrow morning. My guess is that Augusta will have devoured the contents while the paper's still warm from the fax machine."

My aunt fiddled with her earrings. "Plant-based poison? Hmm, that's something female killers are likely to gravitate toward. Most women aren't comfortable with guns or knives. And forget the heavier implements like axes or bats. Too unwieldy. But a nice household-plant-based poison is likely within their comfort zone."

I steepled my fingers and leaned my head into them. "That's an interesting point." Then I looked at Marshall. "Any women on the go-to list?"

"Not really. Not yet. Bowman and Ranston are studying the ballplayers and workers, but so far they're all men. The only woman is Shirley and that's because she discovered the original body dump site before getting wacked in the head with a softball."

"Not the only woman. I really need to find out more about Geraldine Kremler from that Creative Stitchers club. There's only one problem—she lives in Nevada now."

"Who's that?" my aunt asked.

I gave her the CliffsNotes version and she mulled it over quietly for a few seconds before she said anything. "Kremler. Kremler. Why does that name sound familiar? I'll have to ask Louis when he gets home tonight. Seems I've heard it mentioned before. A baritone player? Never mind. If it's of any consequence, my Louis will know."

We ended the night with the usual pub fare, dropped my aunt off at her house, and crawled our way to bed. Morning came early and we were bleary-eyed and exhausted. We took separate cars to the office because the every-other Saturdays I worked, in addition to the Saturdays I used to get caught up, were half days.

Marshall was right about one thing—by the time we got into the office Augusta had inhaled the contents from Bowman's tox screen fax. Most likely the second it left the machine.

"I'll be darned," she announced to Nate, who was halfway to his office with a cup of coffee in hand, and to Marshall and me, who were still in the process of getting ours. "Seemed old Buster succumbed to the mother-in-law's tongue."

"The what?" Marshall turned to me. "I must still be asleep." Then to Augusta, "What's that about a mother-in-law?"

Augusta handed him the paper. "The tongue. The mother-in-law's tongue. Also known as the dumb cane because the plant chokes the words right out of people. It's an effect of the poison. Hmm, I used to have a very pretty one by my kitchen window in Wisconsin but I didn't eat the thing."

"What plant? What pretty plant?" I lifted my hands in the air as I waited for an explanation.

"Dieffenbachia. Lovely decorative green leaves with white spots. You can buy them anywhere. Easy to care for. That's why they're so popular. Every designer magazine has a photo of one of those plants mixed into the décor. Of course, spider plants are popular, too, but you need to hang those. And they're not poisonous to my knowledge. Dieffenbachia. Interesting choice for the killer. They didn't have to look far or mess around with rat poison granules. Could have purchased it at Home Depot, Lowes, Ace, Costco—"

"We get it, Augusta," Nate said. He did a quick spin around and stood directly in front of her, coffee in hand. "Got to admit, it was clever. Easy to chop up those leaves, let them dry and mix them into Buster's tobacco tin."

"Want me to read you Bowman's notes? They're on another page in this fax."

Nate could barely get the *o* out in "No" when Augusta launched into the notes. "It says here the deputies have started searching for the tobacco tin near the scene of the crime. It wasn't found on Buster's body when he was brought to the county morgue."

Nate held out his hand. "Let me see."

"You know what I think, Mr. Williams?" Augusta went on. "That tin either slipped out of his pocket by the golf course path where Shirley first saw the corpse or the killer removed it. I wager those two yahoos are looking around the ball field and not the original dumping ground. 'Course, if you want more of my opinion—"

Nate held out his palm. "That's fine, Augusta. I think we get the picture."

Marshall massaged the back of his neck and moved his head from side to side. "It's been well over a week. Chances are if that tobacco tin *was* near the golf course, it's long gone by now. They keep those grounds pretty darn pristine."

I shook my head. "The grounds, maybe, but unless the landscapers trimmed the bushes, it could very well be nestled under one of them."

"It's worth a look-see. I'll give Bowman a call. The posse station is nearby."

"They won't know the exact area but we do. I'll swing by there this afternoon before I go home. And don't worry, if I do find anything, I'll be sure to pick it up with a Ziploc bag."

Augusta crinkled her nose at Marshall. "You trained her well."

"Nah, she's training us."

Nate glanced at the report again. "Dieffenbachia. A common household plant. Doesn't take a genius to figure out this was premeditated. Now all we need to do is find out who had access to Buster's tobacco tins and who wanted him out of the way."

"My aunt said it was most likely a woman. I know. I know. That's very stereotypical but it does make sense. Poisons aren't messy and it takes weeks until lab reports come in. Unlike guns where bullets can be matched, or knives and the like. Too bloody. And strangulation takes a fair degree of strength. Not to say a woman couldn't pull it off, but still . . . Oh my gosh, I'm getting as bad as my aunt and my mother."

The second I uttered the word *mother*, I froze. "Please don't tell me those news stations are going to specify the poison. My mother will be on the phone with all her friends insisting they toss out any plant that remotely resembles the dieffenbachia. At least I won't have to worry about it appearing on Streetman's neighborhood walking map. It's mostly boxwood beauties, long Johns, ficus, cacti, and lantana around here."

"Oh, they'll specify it, all right," Nate said. "Anything to get the attention of viewers. Then they'll have spinoff segments about growing the plant, trimming the plant, and holiday decorating with the plant. Not to mention warnings about potential poisonings from ingesting the plant. And you know what the worst part is? Every other household has got one, including my elderly aunt's in Sierra Vista. It's not as if we can track down a one-of-a-kind murder weapon where the remnants, like sweat or blood, are still on it."

"And no killer is stupid enough to leave traces of it on the knife he or she used to cut it up," I added. "So now what?"

Marshall smiled. "What we always do—poke around and pry for information and answers. Of course, we haven't officially been called in for that next step, but I have a nagging suspicion we will be. Meanwhile, that fraud case is still looming. Once we get an alert from Rolo, who knows where it will take us?"

"That's right," I said. "The Klingons." Then two thoughts came to me at once, forcing me to reconsider using the Notes section on my phone. At least I'd be compelled to check it out now and again rather than let my ideas slip out of my mind completely.

I never followed through on Karl Creedman, the concession stand owner who had Buster's info on his phone, nor did I get a heads-up from my mother regarding the photo Lyndy took of the two men seated behind us at Herb's baseball game. Their conversation led us to believe they might know who had it in for Buster.

In fairness, it wasn't my fault. Shirley had that awful incident with the GPS, only to find her house was bugged as well. Top that off with learning Buster had gambled away the softball team's equipment money. Those two things alone sent me off in another direction, and what did I accomplish? I may have inadvertently set up my best friend on a date with a killer.

"Are you all right, Phee?" Augusta asked. "You look lost in space."

"Huh? No. I was just thinking. Guess I can do that in my office. With real work."

Nate laughed. "I suppose that's an invitation for all of us to get moving."

And like that, everyone scurried off to their respective offices, leaving Augusta to manage the outer sanctum.

CHAPTER 28

I left the office at a little past noon and drove straight to Sun City West. Well, almost straight if I didn't count the short detour to Wendy's for a burger. It was a glorious Saturday afternoon as long as I remained in my car with the air-conditioning on. For some reason, Septembers in Arizona are the worst. The humidity hangs on and the temperatures refuse to go below the nineties. At least October was coming.

Since Marshall wouldn't be home until later in the day, I figured I'd kill two birds with one stone: stop by my mom's to see if she'd had any luck with the photos I'd forwarded her, and snoop around the bushes by the golf course where Shirley first spied Buster's body.

The entry path to the golf course was off to my right as I pulled into my mother's section of Sun City West. Like the time before, there were no golfers in sight, let alone their carts. But I knew from prior experience that could change in a flash. I'd already concocted a decent fib should anyone ask me what I was looking for.

Without wasting time, I parked my car six or seven yards from the path and doubled back. A few scrubby-looking lantanas graced the area between the golf course and the street. Behind them were some taller rosemary bushes in need of a trim.

Hallelujah! The gardeners haven't arrived yet.

The house on my right, with its faded pinkish-beige stucco, was as unoccupied as it was when Marshall and I first canvassed the area. Snowbirds, no doubt. To my left stood the house where the gentleman we had spoken with told us he didn't hear or see anything because he was too busy watching Netflix.

As I moved closer to the golf course, I watched as a young woman in khakis and a green T-shirt walked down the driveway. Her short platinum hair, streaked with blue wisps, bounced rhythmically as she approached the mailbox. Maybe the man's caregiver? Or a relative living with him? Intent on the contents of the mail, she either didn't notice me or didn't care. Funny, but Marshall and I had made the assumption that the man lived alone. Apparently not, but it didn't make a difference. Had the woman been in the house at the time of our visit, surely the man would have called out to her.

The green and beige awning over their side window made me wonder if perhaps that was something Marshall and I should consider for our rental. The afternoon heat in our guest room/office could be unbearable, even with the shutters drawn. I squinted to take a closer look at the awning and realized it was most likely their kitchen window.

Since the woman had already gone back inside, I moseyed over to take a closer look at the awning, and that's when I noticed the row of plants on the windowsill. I was too far away to be sure, but an educated guess told me I was looking at geraniums, ferns, and dieffenbachia. I squinted to get a better look and then realized I could use my iPhone and blow up the photo later.

Without wasting a second, I snapped off two shots, turned, and walked up the path to where the bushes met the golf course. True, the indoor dieffenbachia were as common as cacti around here, but given the proximity of Buster's corpse, this was one coincidence I didn't want to overlook.

In the distance, two golf carts breezed across the course, but other than that, it was perfectly still when I bent down to peruse the bushes where Shirley had said she saw the body.

A few candy bar wrappers and one empty mini vodka bottle, the kind they sell at the checkout counter at the supermarkets, graced the bottom of a sprawling lantana. Nothing like a quick nip before teeing off, I thought. Moving on to the next few bushes brought more of the same, but only as far as paper wrappers were concerned.

Farther up the path, I spied an old flyer for a missing dog and a chewed-up pencil. Not very encouraging. I'm not sure why, but I crisscrossed to the bushes on the opposite side, closer to the house with the plants on the windowsill. More lantana. More boxwood beauties. More rosemary in need of a good shaping.

Unlike lantana and similar plants, rosemary bushes are thick, and when they get overgrown, the only way to see if there's anything underneath them is to separate the tight leaves and peer between them. Not a fun task. Still, if I expected to find anything, I had no choice. But this wasn't my first encounter with Arizona plant life. I'd come prepared.

A while back I purchased golf sleeves, for lack of a better word, and kept an extra pair in the glove compartment. They were similar to stockings and worn on the arms from the wrist to the underarm so as not to get sunburned when golfing in the heat of the day. I used them for yard work and those unfortunate occasions when I took Streetman to the dog park.

Prior to exiting the car, I'd stuffed them in the pocket of my pants. Now, inches away from those annoying needle-like leaves, I put the sleeves on and pried the branches apart. Nothing. One bush down, two more to go. Taller bushes. Thicker bushes. I mumbled unmentionable obscenities and kept going. Thankfully, I never got to the third bush because the reflection from the bottom half of a round tin nearly blinded me. I had hit pay dirt! Or at least I hoped so. I honestly don't think Flash Gordon could have moved faster.

I snatched the folded Ziploc bag from the same pocket where I had stashed the golf sleeves and turned the bag inside out. Then, like a seasoned forensic lab tech, I reached under the bush, secured the object and sealed the bag. It was only then when I took a closer look.

The tin looked older than Moses and pretty well scraped up. The tops of the letters on the tin were missing but the bottom was clear enough— Copenhagen Long Cut Wintergreen. I prayed to the gods it was Buster's favorite blend.

Energized by my find, I skirted around the other bushes in hopes of locating the lid, but no such luck. It didn't matter. If the tin did indeed belong to Buster, and if it had any remnants of dieffenbachia in it, the lab would be able to tell.

Seconds later, I was in my car with the golf sleeves on the passenger seat so I'd remember to throw them in the wash, and the Copenhagen tin securely nestled in the console. I got ready to send Marshall a happy-face emoji but thought better of it and chose a thumbs-up one instead. But before tapping Send, I changed my mind and sent him a photo of it. With no room for misinterpretation, he and Nate could give Bowman and Ranston the good news.

Next, I was on to my mother's house, less than three minutes away. To prepare her for my unexpected visit, I phoned. Short and simple. "Hey, Mom, I'm down the block and thought I'd stop by for a few minutes."

"Down the block? What happened? Did someone find another body? I didn't hear any sirens. Hold on." Then she shouted, "Herb, did you hear any sirens?" Then back to me. "Herb is changing a lightbulb for me. It's by the cathedral ceiling entrance. He's not afraid of ladders."

I rolled my eyes. "Uh, good. See you in a minute."

Please, dear Lord, do not let Herb mention last night at Tailgators.

I pulled up in front of the house, where my mother stood inside the second security door and the entrance to the house. She had that door installed so Essie wouldn't escape. Marshall referred to it as the vapor lock.

"So?" she asked. "What happened?"

"Nothing happened. The forensics lab identified the poison that killed Buster and it was from the dieffenbachia plant."

"Herb!" my mother shouted. "The poison that killed Buster was from the dieffenbachia plant. Do you have any of those? We used to have one back in Mankato. Along with rhododendrons. I've got to make sure none of the book club ladies have those things in their house. Bad enough I have to worry about those awful sago palms. At least the dieffenbachia is a houseplant. Hmm, a houseplant. Anyone could have snipped a few leaves, mashed them up, and mixed them into Buster's chewing tobacco when he wasn't looking. That should be reason enough for someone to quit that nasty habit."

"Um, I doubt most tobacco-chewing ballplayers worry about being poisoned."

"Well, Buster should have."

By now, Herb was in the kitchen munching on a muffin. "Hey, cutie! Did you drive all this way to announce the murder weapon?"

"Not exactly." When my mother wasn't looking, I mouthed, "Don't talk about Tailgators." Then I said, "Our office got the tox screen, and once we knew what the poison was, we figured the killer must have done exactly what my mother said—chopped up plant leaves and put them in Buster's chewing tobacco tin. I drove over here to the spot where Shirley first saw the body and sure enough, I found the bottom of a Copenhagen tin underneath one of those rosemary bushes. I'll drop it off at the posse station on my way back to the office."

At that moment I felt something brush against the bottom of my leg and looked down. Essie rubbed herself against me with Streetman watching her every move from beneath the coffee table. Her gray fur had grown longer and appeared silkier. She was filling out as well.

"Isn't that the most precious thing?" my mother said. "She's claiming you."

As long as the dog doesn't try that, I'll be fine. Canines claim by lifting their legs.

"Listen, I dropped by because I completely forgot about the photo I sent you that Lyndy took of the two men who sat behind us at the ball field. Were you able to pass it along? Did anyone recognize them?"

"Oy! With everything else going on I never followed up with the book club ladies once I forwarded the picture. Of course, if anyone *did* recognize those men, they would have told me." She glanced at Herb and slapped her hand to her chest. "I meant to send you Phee's snapshot or whatever they call them but must have gotten sidetracked."

"Don't worry about it," I said. "I've got the photo on my phone."

I walked over to the kitchen counter, where Herb was now on his second muffin. "Do you recognize either of these two men?"

He held the screen inches from his nose and grunted. "Sure do. I recognize both of them."

CHAPTER 29

"That's fantastic!" I stopped short of giving Herb a hug. "Who are they?"

"Oh, I don't know their names, but the baby-faced guy with the Cardinals shirt works for some bread delivery company. I've seen him at the ball field's concession stand delivering rolls."

"And the older guy with the dark hair?"

"Works maintenance for Sun City West. Last time I saw him was when he was spreading that new dirt on the field."

"They actually have to spread dirt? I mean, the ground is pretty well bone-dry and sandy as is."

Herb looked at me as if I'd exited a spaceship. "Of course they have to spread dirt. Ball field dirt is special. Some sort of blend of clay, silt, and sand. Minerals, too, but I think that's part of the clay."

"How on earth would you know this?"

"Because I went to one of the budget meetings for the Rec Centers last year when they discussed operating costs. Hey, someone has to keep an eye on expenses. Our dues keep going up like we're all millionaires." Then he looked at my mother. "You should go to one of those meetings, Harriet. Very informative."

"No, thank you. It will only raise my blood pressure."

"Listen, I really need to get going," I said. "I've got to drop off this evidence at the posse station. By the way, how's Shirley doing?"

"Surprisingly well." My mother bent down, picked up Essie and cradled her for a few seconds. "Shirley is certainly resilient considering someone bugged her house and put a tracking device on her car. Not to mention her business card being found on a corpse. Having Thor around gives her a good sense of security. Just like my Streetman. Of course, Thor demands a bit more exercise and chases balls all over Shirley's yard but Streetman has his passions, too."

I glanced at the dog, who now moved to a small area rug near the kitchen and proceeded to furiously clean his paws.

Yep, nothing spells security like a neurotic OCD dog.

"How long will Thor be staying with Shirley? I imagine Gloria will be getting back soon."

"Not that soon. She spoke with Shirley and decided to extend her family visit. The daughter has lots of vacation time so they decided to visit wine country in California as long as they were there."

"Do you think Shirley's home now? I wanted to ask her about

Geraldine Kremler. You remember, the woman from Creative Stitchers who borrowed money from Buster?"

"If you're going to stop by Shirley's house after the posse station, can you bring her a box of mohair fabric I picked up at a garage sale for her? She uses it for those teddy bears."

Before I could respond, my mother opened the small closet by the door and took out a medium-sized cardboard box.

"Um, sure. No problem. I'll give her a quick call to make sure she's home."

"When you get her on the phone, tell her Myrna emailed me a new recipe for Monterrey chicken. It calls for three different cheeses and—"

"Why don't you just call her and see if I can drop in?"

"Good idea."

My mother walked to the kitchen counter near the patio door and reached for the landline. Meanwhile, Herb grabbed a third muffin and started for the door. "Gotta run, Harriet. The guys are coming over for pinochle later this afternoon. By the way, when you buy those muffins again, get the blueberry ones. More flavor than the others."

She waved him on as he opened the door, but before he stepped outside he turned back. "Almost forgot! Mark your calendar for the Cactus Slow-Pitch game a week from today at two. It's one of those softball theme days with extra refreshments, a few of those pom-pom ladies performing and some demonstration from a newly forming juggling club. Naturally my blue team will be playing. Remember, put it on your calendar. With or without the ankle biter in tow."

He smiled and gave me a wink. "Bring your husband. He'll probably need a break from this case. Although maybe by next week Buster's killer will be behind bars."

I followed him to the door and said, "Let's hope so," even though I knew the deputies and Williams Investigations were far from closing in.

My mother hung up the phone and smiled. "Shirley said to come on over. I told her you wanted to know more about Geraldine. I told her about the dieffenbachia and she doesn't have any. Only spider plants and one of those decorative fig trees."

My head spun when I reached my car and put the box of mohair fabric on the passenger seat. Without dawdling, I drove straight to the posse station on Stardust and RH Johnson Boulevards. Minutes later, I stood in front of Deputy Ranston, whose large jowls nearly dropped to the ground when I told him what I had discovered.

"The forensic team scoured that place," he said. "What bush did you say you found it under?"

When I described the area surrounding the golf course entryway, he looked confused. "The golf course? That body was found beside the ball field."

"Yes, but Shirley said she saw it the Sunday before by the golf course. That's where I went to look." I handed him the Ziploc bag and he squinted at it.

"It's a chewing tobacco tin, all right. Wintergreen." He rubbed his chin and took another look. "Wintergreen. That's a pretty strong flavor. Buster probably never noticed the dieffenbachia mixed in."

"Do you think whoever poisoned him might have known his chewing tobacco preference?"

Ranston shrugged. "Hard to say. Could've been a stroke of luck. If indeed this tin has traces of the poison. We'll know soon enough." Again he eyeballed the Ziploc bag. "You didn't get your prints on it, did you?"

"No, I did not. Oh, and lest I forget, I have another present for you. Check your email. I sent you a photo of the bush and surrounding area where I discovered the tin. You can thank Williams Investigations."

Ranston made some sort of a guttural sound and called out for someone to bring him an evidence bag with the appropriate form.

"My office will be in touch," I said. "Have a good afternoon."

With that, I drove over to Shirley's house hoping to fill in the missing pieces regarding Geraldine and a possible motive for murder.

The minute I stepped inside Shirley's house, Thor was at the door sniffing me. A quick lick on the hand and I had passed the test. "I think he remembers me," I said as I handed Shirley the box of mohair fabric.

Shirley patted the Great Dane's head and motioned toward the beige couch. "Watch this. Thor knows how to smile and show all of his teeth when you say 'show teethes.' It's something Gloria taught him."

The minute she said the word, Thor bared his teeth and I recoiled.

"It's fine," Shirley said. "Now he's waiting for a treat. Hold on."

She reached in her pocket and handed him a small dog biscuit. "Most of the dogs I'm familiar with can sit, stay, and shake. Thor can do facial expressions. I don't suppose it will ever come in handy, but you never know. By the way, thank your mother for me. I've still got a few more teddy bears to make for the fall craft show. I imagine your mother's all set with those clay creations of hers."

"To be honest, I saw a few more of them on the credenza but didn't say anything. I know she used Streetman and Essie as models but the end products look more like abstract art to me."

"Good thing abstract art is popular these days." Shirley chuckled. "Sit down. Feel free to move those teddy bears out of your way and make yourself comfortable. Can I get you something to drink? Iced tea? Lemonade? I also have some nice sugar cookies. Store-bought because it's still too hot to use the oven, but tasty nonetheless."

"Thanks, but I'm fine. I only stopped in for a few minutes. I need to know more about Geraldine Kremler and the arrangement she had with Buster. You mentioned she borrowed money from him but he was willing to drop the entire loan if she'd agree to something. Do you recall exactly what that was?"

Shirley took the brightly colored armchair next to the couch. "You have to keep in mind Geraldine was barely making ends meet. No matter how hard people prepare for retirement, the health costs and unexpected economical downturns set them back. I would never judge her."

"What was it she did?"

"I always had a feeling there was more to it than this, but from what she told me, she agreed to have a shared bank account with Buster so that the money he collected from his bets would go into that account but the tax number on that account was hers. She held the legal obligation for taxes."

"Whoa. That would be motive for murder if she wanted to end the deal."

"It would be, except for one thing. She's in Nevada."

"Shirley, Nevada is only a few hours driving time from here. And less than an hour by plane from some cities."

"Geraldine's in her early eighties with arthritis. She'd hardly have the stamina. And it still wouldn't explain who had it in for me."

"What about her son? The one she's living with. Maybe he considered you a loose end that needed to . . . well, you know."

"She may live with him and his family but Geraldine is a very private person. I doubt her son even knew about the financial arrangement she made with Buster. Or the fact that I was aware of it. Only a few of us in Creative Stitchers knew. She told me she wrung her hands pondering his offer and, in the end, had little choice. That louse would've made it impossible for her to survive. Imagine choosing between paying for your food or your prescriptions. Worse yet, juggling utility bills against everything else."

"Weren't there any other resources for your friend?"

"She was over the income threshold by a hair and didn't qualify for government assistance. And like I said, even if she did, she was way too proud."

"Guess we can all understand that," I said. "Um, have you heard anything more from the deputies about the bugging device or the GPS?"

Shirley shook her head. "Only that they're working on it. And I'm trying to work at it, too, Phee. I keep pushing myself to remember anything out of the ordinary that Sunday when I discovered Buster's body. So far I keep hitting a wall."

"Don't push yourself. If there's something in the recesses of your mind, it'll come through. Give it time."

"I'm scared if you want the honest truth." At that moment, the dog bumped against her leg and she bent down to rub its head. "Thor is a comfort even though I have to make sure every little bit of food is in the pantry or the fridge. He goes especially wild over cold cuts and processed meats. Unfortunately, he can't stay here forever. Probably a good thing because I'm getting attached to him."

"I can see that."

"Lordy, I have to know who's behind that murder and what they want from me."

I reached for her hand and gave it a squeeze. "You will. Be patient."

CHAPTER 30

"I don't think the attack on Shirley behind the ball field had anything to do with what she knew about Geraldine Kremler," I told Marshall that night.

We sat across from each other at the kitchen table eating a hodgepodge of leftovers—chicken tenders, rigatoni with Ragú sauce, day-old Caesar salad, and reheated quesadillas. Growing up in Harriet Plunkett's house meant never throwing out anything from the fridge unless the mold made it unrecognizable.

"Go on." He washed the chicken down with a sip of Coke and reached for a quesadilla.

"For starters, it seemed Geraldine had shared that information with other members of the Creative Stitchers club and none of them experienced anything like what Shirley did. Also, having that knowledge about a shared bank account doesn't rise to that occasion. And why now?"

I took a bite of a chicken tender and spooned some of the pasta onto my plate. "Besides, from what I heard, Buster was a small-time operator. Sure, his earnings were as illegal as hell but they couldn't be that much, could they? The money he took in could have blended into his regular retirement earnings and gone unnoticed."

Marshall shook his head. "Maybe not. From what you told me earlier, Paul insinuated the guy had added blackmail to his repertoire."

"That's true. He mentioned betting, bookmaking, and blackmail, but no specifics except that the action revolved around the concession stand. I think if he knew more, he would have said so. Yeesh. His gossip could be anything. All sorts of people gather there and yank."

"Bowman and Ranston interviewed the owner but I'll look into a second go-around with him."

"Good idea." I looked at the wall clock behind me and grimaced. "Lyndy's probably on her dinner date with Lyman by now. I hope I didn't inadvertently get her mixed up with the wrong guy."

"Oops. I meant to tell you—I knew you'd be concerned so I ran a background check on Lyman Neal. Looks pretty darn clean. The guy's fifty-six, married thirty years ago but the wife passed away, no kids. No arrest record in Arizona or Wyoming, where he's originally from."

"What did he do in Wyoming?"

"Worked for the department of health and human services. That was after he retired as a firefighter."

I scooped more pasta but tossed it around on my plate. "Okay, so maybe she's not out with Jack the Ripper."

"I think Lyndy can take care of herself. *And* us."

"Us?"

"She's worked the sidelines on your sleuthing before. Now she's about to go full center stage. I watched her expressions last night. She likes Lyman, all right, but something tells me she'll do what she can to eke out more information on Buster."

"At least she's discreet. Not like my mother's yenta klatch. Or worse yet, Herb's cronies. Oh, speaking of Herb, his team is playing in some Cactus Slow-Pitch game a week from today. At two. Wants everyone to show up."

"A week from today, huh? Maybe we'll have Buster's killer behind bars by then. Not to mention that dangling thread from the insurance fraud case."

"Was Rolo able to find out more?"

"Lamentably, yes. And I say *lamentably* because the more he found out, the deeper and more twisted the case became. And just when we thought it was over. Aargh. Rolo had us call him on one of our burner phones this afternoon and spoke for less than a minute. The person orchestrating the insurance fraud faked his own death on more than one occasion. Not only that, but moved around like a chameleon. Duped people into helping him by putting their names as beneficiaries on the policies."

"If Rolo knows that, why can't he track down the cheat?"

"He's trying. He's got the bank routing numbers and all sorts of connections, but when he gets close, the guy vanishes."

"Wow. Just like Shirley's body did. But then again, Buster showed up later, deader than ever."

"One good thing about that—a body's tangible. The fraud case feels as if we're trying to catch wind in our hands."

We cleared the table and I reached for a sponge to wipe it down when the landline rang.

"Ugh. Probably my mother." I looked at the ID and picked up the phone. "It's my aunt," I said. Then I braced myself for her voice.

"Phee! I'll only keep you a minute. If nothing else, you did a wonderful job matchmaking last night."

"I was trying to solve a murder."

"Yes, yes, that's why I called. Remember when I said the name Geraldine Kremler sounded familiar? Well, I was partially right. She *did* play the baritone. But her name was Bernadine Kreppler and she passed away last year at age ninety-four in Boca Raton. Played on the cruise ships with Louis."

"At least you tried. And I appreciate your help with Lyndy. Who knows? Maybe she'll be able to find out more on her own."

"Wait. Before you hang up, I have more news. Louis got to chatting with one of the party guests last night. Nice man according to Louis. I meant to call you sooner but we went shopping today at Costco's in Surprise and you can't imagine what an ordeal that was. We came home exhausted, and even though we spent a fortune on groceries, we ordered take-out."

I looked up at the ceiling as if some celestial force might bring my aunt back to her original thought but instead, she started to tell me what she ordered from the Texas Roadhouse.

"Uh, sounds delicious, but what was it you were going to tell me about that conversation my uncle had?"

"Oh, goodness, yes. The man lives in Sun City West and knew all about Buster's murder. Mentioned he had seen him play numerous times in the past year. Then, he told Louis to watch out for expired meats and rolls if he went to the concession stand. Referred to the owner as Karl Greedman, not Creedman, and said the guy all but lived in that place."

"How would someone know if the products were expired? I suppose the rolls might taste stale but once the burgers and hot dogs are cooked and covered with all those condiments, it would be hard to tell."

"Said if the stuff tasted bad, ask to see the packaging. Said that happened to him on more than one instance and the owner made him a new meal and opened the products right in front of him. Didn't use the ones that were already there."

"Hmm, that's suspicious but I'm not sure what that would have to do with Buster."

"Maybe he had a bad meal and it escalated. Flared tempers can turn into murder. Now, in Feterina Pulnetski's novel *The Blood-Soaked Hand*, the killer lunged out at his victim over a disagreement about cheating at cards."

"Uh, very interesting." *Fictional, too.* "The evidence, however, points to something deliberate. Most poisonings do. I seriously doubt someone became incensed at Buster, went home, chopped up some leaves from his or her dieffenbachia plant and found a way to get them into the man's chewing tobacco tin."

"You may already have an answer, Phee."

"What do you mean?"

"Find out who had the opportunity to do such a thing. You're partway there. You already know the means they used, and once you nab the killer, you'll find out the motive."

"Usually the deputies interview suspects, witnesses, and anyone who might know anything about the case. Next, they look for motive and pull things together."

"That's why they're still looking. Listen to me. Find out who had the chance to mess with the chewing tobacco. I should know. Your uncle calls me the chair-side sleuth. Maybe one of these days I'll trade those comfortable cushions for a good pair of walking shoes and a magnifying glass."

Oh, heaven help all of us!

"There's a lot to be said for chair-side sleuthing. Don't underestimate its value. I'll keep you posted, Aunt Ina. Have a great weekend."

Having finished washing the leftover bowls, Marshall dried them and put them back in the cabinet next to the sink. "What was that all about? Sounds like your aunt has a theory about Buster's poisoning."

"Not a theory. More like a roadmap. She thinks we should turn our attention to *opportunity*. Who would have had the chance to swap out his tobacco tin, or even add the dieffenbachia grounds to his existing chewing tobacco?"

"It goes back to the time line. Based on the coroner's finding regarding state of decay and approximate time of death, the body Shirley saw was most likely Buster's. And *if* it wasn't his, then Buster's corpse was lying around somewhere. So, to be clear, whoever swapped out the chewing tobacco had to have done it earlier on Sunday, or possibly the night before, given what we know about our victim."

"Which is?"

"Buster was a regular chewing tobacco addict. Everyone we interviewed without exception said as much. That stuff was always wadded up in his mouth."

"Then all you need to do is find out his whereabouts that Sunday."

"Yep. Easier said than done."

CHAPTER 31

"What about his calendar?" I asked Marshall. "Bowman and Ranston were able to scope out his house, weren't they?"

"That was one of the first things they did once they declared it part of the crime scene. A regular rat's nest, according to Bowman. Papers strewn everywhere on Buster's desk, kitchen table, and dining room table. The place wasn't a pigsty, Bowman's exact words, but it was as disorganized as a stockroom after a tornado."

"I take it they didn't find anything that linked him to illicit gambling or loan-sharking."

"The only thing they linked him to was dirty laundry and chewing tobacco. They found other tins and sent them to the lab with a rush on it but they all came back clean."

"And no notes on any of his calendars?"

"Nothing that raised an eyebrow. Only an annotation that said 'rent due this week' and notations for baseball game days. That sent them back to the wadded-up papers and notes."

"And?"

"Nate and I have a bet as to when they wind up in our office for review. My lucky day is Tuesday. Meanwhile, we'll compare interview notes with the deputies on Monday to see if anything stands out. At least we'll have tomorrow to ourselves. I've been hankering for pancakes at the nearest IHOP."

"Sounds good. Just the two of us and a giant stack of blueberry pancakes. No crazy book club chatter, no yahooing from Herb and his crew, and no shenanigans from my aunt and uncle. I can almost taste the syrup already."

When I closed my eyes for the night, I pictured two things—pouring syrup on a stack of pancakes and Lyndy running for her life. In spite of the background check, I still had my concerns. At least I didn't have to wait too long for either of them.

• • •

Lyndy's text interrupted our lazy morning in bed and I had to stretch my arm at a really uncomfortable angle to retrieve my iPhone from the nightstand. *TY, TY, TY, A++ date*, the text read.

"We can relax," I said. "Lyndy survived her date with Lyman."

Marshall propped his head on his elbow. "Survived?"

"Actually, she gave it, or him, an A++. I'll catch up with her later."

"Too bad we'll never know how that waitress got through Friday night."

"Probably with a long shower and lots of body wash and shampoo."

"Yeesh."

We moseyed to the shower, dressed, and headed out to the IHOP on Bell Road in Surprise. The one near us was undergoing a renovation so we trekked the extra few miles.

"Is that Shirley's Buick?" I asked as Marshall pulled into the parking lot in search of a spot.

"There's like a zillion Buicks in here. Doubt it."

We stepped back as a man and woman with a large baby carrier in tow exited the restaurant. I stared at the contraption wondering how I ever managed all those years ago with Kalese. Going out to eat two decades ago meant a stroller, a baby seat, and a tote bag the size of Mount Rushmore.

Thankfully, there was no wait and the hostess greeted us as soon as we got inside.

"Good timing," Marshall whispered. "Another month and we'd never get in with all the snowbirds."

We were ushered to a booth at the far end of the larger dining room, but no sooner did our butts hit the orange cushions when a woman brushed by our table with her eyes fixed directly ahead. Black skirt, clunky black shoes, white blouse, black cardigan.

"Oh, no," I muttered. "Only one person I know dresses like that— Cecilia. Thank goodness she didn't see us. Let's pray she's meeting with her church group, otherwise—"

I never finished my sentence. Directly behind Cecilia were Myrna and Louise, who spotted us immediately.

"Phee, Marshall," Myrna exclaimed. "Join us. Cecilia called us when her morning services ended. Your mother and Shirley are on their way as well."

I swallowed. "Herb, too?"

Myrna shook her head. "Shh. There's only so much of Herb we can take at one sitting."

"Thanks, Myrna," Marshall said. "We just got settled. Why don't you tell everyone at your table we'll join them for a coffee when we're done?"

"Okey-dokey."

With a quick wave, Myrna and Louise took off and I breathed a sigh of relief. "It's going to be a *very* quick cup of coffee. There's only so much of *them* I can take at one sitting."

Marshall laughed as he picked up the menu.

My mother waved us over when we exited our table after eating. The book club ladies had a large corner table with plenty of room for us to plunk ourselves down.

"Any news?" Shirley asked as soon as we approached.

"Still tracking down leads," Marshall said. "But now that we're here, would you mind going over the time line with me again? The tiniest detail could be the very thing we need."

Shirley added a spoonful of sugar to her coffee and took a sip. "I'll try." Then she pointed to the table. "The waitress left extra cups and two carafes. Help yourselves."

I poured coffee from the one marked *Regular* and passed it Marshall's way. "I may float out of here, but what the heck."

"I remember the white van whizzing past me," Shirley said, "but not much else. No one was on the golf course. At least not from my vantage point."

Marshall leaned an elbow on the table and rubbed his chin. "What about before that? Before you even turned off RH Johnson into the neighborhood?"

"Not before I made the turn, but now that you mention it, I did see one of those maintenance golf carts, or whatever those things are called, on the golf course roadway on the other side. The side closest to Grand Avenue and the railroad tracks. It seemed so inconsequential that I forgot all about it. And it was on the opposite side of the street from the body. The cart was gone by the time that white van went by."

Opposite side of the street? Easy to zip across to the other part of the golf course.

Marshall gave me a quick look but neither of us said anything. I wondered if he thought the same thing I did—that someone could have very well gotten nervous, dumped Buster's body and then came back to retrieve it once the coast was clear. It would still beg the question—"Where did they store it for two whole days before it reappeared right where Shirley got that blow to the head?"

"If I think of anything else," Shirley said, "I'll let you know."

"No chance you could have seen who drove that maintenance cart?" I asked.

She shook her head. "It was too far away. Like a blurred image."

Shirley couldn't have phrased it better if she tried. Everything seemed to be a blurred image. Bits and pieces of this and that with nothing adding up. Nate once told me that's how it is with investigations until some minor detail emerges and bam! Everything falls into place. Or in this case, the image sharpens up.

On the ride home I turned to Marshall. "I don't suppose Bowman and Ranston can check for DNA on those maintenance golf carts from the Rec Centers, can they?"

"I doubt it. It's been close to two weeks. Trace or touch DNA fades after that time frame. Not to mention, there must be at least a dozen or more of those things. And even if Buster's DNA was found, who's to say he didn't take a ride with one of his buddies? From what you said, the maintenance worker who sat behind you and Lyndy seemed pretty familiar with him. If that's the case, I wouldn't be surprised if the same held true for the others in the maintenance department."

Then Marshall grinned. "Guess the case is moving on. It's time we got to know who that maintenance worker is. Of course, you know how this will end up, don't you?"

"What are you saying?"

"The minute I mention this recent recollection of Shirley's to the deputies, it will be tantamount to me offering up our services for *seek and find*."

"You said it was only a matter of time for the inevitable."

"True, but with that insurance fraud case dangling over our heads, I hoped the inevitable would come at a later time."

• • •

As luck would have it, the inevitable came, all right. But not from Bowman and Ranston. From Rolo Barnes at a minute or two before nine the following morning. Augusta had just put the *Open* sign on the door when the phone rang.

"They always know when I'm not seated at my desk," she said as Nate, Marshall, and I jockeyed for positions at the Keurig. A second later she announced, "It's Rolo. I'm saving myself a headache and putting this on speakerphone."

One tap and Rolo's guttural voice filled the room. "You're still using Sfax, aren't you?"

Nate responded, "You didn't leave us much choice the last time."

"Can't be too safe. The Public Switched Telephone Network has its advantages but nothing beats higher-level data encryption. Okay then. Sit back. I'm sending you a fax. Call me on a burner phone once you read it. Hey, I'm adding collagen peptides to my diet. Bye."

Augusta widened her eyes and shook her head. "If I have to decipher this like the last time, I want a raise."

The mechanical sound of the fax machine silenced all of us. We watched it as if it was a space shuttle launch. Before Augusta could snatch the paper from the machine, Nate latched on to it and gave a thumbs-up. "Doesn't need to be deciphered."

He held the paper at arm's length and gulped. "Better hope this doesn't turn out to be a trilogy." Then he read it aloud. "Computer files in Gilbert document bait-and-switch for product billing. Small potatoes. Three suspects caught but the kingpin's on the run. Fakes his own death for insurance payoff with bogus beneficiaries. Gotcha! Lamont Rooney's the name. Allegedly died two years ago in a boating accident at Lake Pleasant. Lucky break. Your neck of the woods. Never found the body. Money trail recently took him to Laughlin, Nevada. Call me on the burner."

With that, he winked at Marshall and I knew in that split second hunting down a maintenance guy in Sun City West would be the last thing on their agenda for a while.

CHAPTER 32

R olo detailed a list of the man's prior aliases along with his last known address. It was enough to put Augusta in a tailspin shuffling Nate's and Marshall's schedules so they could track down the elusive flimflam man.

"If all goes well, this should only take two or three days tops," Marshall said when he came into my office and closed the door behind him. It was a little after eleven and he had informed Deputies Bowman and Ranston that he and Nate would be unavailable for a few days.

"Listen, we all want to expedite the investigation into Buster's death, especially since there may be a link to Shirley's situation, but whatever you do, don't go off on your own. Let Bowman and Ranston do what they're trained to do. I'll give them the rundown on that maintenance vehicle. Most likely, they'll have another conversation with Shirley and then poke around the Rec Centers' utility area."

I tried not to sound anxious. "Two or three days, huh?"

"We'll get on the road early tomorrow. Laughlin's only a few hours away. And don't worry, we'll steer clear of the gambling."

"Lucky for you Uncle Louis doesn't know or he'll offer to tag along."

He gave me a hug, tussled my hair and snuck in a quick kiss before Augusta banged on the door. "I'm taking lunch orders for the deli. Wanted to get ours in early before they get backed up."

Four Rueben sandwiches later, we were no closer to figuring out why someone would go to the trouble to bug Shirley's house, put a GPS tracker on her car, and whop her in the head with a softball. And one that didn't yield any prints, for that matter.

It was the usual thing we did when the four of us were able to grab lunch together—toss around theories to see if anything would stick. In this case, nothing did. And everything would have to wait until the guys got back from Laughlin. Truth be known, none of us had much faith in the Bowman-Ranston end of the deal.

That night, as I helped Marshall put together some changes of clothes and more than two pairs of underwear, I went through my own murder suspect list again. Much as I hated to admit it, Lyman still held a top place. He did, after all, have a visible verbal altercation with Buster over the chewing tobacco, which meant he was familiar with the product. Then, getting stiffed on that equipment money. Anger and revenge can equal murder if someone fumes long enough.

Geraldine was also a player but not a likely one. Then again, that didn't leave out her prodigy. It was quite possible that her son found out about

Buster's little deal with his mother and didn't take it lightly.

As far as the ballplayers went, Herb told me some of them got ramrodded by Buster but not to the extent that would result in a firestorm of sorts.

"I'm hopping in the shower, hon," Marshall said. "It'll save me some time in the morning. Nate's picking me up at five. We'll take Route 60 till it becomes 93, then west on 40 into Laughlin. Looks good on the map, but up close and personal those curves are contentious. We want to give ourselves plenty of time."

"Um, I know Rolo found your guy's last known address, but what if it turns out to be a bust?"

"It will lead us to more contacts and more information. That's how it goes and that's why we estimated two to three days. Nate already had a nice conversation with the Nevada county sheriff's office, so if things were to go awry, they'll be familiar with the situation."

"You're not making this sound good. Especially after that last encounter in Gilbert."

"We'll be fine. It's you I worry about. Keep your sleuthing to paper chases right now. Please?"

I nodded but felt like I was back in junior high crisscrossing my fingers behind my back. That was the moment I realized I had overlooked the obvious. The second I heard Marshall turn on the water, I grabbed my murder notebook and turned to a clean page. This time I needed to profile Buster's killer.

Having never worked backward like this before, I brainstormed words that matched what I held to be the character and/or personality traits the killer had. Five minutes later, I perused my list: *meticulous, conversant with plant-based poisons, attention to detail, a planner, possible second-guesser* or, *easily spooked*. I added the "second-guesser/easily spooked" part to my list because Buster's body was first dumped in one place but found in another. And, like Marshall, I didn't think it was the same body Shirley saw right before she got lobbed in the head. I think that body was alive and well, and a setup. Shirley would have had to slow down to give it a good look-see, allowing her assailant a better opportunity to aim the softball her way.

Then, it hit me like a thunderclap—Buster didn't have one killer, he had a pair. If Marshall was right about his gaslighting theory, that took two people. And two people could have easily wrangled a body from a maintenance vehicle. The trouble was . . . which two?

Obviously, there had to be a planner. That much I'd already figured out. But what about the sidekick? I had no way to figure out that accomplice's traits.

• • •

Marshall was up by four and fortifying himself with deep-roasted coffee the following morning. I kept him company sleepy-eyed and semiconscious until Nate arrived at four fifty-five. Having given Marshall as passionate a kiss as I could muster at that hour, I waved goodbye to both of them and went back to bed for another hour of sleep. When I got up at a little past seven, the dull headache I had was replaced by hunger and thirst, two things I could easily remedy.

By eight fifteen, I had my wits about me and decided upon a plan of action to find out who drove the maintenance cart the day Shirley first spied Buster. All I needed to do was meander down to the maintenance work area between the bocce court activity building and the fitness center at the large Rec Center complex. However, it wasn't exactly a place where most people meander. That meant I needed a foil, or in this case, a neurotic chiweenie.

I knew Streetman got my mother up at the crack of dawn, so picking up the phone to call her wouldn't be an issue. Or so I thought.

"What happened? Why are you calling me so early? Was there another murder? Did something happen to Shirley?"

"Nothing happened. No murder." *Boy, am I going to regret what I'm about to ask.* "Can I take Streetman to the dog park tomorrow morning? And maybe for a short walk around the complex?"

"Aha! You're finally taking my advice about chatting with Cindy Dolton." Then to Streetman, "Guess what? Your sister is going to take you to the doggie park tomorrow."

"Good Lord, mother, I'm not his sister."

"In his dog mind, Phee, you are. Don't confuse him. And why would you want to walk him if you're taking him to the park?"

"Shirley remembered seeing a Rec Center maintenance cart on the day she found Buster's body. Um, before it vanished. Anyway, I thought I'd do a little snooping around that utility area. With Streetman on a leash, no one will question it. Unless he still growls at car tires."

"He hasn't done that in months. What do you expect to find?"

"Actually, nothing. I expect to strike up a conversation with someone and find out who was in that area that day."

"Why aren't those deputies doing that? Or Williams Investigations?"

"Our office was only called in to assist with the interviews. Besides, Nate and Marshall will be in Laughlin for the next two or three days on that insurance fraud case."

"I thought it was solved."

"Partially solved. The head honcho is still at large apparently."

"Laughlin, huh? Don't mention that to your uncle Louis. He'll want to tag along and go to the casinos."

"Too late. The men already left. And I had the same thought about Uncle Louis, too."

"I'll have my little prince ready by six tomorrow. Want me to make a cup of coffee for you?"

Visions of heated-up leftover coffee gave me heartburn. "Nah. I'll get something at Dunkin' or Starbucks. Thanks, Mom. See you in the morning."

Augusta was busy with filing when I walked into the office. She looked up and motioned to the counter. "I brought in some caramelized sweet rolls from a new farmers market by my house. Figured we'd give them a try. Not bad."

I reached for a roll, took a bite and closed my eyes. "Wow. Best part of the morning ever."

"Honeymoon over that fast?"

"Very funny. Marshall was up and out before I could pry my eyes open."

"Yep. Laughlin. Good thing they're seasoned detectives and not gamblers. Do you think Bowman and Ranston will make any progress while they're gone?"

"I don't know about them, but I hope I will. Even if it means the dreaded dog park."

I went on to tell Augusta about the maintenance area, my profile sketches for the killer, and my latest revelation that we were dealing with more than one suspect. Then she blurted out the very thought I'd been keeping under wraps—"What if it's Lyman Neal?"

Augusta shared the same unsettling thought about Lyman but Lyndy sure didn't. She called me during my break time, which happened to coincide with hers, to tell me all about their dates. Plural. More reason for me to worry.

"He's an absolute gentleman, Phee, and that's not all." Her voice was as chipper as could be. "He's smart, funny, and definitely attractive. He called me Sunday morning, right after I texted you, and wondered if I'd want to poke around Old Town Scottsdale with him that afternoon. We wound up checking out a few galleries before eating at Citizen Public House. First time I'd ever been to an award-winning restaurant. Usually it's chain restaurants or fast food. Oh my gosh, I'm babbling like an idiot. I wanted to call you yesterday but got mired under with work and was too exhausted to think."

"Uh, wow. That's great. Really great. I take it you'll be seeing more of him?"

"Naturally he wants me to watch the Blue Team play at that Cactus game on Saturday and thought maybe we could grab dinner out on Thursday or Friday, depending on how their practices go."

"Sounds good. Keep me posted." *And keep one of Myrna's Screamer devices in your bag just in case. Much better than mace.*

"She's falling hook, line, and sinker," I said to Augusta over lunch. Since it was Tuesday, we ordered street tacos and nachos from the Mexican restaurant around the corner and wasted no time getting into them.

Augusta added two packets of extra hot sauce to her taco and nodded. "Yep. Nothing worse than a whirlwind relationship. My aunt Beula-Mae, the one I told you about who was in Chicago during that Tylenol catastrophe, always said, 'Too much, too soon, and it's over.' Let me tell you, she drilled it into all of our heads. Not that any of us listened seeing as she was a diehard spinster and all."

"Still, that's kind of good advice, but far be it from me to interfere with Lyndy's social life. Let her enjoy a fun week with Lyman."

Bite my tongue, because there was nothing fun about the week Lyndy had, or the rest of us, for that matter.

CHAPTER 33

Marshall phoned me in the early afternoon to let me know they arrived safely in Laughlin, checked into a motel, and were fast at work tracking down leads. All I could tell him was that our street tacos were good and Lyndy hit it off with Lyman.

He promised to keep us posted but reiterated what I already knew—if there's radio silence, call Rolo on a burner phone.

I was up at an ungodly hour the next morning and had no one to blame but myself. It was my imbecilic idea to scout around the maintenance area and wallow in the gossip mire with Cindy. After a hasty retreat from my mother's house, with Streetman spinning in circles to get into my car, I headed to the dog park.

My pumpkin spice latte was securely nestled in the car's cupholder between the driver's side of the car and the passenger's. Thankfully, Streetman showed little interest in it. He was more concerned with a rabbit that darted across the road and into some bushes as we neared the Rec complex. I made a mental note to double loop his leash upon exiting the vehicle.

Cindy was at her usual place by the fence with Bundles, her fluffy little well-behaved dog. When Streetman charged into the park, I heard people shout for their dogs as if a tribe of Mongols had arrived. I closed my eyes for a split second and prayed to the gods he wouldn't get amorous.

"Phee!" Cindy called out. "I thought I'd see you here days ago. Everyone's been talking about Buster's death. And poison, no less. Under normal circumstances I'd say that was a jilted lover seeking revenge but the only thing that man loved was money. Or scamming it out of others."

I moved closer to where she stood even though her voice carried like nobody's business. To be on the safe side, I kept mine low. "Yeah, I was kind of hoping you might be able to fill in some blanks. The deputies don't seem to be getting anywhere and somehow Shirley Johnson's become a target for some lunatic. The cases may be linked."

"I know. I heard about that from my friends in the Creative Stitchers club and the Rip 'n' Sew. Word travels fast."

Cindy went on to tell me what I already knew about Buster with one tidbit that had escaped all of us—the position of third baseman was taken away from some other guy and bestowed upon Buster since he had more talent and skill than the prior player.

"You don't think that's a motive for murder, do you?" Cindy asked.

"Aargh. Seems like everything's a motive these days. Do you know the guy's name?"

"No, but I can tell you he works for the Rec Center's maintenance department."

"How do you know?"

Cindy pointed to a large placard outside the gate. "He's the one who posted that sign about the October reseeding for the dog park. I was here that morning and overheard him complaining to the lady who checks our rec cards. He was pretty loud about getting booted out of his softball position thanks to Buster."

My brain did flipflops at the possibility Buster's killer could be that maintenance worker. Especially if Buster's corpse was dumped from a Rec Center utility cart driven by that man. Like Marshall said, "Too late for trace DNA," but in my mind, not too late for chitchat.

"My next stop is actually their maintenance area. I have a theory and wanted to poke around there. Maybe pick up some clues."

"Or ruffle some feathers. Especially with Streetman."

"Don't remind me, but I'll be quick. I also have to get to work."

Suddenly I remembered that photo Lyndy took of the men seated behind us at Herb's game. It was a long shot but maybe the man Herb identified as the maintenance worker was the very one who got kicked to the curb so Buster would man third base. Without wasting a second, I pulled out my phone, made a few taps and all but shoved it under Cindy's nose.

"Is that him? Is that the man? Not the one who looks like Beaver Cleaver, the other one."

Cindy squinted and stepped back. "It could be. Kind of looks like him. I'm not sure. The guy I saw wasn't facing me directly."

I knew I might have been putting two and two together and coming up with five, but it didn't matter. I was on a roll and unstoppable. A few yards from me, Streetman was on a roll, too. Only in the freshly mowed grass.

"Stop that!" I rushed over to him and saw greenish wet slime on his back. "Stand still while I wipe this off of you." I reached into my bag, grabbed a few tissues and removed whatever wetness I could. "Guess that'll have to do."

Cindy walked to where I stood and laughed. "They usually do that after a bath. Hey, look now. At least he's doing what he's supposed to." Without pausing, she handed me a doggie bag and I immediately cleaned up.

"Thanks. I'm going to hightail it to the maintenance area. Maybe I'll get lucky. You've been a terrific help."

She smiled. "You know where to find me."

A minute or so later, with Streetman on his leash, I was on the sidewalk headed to the utility area. I wasn't sure what I was going to say to any of the workers but I bit my lip and prayed for an epiphany.

Two large work trucks flanked the left side of the small interior parking lot that housed the small utility building. Only one maintenance golf cart was parked in the lot, but seconds later another one, much larger, pulled in. The man behind the wheel appeared to be in his forties, rotund, with short brown hair and day-old stubble. His physique made Herb Garrett's look like Aaron Judge from the New York Yankees. I took a breath and approached the man.

"Hi!" I said as I quickly shoved my leash hand into the pocket of my pants so my wedding ring wouldn't be visible. "Can you tell me if the department keeps a record of the whereabouts of these golf carts during the day? This is kind of personal, but I have a feeling my boyfriend's cheating on me. He works for this department and swears up and down he was on Grandview and Trail Ridge Golf Courses two weeks ago last Sunday but a friend of mine swore she saw him with another woman locking lips in one of these vehicles behind Kuentz Rec Center."

"What's his name?"

I gripped Streetman's leash tighter and glanced at the little chiweenie. So far, so good. He busied himself sniffing the ground. "I'm sorry. That's the last thing I want to divulge. Yes or no? Can you tell me if a record is kept on file?"

The man got out of the golf cart and didn't say a word for what seemed like forever. Finally, he spoke. "Yeah, I get it. I've been on the raw end of cheating myself. It's a bummer. Look, I'm not supposed to do this, but give me a sec. I'll go inside, check the record book and let you know who had a vehicle signed out for one of the golf courses."

"Oh my gosh. I can't thank you enough."

I tried to act nonchalant as I watched him walk into the building. Meanwhile, Streetman gave the performance of a lifetime impersonating a bloodhound in the parking lot. At least he didn't do any damage.

"Cute little guy," the man said when he returned. He bent down to pet Streetman and I froze. *Do not have a neurotic episode, dog, whatever you do.*

Thankfully, the dog was in a pleasant mood and actually nuzzled against the man's hand.

"You must have a dog at home," I said.

"Nope. Four spoiled cats."

"Ah, that's what he smells. He lives with a cat, too."

"Here you go," he said. He handed me a notecard that I grabbed with my free hand. Then he looked around. "We never had this conversation, but I think you'll find what you need."

"I really appreciate it. Really!"

"No problem."

He returned to the utility room and I hustled back to my car where it was parked adjacent to the dog park. By now, the place had really filled up and I could hear the familiar shouts of "Poop alert!" and "Hey, pick up!"

I was dying to read the note but knew better than to do it right then and there. Instead, I waited until I was in front of my mother's house before setting my eyes on it. When I did, I could have turned cartwheels.

Six club car golf carts were signed out for golf courses that day. I immediately eliminated three of them because they were for the opposite side of the community. Nowhere near the disappearing body in question. The remaining three had been signed out for Echo Mesa, Grandview, and Trail Ridge, all within a reasonable distance.

The names listed next to the vehicles were unfamiliar, but I expected as much. However, *unfamiliar* to me didn't necessarily apply to my mother, her friends, or Herb's crew. Not to mention Paul. He seemed to know everyone.

Three maintenance workers. Three utility golf carts. Not bad odds.

CHAPTER 34

Streetman pawed at the car door and I couldn't hold off any longer. With the leash all but permanently attached to my hand, I walked to the front door and rang the bell. It took my mother a few minutes to be sure her "vapor lock" was all set before she opened the first security door.

"My little man!" she exclaimed. "Were you the perfect prince?"

Streetman bumped her leg and charged into the house once she opened the remaining two doors. I peered inside and watched as he made a beeline for Essie and licked her furiously.

"He was fine. Did his business and didn't get into trouble."

"I told you he was making progress with socialization. I think having the cat helps."

I rolled my eyes when she turned to look at her little darlings. "Cindy told me Buster replaced someone who was on the team. Not by that player's choice. And, here's the best part—that guy works for the Rec Center's maintenance department. Could be he held a grudge and found the perfect opportunity to eliminate Buster." Then, I had the most god-awful thought and couldn't hold it in. "You don't think if that's the guy, he'd be going after Herb next, do you? And why didn't Lyman put him back on third base rather than asking Herb?"

My mother ushered me into the kitchen and pointed to her coffeepot. "Maybe he didn't want to go back to the team. People have their pride, after all. And I wouldn't worry too much about Herb. If something was going to happen, it would have already happened."

I winced at her wording. "Okay, so maybe revenge trumps pride. But why kill Buster when it was Lyman who gave the guy the boot? Anyway, I was able to find out which maintenance workers were driving utility golf carts the day Shirley first saw the body."

My mother poured herself a cup of coffee and showed me an empty cup. I shook my head and kept talking. "Shirley finally remembered seeing one of those vehicles on the opposite side of the street. Now I just need to figure out which one. I've narrowed it down to three possibilities. Uncle Louis would say those are good odds."

"Everything's 'good odds' with your uncle. I take it you spoke to someone at the utility maintenance area. Was my Streetman a big help?"

"I wouldn't exactly say he was a big help, but he wasn't a hindrance either. Believe it or not, your upfront and honest daughter lied like a rug in order to get the information. Cecilia would be aghast at the way my moral scruples went down the toilet."

"Oh, for heaven's sake, Phee, it's an investigation. All of those detectives disguise themselves and fabricate all sorts of things."

"Yes. Detectives. Not bookkeeper/accountants posing as actual sleuths."

"You're doing the right thing."

"Kind of like the end justifies the means?"

"Kind of like if you don't find out who's behind this, Shirley may be the next victim. Who knows what that maniac has in mind? And that doesn't include the murder that he already committed."

It was one of those rare moments when I knew my mother was right. I reached for my bag. "Let me jot down the three names of those maintenance workers. Ask around but try to be low-keyed. I don't need you to draw attention to this because Bowman and Ranston will pitch a fit. Geez, of all the times for Nate and Marshall to be out of town on a case."

I grabbed a pen and wrote the names down on the back of a business card advertising home insurance. I had truly become my mother's daughter using unwanted business cards as notepaper. "Talk to you later, Mom. I've got to get to work."

She spun around and called out to the dog, "Give your sister kissies before she leaves."

Streetman froze.

"That's okay." I hurried to the front door and was outside before she had a chance to coax the dog again. Kissies were the last thing I needed.

"I'm so close I can feel it," I said to Augusta the minute I got into the office. "If these little clues I've gathered fall into place, I will have rooted out the murderer."

"Must be the morning for rooting out. Your boss called a few minutes ago. Kept it short and sweet. Said their clues are lining up, too. Harrumph. Sounds like a regular board game to me. Better hope someone doesn't knock it over."

"Did Nate say anything else?"

"Only that your husband will call you tonight."

I smiled. "Want to hear what I found out?"

"You're going to tell me anyway, so start talking."

"The third baseman, who happens to work for the maintenance department, got axed and was replaced by Buster. Right before Shirley found Buster's lifeless body, she saw a Rec Center maintenance vehicle driving into the other side of the golf course from where she made her discovery. Come on, Augusta, put two and two together. The timing is perfect for a body dump. With revenge as the motive for murder, the killer could have easily doctored up Buster's chewing tobacco, or better yet, switched the one he had with the poisoned one. When Buster succumbed, all the killer had to do was roll him out of the cart."

"That's assuming Buster was in the golf cart with him."

"It's feasible. Maybe the guy told Buster he wanted to share some information about the team. Or, better still, maybe he knew about Buster's sideline and used that as a ruse. Loan sharks and gamblers don't turn away from opportunities."

"Pull up on those reins, girl. You're going to need ironclad evidence, the kind those deputies are supposed to find."

"Ugh. Don't remind me. The good news is that I've got three names of employees who checked out maintenance golf carts that morning. And, *here's the best part*, if one of them turns out to be the maintenance worker who sat behind Lyndy and me at that ball game, I've got more than a link. I've got a solid lock in place!"

"How much coffee have you had this morning?"

"Not enough. I'll need another cup before I tackle my real job."

With that, I popped in a K-Cup, waited for it to brew, and trotted off to my office with Augusta shaking her head behind me. To say I was ecstatic would have been an understatement, but all of that ended with Lyndy's phone call an hour later.

Her voice was garbled and it sounded as if she'd been crying. "I know it's not your break time but I had to call."

"What's the matter? Are you at work? Are you okay?"

"I'm fine. I'm in the ladies' room at work. No one can hear me. I can't believe this—Lyman's been arrested under suspicion of murder. He called his attorney, who specializes in wills and codicils, and asked for a recommendation for a criminal defense attorney. His attorney did some of the legwork so Lyman will be able to meet with the defense attorney this afternoon."

"Is Lyman at the posse station?"

"Until the end of the day. Won't get a preliminary hearing until tomorrow if he's lucky. That means—"

"I know. The Fourth Avenue Jail. I could drive there blindfolded. How was he able to call you? I thought they only allowed one phone call."

"Apparently they allow for exceptions. At least they did in his case."

"Can you tell me what happened? What probable cause did the arresting deputies have?"

"They got an anonymous phone call telling them they'd find a tin of Wintergreen chewing tobacco underneath the driver's seat of Lyman's car."

"So what? That's not illegal."

"It is if the prints belonged to Buster LaRoo. They sent the tin to the lab on a rush order. The deputies believe Lyman swapped out Buster's original tin with the poisoned one. Oh my gosh, Phee. This is horrible. I don't believe for one second he's culpable."

"Is that all they found? The tin in Lyman's car?"

"That, and a dieffenbachia plant in the corner of his patio. He swore up and down he didn't have *any* plants there. Said he had a brown thumb and killed them off. Oh my gosh. The only one killed off was Buster. I can't believe this. The first man I've met in a decade who didn't turn me off and now what?"

I took a breath and tried to think. "Calm down. It will be fine. You said he got a defense attorney. That's a good thing. They'll sort through things. Um, did the deputies mention motive?"

"Uh-huh. They kept asking Lyman if he got even with Buster over the equipment loss. Lyman told me he kept insisting he had nothing to do with Buster's murder but that the deputies refused to believe him. Asked instead about the evidence they found."

"And?"

"According to Lyman, the tin under his driver's seat was a no-brainer. He leaves his car unlocked half the time."

"At least the plant was found outdoors. Anyone could have put it there. Does Lyman have a security system?"

"No, he always felt Sun City West was safe."

"It's safe, all right, except of course for the real killer who's lurking around."

"I hate to ask this, but can Nate and Marshall help?"

"I'm sure they'd want to, but they're up in Laughlin on that insurance fraud case. Listen, we'll figure something out. Meanwhile, try to get through your day. I'll call you when I get home. It'll work out. I'm sure it will."

"It'll work out?" Who says such a thing? I have no idea if it will work out. For all I know, they'll issue me a permanent visitor's pass to the Fourth Avenue Jail.

CHAPTER 35

"My time line to find out who axed Buster got cranked up a notch," I said to Augusta the minute I got off the phone with Lyndy. "Did I say notch? More like an entire belt. This is spiraling out of control and I can't very well take Nate and Marshall away from their investigation."

Augusta removed her tortoiseshell glasses and rubbed the bridge of her nose. "Give me the condensed version. Which drama queen called you this time? Your mother? Your aunt? Please don't tell me it was the woman who could pass as a nun."

"Worse yet. It was Lyndy. Lyman's been arrested on suspicion of murder."

"So much for casual dating in the modern age."

"She doesn't believe he did it and neither do I. True, there were some wishy-washy motives but nothing that would call for such an extreme measure. Short of plastering flyers all over town with that cell phone photo we took at the ballpark and the caption, *Do you recognize that man?*, I don't know what else to do at this point. I've already got everyone I know looking into it."

"Then look into something else. You always complain that those deputies are myopic when it comes to investigations and reaching conclusions. What if the maintenance man in that photo doesn't give a hoot about Buster or his unfortunate demise? Think back. There must be other suspects."

I clasped my hands together and nearly cut off the circulation to my fingers. "Hmm, now that you mention it, when Lyndy and I ran into Paul the evening we watched that ball game, he mentioned the concession stand. Said he heard his fair share of gossip and that Buster had hit the three B's—betting, bookmaking, and blackmail. I never got to ask him what else he knew."

Augusta rubbed her chin and smiled.

"Don't you dare suggest I offer to go fishing with him in order to find out what he knows. I'll never be able to get that incident at Tailgators out of my mind."

"A few fins and tails are going to prevent you from finding a killer?"

"Aargh, if you put it *that* way. But it doesn't necessarily mean a fishing excursion. I'll give Herb a call and see if he knows where Paul hangs out when he's not at a lake, on the radio, or cutting bait."

"Probably Cabela's. Which reminds me, they've got a nice Ruger standard-bolt rifle I've been eyeing. I should stop by."

"If I do wind up meeting him at Cabela's I guarantee it'll be in the pro-fishing shop."

"That, or the aquarium exhibit. Nothing like looking at those walleye, carp, and bass up front and personal."

I cringed and walked back to my office. "Maybe I can talk him into Starbucks."

"What's today? Wednesday?" Herb asked when I got him on the phone a few minutes later. "Paul's at the men's club, why? Is Tailgators hunting him down? That'll be the second piece of gossip I heard today and it's not even noon."

I closed my eyes and prayed that the first piece of chin-wagging didn't involve Lyman. *Who am I kidding? Of course it involves Lyman.* I took a breath and waited for Herb to dish the dirt.

"Wayne was in the posse station this morning to pick up some neighborhood watch signs and you'll never guess who they arrested—Lyman Neal. It has to be for Buster's murder. What else could it be? Wayne was in the outer room but he could see Lyman in that little interrogation room and overheard him demanding to call his attorney."

"That's how rumors get started. For all anyone knows, it could have been a traffic violation."

"Not when someone says, 'I didn't kill him.'"

I rolled my eyes and took a breath. "Does my mother know?"

"I haven't called her yet, if that's what you're asking. I'm trying to get a few loads of laundry done. Ran out of clean underwear and had to—"

"That's okay, I get it. Look, whatever you do, don't call my mother. She'll spread that news like a California wildfire. I need to talk to her first. And don't worry, she'll know soon enough." *Along with the entire West Coast.*

"Fine. Why do you need Paul? You and Marshall aren't taking up fishing, are you?"

"Ek! No! I think Paul might know something about the goings-on at that concession stand at the ball field. And who really killed Buster."

"Yeah, I had a hard time wrapping my head around Lyman as a murderer. Paul's playing euchre and he should be done any minute. Then, it's anyone's guess. If I were you, I'd mention lunch. That guy has an appetite. He's probably going out somewhere."

And sure enough, Herb was right. I thanked him and dialed the men's club in time to find out that Paul left for Long John Silver's in Peoria, all but walking distance from here. Well, marathon walking . . . I saved the spreadsheet I was working on, grabbed my bag and rushed out of my office.

"Early lunch today, Augusta. Want me to bring you back some fish?"

"I've been to Cabela's. Thanks."

"No, Long John Silver's. Paul is on his way over there. Besides, I haven't had a fish sandwich in who knows how long. And while I'm biting into fried haddock and tartar sauce, I'll see what I can weasel out of Paul. Myopic vision, my you-know-what. You were right. Time to chase another clue."

"Just be sure to wash it down with enough soda or iced tea. And thanks for the offer but I'll pass on the fried fish."

Long John Silver's and Taco Bell shared the same building on 83rd and Peoria Avenue. It was a strange combination as far as my food tastes were concerned, but it wasn't food I was after. I had beaten the lunch crowd but not by much. Many of the booths and tables were already occupied and it was impossible to locate Paul without walking all over the place. Unfortunately, I located Myrna Mittleson without even trying.

She stood in a short line of two people and spotted me immediately. "Phee! What brings you here? Oh, goodness, I should know better. Your office isn't too far away. Had a hankering for fried fish? I did. Not that I drove all this way just for fish, mind you, but I had an appointment with my chiropractor at his Peoria office. He's only in Sun City West on Mondays and I have bocce practice then, so naturally I had to drive all the way over here."

I looked at the line and it moved slowly. Way too slowly. That meant I was stuck listening to Myrna ramble on about bocce and chiropractors and who knows what else. At least she hadn't heard about Lyman or he would have become number three on her conversation list.

"Um, actually, I was hoping to run into Paul. Herb told me he was here."

Myrna looked stricken. "Paul? *Our* Paul? Fish-talking Paul?"

"Uh-huh."

"Why?"

I kept my voice as low as possible and told her I needed to track down some information he might have regarding Buster's murder.

"Well," she said, "you won't have far to track. Isn't that him coming out of the restroom?"

Sure enough, Paul exited the restroom corridor and made a beeline for a booth that had no occupants but a table full of fried fish and all sorts of side dishes.

"Thanks, Myrna. I'd better get over there."

"Aren't you going to order something first?"

I shook my head. "Paul's a fast eater. He might be done by the time I get to the front of the line. Enjoy your fish."

"If he's still eating, I'll join the both of you. It's much more fun to dine with someone."

True, and it was a matter of semantics, but nothing at all smacked of "dining" in these fast-food places. I mumbled something and charged over to Paul's table.

"Hey, Paul, what a coincidence finding you and Myrna here," I said. "It's my lunch hour." *More or less.*

"What? Myrna's here? Don't tell me she wants to talk about our radio show. And how'd she find out I was here in the first place?"

"Uh, she didn't. She stopped in for lunch after a doctor's appointment."

"Good, because I have this week's program all set. I plan to talk about lures. I've had good luck with the Mepps Hot Trout Kit and thought I'd pass that on to listeners. Of course, nothing beats the Rapala Floating Lure but sometimes you got to mix it up a bit."

Oh, crap. He's going to binge talk about fishing lures.

"Of course," he continued, "Myrna and your mother are going to cut in and yammer about some cutesy cozy mystery novel that features cupcakes or petit fours, but if you ask me, listeners want something they can sink their teeth into, like a grilled lake trout."

"I don't know many cozy mysteries that feature lake trout but I need your help with the one that features a certain third baseman who choked on tainted chewing tobacco."

"Huh?"

"The last time we spoke, other than that fiasco at Tailgators, which I'd like to forget, you mentioned the concession stand at the ball field. I was with my friend Lyndy and you said something about Buster and blackmail. Care to be more specific?"

Paul looked around as if the place was bugged. Then he motioned for me to take a seat. I glanced at the line and Myrna still had one person in front of her.

"Okay, I'm seated," I said. "What's with the blackmail?"

"Buster was blackmailing someone in that business. Those kinds of secrets don't stay secrets for long in Sun City West."

"What do you mean *someone*? I thought Karl Creedman was the owner of the concession stand."

"Ever hear of silent partners?"

And then, the polar opposite of the word *silent*. Myrna tromped over to Paul's booth, placed a pile of fried fish and chips on the table and announced in the loudest voice possible, "So, what is it you've been keeping to yourself about Buster LaRoo's murder?"

CHAPTER 36

I immediately looked to see if anyone heard her, and if so, reacted. Thankfully Long John Silver's was not located in a retirement community, hence no one's ears perked up. Instead, I noticed parents dealing with toddlers who did everything possible with their fish except to eat it. The few patrons who didn't have children with them were either scrolling on their cell phones or listening to something with their earbuds.

"Shh," I said. "We don't want to call attention to this." Then I looked at Paul. "Who was the silent partner? Are you saying it was Karl's partner who was being blackmailed?"

Myrna opened a packet of tartar sauce and glopped it on a piece of fish. "Who's blackmailing the partner? And who's Karl? Is this about the"—and then she lowered her voice—"murder?"

Paul reiterated that he had heard Buster was blackmailing someone who was involved with the concession stand but he couldn't substantiate it. Only that he had heard it from more than one "reliable" source. With that, he took a giant bite of his Pacific cod sandwich and all but swallowed it whole before he spoke. "You're married to a detective, Phee. This should be right up your alley."

"Huh? What's right up my alley?"

"Sneaking into that concession stand when no one's around so you can find evidence of blackmail."

"Find evidence? The only thing I'll find is an arrest warrant for breaking and entering. Are you nuts?"

"I didn't say 'breaking and entering.' And if you're going to do it, tonight's your lucky night."

"Define 'lucky.'"

"Yeah," Myrna chimed in. "Why is it her lucky night?"

"Because I happen to know for a fact that Karl couldn't turn down a certain poker game in Surprise and he's got his high school nephew holding down the fort. The kid couldn't hold down a fifteen-pound rock, if you catch my drift. Too busy playing video games. Karl asked around if any of us would be willing to step in and help. Offered to pay minimum wage. Whoop-de-do. I'd say Karl's probably a bit desperate by now."

Myrna poked me in the arm. "Pay *him* the minimum wage and snoop around."

"How am I going to snoop around if I'm busy making hot dogs and hamburgers?"

Myna opened another packet of tartar sauce. "We'll get reinforcements. Louise worked as a short-order cook for F.W. Woolworth when she was in high school. And no one can make tamales and tacos like Lucinda."

Three mental eye rolls came and went in my head. "They don't serve tamales and tacos. Only hot dogs and the like. Besides, once word gets out, your entire book club will show up."

I pictured someone opening a drawer and yelling, "Does this look like a payoff slip for blackmail?" Or, worse yet, "Have you found any extortion letters in here?"

"Hmm," Myrna said. "You make a good point. Some of those women don't understand the definition of *subtle.*"

Or irony, for that matter . . .

I propped my elbow on the table and leaned on it, my eyes fixed on Paul. "What about the so-called silent partner? Can't he or she flip hot dogs or burgers?"

Paul shoved the remainder of his sandwich into his mouth and wiped his lips with the backside of his hand. "Not if they're silent. Geez."

"So?" Myrna asked. "Should I call Louise and Lucinda?"

"No. No. I need a few minutes to think." I closed my eyes and pressed my fingertips to my temples. I couldn't very well ask Lyndy to step in again. And words like *ransacked* and *plundered* came to mind at the mere thought of the Booked 4 Murder book club ladies offering their culinary assistance. Instead, I opted for the nuclear solution.

I clapped my hands together with enough force so that Paul's Coke shook in its glass. "Only one way around this. You'll need to man that grill while I make sure the nephew doesn't budge from his video entertainment. That way, I can seamlessly poke around for any correspondence that may be floating around. The way I see it, you owe me for that disaster the other night."

Paul widened his eyes. "Me? You expect *me* to grill meat?"

"Oh, for goodness sake," Myrna said. "Think of it as pretty little pink fish without the fins."

I tried not to laugh. "What time tonight?"

Paul looked defeated. "The game starts at seven thirty. Red Team opposite the Sun City Stokes. Meet me at the concession stand at six thirty. I'll let Karl know his nephew will have backup."

"Backup? He'll have the whole night to himself on cyberspace." With that, I stood and edged out of the booth.

"Phee," Myrna said, "you haven't even eaten. Here, take this fried fillet of cod with you."

She reached for a napkin as I stepped back from the table. "I'm fine. Really, I am. Had a big breakfast." When I was a good yard or two from the table I called back, "Sixty thirty. See you then, Paul."

I was positive my clothing reeked of fried fish but there was nothing I could do about it. In fact, I wouldn't even have time to go home after work, change, and get to the concession stand by six thirty. At least the fabric in my shirt and pants would absorb new odors—grilled meat.

Although I intended to grab a sandwich at Long John Silver's, I lost the appetite for it while watching Paul stuff fish into his mouth and Myrna chomp away. Now starving, I pulled into a Wendy's drive-through so I could munch on a burger when I got back to the office. What I didn't expect was the news Augusta delivered the second I opened the door.

"It darn well took them long enough," she said. "It's been what? Nine or ten days since they rooted around Shirley's house?"

"Huh? Who are we talking about? And by the way, keep a distance. I smell like fish grease."

"Could be worse. Paul could have been preparing bait."

I winced. "Tell me, what's been nine or ten days?"

"Here, see for yourself. The fax is addressed to Mr. Williams and/or Mr. Gregory but someone had to remove it from the machine. It's from the Maricopa County Sheriff's Office. It's a copy of the forensic report their lab sent to Deputies Bowman and Ranston."

I took the paper from Augusta's hand and read it. "It's the analysis of the dirt they found on Shirley's Swiffer. Wow, if that isn't a smoking gun, I don't know what is. That dirt had to have come from the ball field. It says it's a combination of sand, silt, and clay minerals. That's what Herb said was in ballpark dirt. You know what this means, don't you?"

"Yep. Someone didn't wipe their feet. Can't teach manners soon enough."

"Very funny. Whoever was in Shirley's house to plant that bugging device was also on the ball field. Trouble is, how does that get narrowed down?"

"You tell me. What did you find out from Paul? Does he have a viable suspect other than the mysterious maintenance man you've been chasing?"

"Um, we may find out tonight. If we don't mess up."

"Uh-oh. I'm not liking the sound of this."

"Heck, I'm not liking any of it but someone has to do something, and with Nate and Marshall out of town, I have a one-chance opportunity to find out more about that concession stand owner. Besides, this was your idea, remember? You said to find out what Paul knew."

"From a conversation, not something that sounds a little off-kilter."

"It's a well-thought-out plan. And it's not as if I'm sneaking behind my husband's back, or my boss for that matter. They're up in Laughlin."

Augusta listened intently for the next two or three minutes while I told her my intentions. Then, she pursed her lips and furrowed her brow. "Let me get this straight. You and Paul are going to take over the concession stand tonight so Karl can lose his shirt at poker, Paul can overcook the meat, and you can snoop around for any evidence that might connect Karl to Buster's murder. Have I got it right?"

"Pretty much. We just need to get rid of the nephew or keep him otherwise occupied."

"Point him to a Wi-Fi hotspot and you should be all set."

"Hmm, good point. The Rec Center by the ball field has an outdoor patio area with one."

"See, problem solved."

The problem may have been solved for Augusta, but truth be known, I wasn't quite sure what I was looking for, only that rumors abounded when it came to Karl. Especially since Paul bandied about the word *blackmail* worse than my mother's friends did when they thought they were on to something. Still, the concept of blackmail narrowed it down a bit. Except of course for the reason.

I rationalized that blackmailing could come in one of two forms—a verbal threat or a written one. Since I was after solid evidence, I needed to find written proof somewhere in that concession stand. From what my uncle Louis found out at that gig of his, the concession stand building was Karl's home base. If so, I imagined his records were stashed somewhere behind the door marked *Office, Employees Only*. If nothing else, it was a start.

Augusta did me a favor and called out for deli sandwiches a little after four. She said she wouldn't have time for dinner since she had a busy evening planned with some of her canasta friends, but I knew better. She didn't want me to starve to death poking around the concession stand while Paul made an attempt at grilling.

If I didn't know Karl's nephew was in high school, I would have mistaken him for a sixth-grader. Seventh grade tops. He was seated a few feet away from the serving counter on the steps of the concession stand. Thin, gawky, with chin-length hair, freckles, and round "John Lennon" glasses. His head was buried in an iPad and he didn't notice me at first. It was six fifteen and I was early.

I cleared my throat as I approached. "Hi! You must be Karl's nephew. I'm Phee. I'm supposed to be helping you tonight."

"Blaine. And the big guy in there said I didn't have to work but maybe I will. The Wi-Fi sucks around here."

"Not if you walk over to that courtyard by the side of the Rec Building. If anyone asks, tell them you're waiting for your uncle, but I don't think anyone will bother you."

He stood and looked at the courtyard. "Sweet. Thanks."

Three seconds later and he was off. A few people had staked out their spots in the stands but I didn't expect the place to fill up for at least another half hour. Still, Paul needed a head start to prepare everything in case there was an onslaught of customers.

I bolted up the steps, turned the doorknob and walked inside the place. Paul lugged a bin from the refrigerator and announced, "Chopped onion, relish, you name it. The nephew gave me the rundown before his phone buzzed. Next thing I knew he raced outside."

"His name's Blaine and he didn't go far. I met him on the steps and sent him to the Rec Center courtyard for better Wi-Fi. Um, it looks like you know what you're doing, so if you don't mind, I'm going to poke around Karl's office before we get hammered."

"Good luck. The door's locked."

I stared at the *Office, Employees Only* sign for a minute and perused the rest of the work area. "Either Karl locked that door on our account or because he didn't want Blaine nosing around in there. Either way, it was probably a last-minute thought and the key is most likely stashed close by."

Much as I hated to admit it, this wasn't my first time poking around places that were clearly off-limits. In the few short years since I'd come to Sun City West, I moved from Dumpster diving to prying around people's residences and even rooting through dressers in an effort to flush out a killer. A locked concession stand office was not about to deter me.

"Which of those drawers in front of you has the cutlery?"

"The what?"

"Knifes and forks, for heaven's sake!"

Paul opened two drawers. "Mostly serving utensils. The knives and forks are plastic and they're in those cardboard boxes near the fridge. And by the way, I'm only doing this to square up for that little mishap at Tailgators."

"Understood." *Mishap, my foot. It's right up there with* The Titanic *and* The Hindenburg. I walked to where he stood and moved a few spatulas and prongs off to the side before finding a small key on a plastic fob that read *Melvin's Plumbing* and another key with a white paper tag that read *Freezer*.

Like Cinderella's slipper, the key on the plastic fob fit perfectly in the office door, but that's where my luck ended. At least for the next half hour. While Paul cussed and moaned on the other side of the door, I slipped on the pair of food-handler gloves I kept in my bag. Then I studied Karl's impeccably neat desk with its relic of a computer and realized I'd have to be sure everything on the desk was exactly as he'd left it. Not willing to risk anything to memory, I pulled out my phone and took a photo of it. Then, I sat in his chair and booted up the computer.

A small box demanding a password appeared but Karl wasn't like the book club ladies, whose passwords were their names. And to my knowledge he didn't have any pets. I had no idea when he was born or where, so that left two other viable choices out of the picture.

I stood and walked to the kitchen area. Paul had moved the boxes of hot dog and hamburger rolls closer to the grill and had two platefuls of hot dogs and hamburger patties precariously positioned near the griddle.

"I think those cardboard boxes are too close to the grill," I said. "And the meats look as if they might fall at any second."

"I've got it under control."

In retrospect I should have stepped in right then and there, but I had my own problem to deal with—finding that darn password.

CHAPTER 37

"Fine," I said, "but I'd keep an eye on those things if I were you."

"What about you? Did you find anything yet?"

"I can't get into his computer without a password."

"Try 'Ballpark Dogs.' It's the name of this place."

"It is? There's no sign or anything. And there was no mention of it anywhere. How do you know?"

"Because I found it on this invoice for ketchup and mustard that was on the floor. It must have dropped."

Paul handed me the slip of paper and I wondered why the vendor hadn't simply emailed it. Then I realized it was probably a receipt copy that went along with the goods.

"Thanks." I made a mad dash for Karl's computer, and within seconds I was home free. "Got it!" I shouted.

"Work fast because the place is filling up and we've got to get moving in here."

I rolled my eyes and searched for the two programs that were bound to house information: Microsoft Word and Excel. Without dawdling, I took out the thumb drive I'd put in my bag earlier in the day and began to copy the files. I'd learned from experience that time pretty much quadruples when conducting computer searches on someone else's device. Besides, I wasn't all that convinced Karl housed the kind of information I was looking for on his computer. Still, it was a logical first step.

When Aunt Ina and I had to ferret out information at my uncle Louis's place before they were married, I was astonished to find little slips of paper and tiny wads of notes stashed in places I'd rather not think about. Louis was a gambler and Karl, I believed, was also a member of that club. I reasoned that if I were to find anything that smacked of blackmail, it wouldn't be on a computer, but rather, at the bottom of a desk drawer somewhere waiting for me to get my clutches on it.

While Paul continued to spout expletives in the kitchen area, I began my search in earnest, beginning with the desk drawers. Again, the obsessive neatness. It was almost frightening. Like the kind of stuff one reads about after a crazed serial killer has been apprehended. Then again, my mother's friends leaned in that clean-freak direction as well.

Nothing of interest in the three drawers to the right of his desk. And no file cabinets in the small room. I imagined the business transactions were all documented in the spreadsheets I'd copied.

I leaned toward the computer screen with my fingers on the edge of the desk and my thumbs hanging down. Oddly enough, my thumbs didn't touch the edge of the desk, so I bent down to see why. There was a panel but no pull knob. My immediate assumption was that the desk was built to look as if it had a fourth drawer when it didn't, much like the panels under kitchen and bathroom sinks.

In a flash I remembered my Aunt Ina's mahogany roll-top desk with the hidden compartment in the center. In order to open it, she had to find a tiny hole underneath the front drawer and push on it. With nothing to lose, I felt underneath the desk, and sure enough my finger located the release button.

I don't remember holding my breath but I must have because as soon as the drawer released, I let it out for what seemed like minutes instead of seconds. I stared at the opened horizontal drawer and couldn't believe what was in front of me—the epitome of every noir movie and 1930s crime novel I'd ever read.

It was a well-worn black notebook that couldn't have been more than five by eight inches. Images of hit lists and payoffs immediately sprang to mind. Just then, Paul called out, "Hey, can you give me a hand in here? I may have a situation."

We all have situations. Deal with it.

"What kind of a situation? I'm in the middle of something."

"Hurry up."

I wasn't sure if Paul's idea of a situation meant he couldn't find tartar sauce or something more drastic like catching those cardboard boxes on fire with splattered grease from the grill. It didn't matter, no way was there time for me to peruse the little black book. At least not then and there.

Without pausing to inhale, I whipped out my iPhone again and page by page took carefully centered photos of the book's contents with two pages on each photo. I was halfway through when I heard Paul yell, "Oh, crap!"

I was so engrossed with my discovery that I didn't smell the smoke until it was too late. I all but flew from the chair and charged into the kitchen. "What's on fire? What did you do?"

"Nothing's on fire. It's just smoke coming out of the microwave. I forgot I put hot dogs in there."

"What? Why on earth did you put hot dogs in the microwave? They're supposed to be grilled."

Paul rolled his neck and pointed to the floor. "They sort of fell off the plate by the grill and I thought if I microwaved them first, I'd get rid of any germs that were on the floor. Guess I cooked them for too long."

By now, the localized smoke near the microwave seemed to be all over the place and the hot dogs that Paul overcooked had exploded in the microwave. Pieces of leathery pink meat stuck to the sides, top, and bottom of the oven. It would take the scrubbing strength of a bench presser to clean it up. I managed to remove the larger chucks but the rest of the mess would have to wait. "We'll have to dump this debris outside when we're—"

And that was the last word I uttered before the smoke alarm went off. "Quick!" I tossed him a towel and threw the meat into the small trash bin under the sink. "Open the side windows! Blow that smoke out." Unfortunately, it was too late. The alarm wouldn't quit. "Is there a stepladder around here?" I asked. "You need to disable the battery."

"I'm looking. I'm looking." Paul sounded frantic but not as frantic as the voices outside the concession stand.

"The concession stand is on fire!"

"Someone dial nine-one-one!"

"The fire station is across the street! Pound on their door!"

"Is anyone trapped? Call nine-one-one."

The last thing I needed was the Sun City West fire crew to respond to Paul's microwave blunder. Those firefighters would be trampling all over the place, including Karl's office, where they'd spy that open drawer and word would get back to Karl. I had to think fast but it was as if my brain froze.

If that wasn't all, the clamor and voices must have dislodged Blaine from his electronic device, and next thing I knew he added his two cents to the crowd that had now gathered in front of the concession stand. "Is the damn place on fire? My uncle's going to kill me!"

"See what you've done," I muttered to Paul. "Can't you get that alarm to stop sounding? The smoke's just about gone. Why doesn't it shut off?"

"They never do."

Paul found a folding chair somewhere in the place and thankfully managed to stand on it without killing himself. Then he removed the battery from the smoke alarm and announced, "I'd say we're even for Tailgators."

"Even?" I couldn't contain my voice. "This mess is all your fault. Keep your fingers crossed the fire department doesn't show up." Then, I stepped outside and scanned the crowd. At least twenty people. Possibly more.

"Everything's fine," I said. "Minor cooking mishap. No fire. We'll be ready with refreshments in a few minutes." And like that, the comments changed. Except for Blaine's.

"How dead am I going to be?"

"Not very," I said and gulped. "You can go back to your game or whatever it is you're doing. Everything here is under control."

He mumbled "cool" or something like that and took off. The crowd, however, didn't budge. Instead, they made demands, and lots of them.

"I'm starving. Those hot dogs better be hot and ready. And the chili sauce, too."

"I'll put in my order now for double nachos."

"Last time my burger was too well-done. Get it right this time."

I nodded and went back inside, making sure to close the door behind me. "Did you know about the chili sauce?" I asked Paul.

"Uh, yeah, it's premade and on a pot on the stove. Only . . . only . . ."

"Only what?"

"I forgot to heat it up."

I rolled my eyes. "That's what microwaves are for." Then I remembered what was last in the microwave and winced. "The crowd can wait a few minutes. I need to finish up in Karl's office and then I'll help you. In the meantime, get some hot dogs on the grill and don't burn them."

My cell phone and Karl's little black book were right where I left them, on the top of his desk. Without wasting another second, I picked up where I left off and used the phone's camera to take pictures of the remaining pages in the book. Then, because I feared something might happen to the phone, like Paul stepping on it, I made sure to keep it tucked safe in my possession and once home, I'd email the photos I'd taken to the email address for the office.

As frantic as I was, I made sure to hit the icon for email and not Airdrop, Messenger, Facebook, or any of the other social media spots so that when I got home, I'd be set.

"What's taking you so long?" Paul's voice all but shook the wall that separated us.

"One more second."

Uploading photos to email is a tedious process, especially when it involves lots of them. Worse yet, there's a risk of putting too many photos on one email, causing it to foul up and not send the message. I wasn't about to take that chance. I made sure I had all the photos I needed and would send the entire contents to the office piecemeal. When I was positive I had everything, I put the notebook back in the drawer, centered the way he had it, and made sure the drawer was closed tightly. Then, I shut down his computer and studied the photo I'd taken of his desk.

With the precision of a watchmaker, I placed every pen, pencil and object just the way Karl had them when I entered the room. Seconds later, I closed the door, locked it and returned the key to the utility drawer. All with food handler gloves still on.

Paul opened the serving window and turned to me. "The natives are getting restless. Guess we can wing it."

Twenty minutes into serving and we were out of meat.

"Check the fridge and those freezers," I said. "Hopefully there's enough in the fridge so we won't have to defrost anything from one of the freezers, but the key to the big freezer is in the utensil drawer, the same place where I found the office key."

A few seconds later, Paul's voice shook the walls. "We're okay. I checked the freezers anyway just to be sure. Get this—lots of frozen hot dog and hamburger buns in the little freezer along with boxes of hot dogs and hamburger patties, but the big freezer is empty. Absolutely empty."

"Maybe it stopped working."

"Nope. Colder than Siberia. Go figure."

"Forget about the freezer. As long as we have the meat, we'll be fine."

Wishful thinking at its best.

CHAPTER 38

There was chili splatter in my hair when I got home, and the smoky grease from the grill, combined with the stale fish odors, permeated my clothing to the extent that I actually undressed in the garage and tossed my outfit into the wash. It would have been one of the worst nights of my life except for one small detail—I had all the evidence I needed on my cell phone to find out exactly what Karl Creedman had been up to. *If* the rumors and murmurings were true.

I headed for the shower, when I glanced at the landline and saw there was a message on the answering machine. Marshall had called the day before to let me know they'd arrived safely and would be perusing leads. Then Nate had told August that Marshall would be calling me tonight at home and not on the cell. I imagined it was because of something Rolo had told him about calls being traced. Drat! I'd missed his call.

My finger couldn't tap the playback button fast enough. The one thing that could be said for landlines was that the reception was crystal-clear and it sounded as if Marshall was a few feet from me and not in the next state.

"Sorry I missed you, hon. It's a little after nine and I'll try again around eleven. I imagine you're either swimming with Lyndy or dining out." *Guess again.* "Very strange scenario here. Found Lamont Rooney, all right, but only on paper. I'll tell you about it later when I call back. Hope you had a good swim. Miss you."

At least I knew he and Nate were fine and not in a dangerous situation. I plopped the thumb drive from Karl's computer into my own for a virus scan and then got into the shower as fast as I could. My hair needed a good shampooing and I wasn't about to wait another minute. When I had pretty much toweled dried and tossed on some sweats, the phone rang again. Figuring it was Marshall, I picked up right away.

Shirley's voice took me completely by surprise given the hour. Suddenly I was on high alert for fear something bad had happened. "Phee? Thank goodness you're home. I tried earlier but there was no answer and I couldn't remember where I'd written down your cell phone number."

"Are you all right? Did someone try to break in?"

"Lordy, no. I didn't mean to scare you but I got the strangest phone call from Geraldine Kremler. She said she had to talk to someone and I was the only one she could trust. Said she heard Buster was dead and asked if it was true. Asked if a body had been found or if it was assumed he was dead from maybe a fire, or a drowning. Now that's an odd thing to ask, wouldn't you say?"

"I, um, er—"

"Well, it doesn't matter. I told her he was as dead as a doornail and that I'd seen his corpse on at least two occasions. Before I could give her the details, she started muttering things like 'the family could really use the money.' When I asked her what she was talking about, she asked again if I was positive Buster was really dead, and when I said yes, she indicated she would write the county for a death certificate."

"Uh, yeah. That really is strange."

"She must have been referring to that shared bank account of theirs. It's in both names. I suppose a death certificate would tidy things up and she could get her hands on that money without question."

"That makes sense. I suppose she must have felt some relief knowing he couldn't hold anything over her anymore."

"There's something else, Phee."

"What?"

"Maybe it was the connection or my ears played tricks on me, but I swore I heard her mumble to herself, 'He's really dead,' before we ended the call."

"Did you ever find out where Geraldine lives in Nevada?"

"Oh, yes. Her son's family lives in a residential community off of Needles Highway in Laughlin. He and his wife both teach at William G. Bennett Elementary School. Talk about convenient."

Talk about coincidence . . . Then again, maybe my mind is playing tricks.

"Shirley, did you tell Geraldine about your house being bugged and that hit on the head you got?"

"No, I never got the chance. She had to end the call quickly because she didn't want her son or his wife to hear anything. Lordy, I could never live like that. Imagine, not being able to have a private conversation in your own home. I'm still having the heebie-jeebies just thinking about my own house being bugged."

"Speaking of which, did those deputies tell you anything about the evidence they found on your Swiffer?"

"They found something? What? When?"

I cringed. I never should have said a word and now I was stuck. Rather than dig myself into a hole, I told her about the fax our office received that afternoon. "All it really means," I said, "is that whoever was inside your house most likely had something to do with the ballpark. And frankly, we already figured out that much."

"As long as Thor is here, I think I'll be fine. By the way, I plan to bring him to that Cactus ball game on Saturday. All of the book club ladies are going, including your aunt."

"At least you won't have to put him in a stroller like my mother does with Streetman."

We both laughed and I thanked her for letting me know about her bizarre call from Geraldine. I couldn't remember who it was who said there was no such thing as coincidence and I began to think they were right. I grabbed the pencil and pad next to the phone and drew a circle with three names in it—Buster, Geraldine, and Laughlin. Then, I wrote out Buster's full name and stared at the letters.

The nebulous thoughts clouding up my mind began to gel but I knew I was a good way off before I could make sense of them. Instead, I got busy with the one thing that would make sense—Karl's spreadsheets. It was ten thirty and I was already on edge waiting for Marshall's call. I had to keep occupied and I wasn't in the mood to channel surf or watch the news.

Pulling up an Excel spreadsheet was second nature to me and I immediately dove into the file marked "Business Accounts." The only other file was labeled "Misc. Documents" and it sounded like a Word doc from Microsoft. I figured it was a hodgepodge of stuff that could wait.

Karl's spreadsheet was a simple enough setup consisting of monthly income and expenses. Income was generated from sales of goods, namely foods purchased at the concession stand. No sale of tangible property, other than the food, of course.

Expenses included utilities, licensing fees, advertising, goods purchased, legal/professional, and taxes. Karl also had a column for travel but there were no entries. At first glance, nothing stood out, but I knew that in order for the business to be on the up and up, the food expenses would have to reconcile with the income. That meant a painstaking look line by line, month by month, product by product.

I began with January and took a hard look at the products: ground beef patties, ground beef, canned nacho cheese sauce, hot dogs, hot dog and hamburger rolls, ketchup, mustard, relish, onions, peppers, canned chili sauce, Frank's hot sauce, nacho chips, napkins, plastic utensils, salt, pepper, and Band-Aids. I imagined his major purchases such as pots and pans had been made prior.

Quantities were based on cartons for the most part, and I had to do some quick thinking. Too bad my mother wasn't here. She could nail a product down to the penny on *The Price Is Right*. As for me, I was always a few dollars off. However, I wasn't *that* far off to find a discrepancy. Either that, or to spy the deal of the century on hot dog and hamburger rolls for the month of January.

Granted, consumers save money on large quantity purchases, but still, packages of those rolls usually run $2.50–$2.99 a bag, not less than a dollar. Again, maybe there was some deal going on from his distributor that month.

Chalking it up to an anomaly, I moved on to February, and that's when the phone rang. I couldn't reach it fast enough, and hearing Marshall's greeting alleviated the tension that had caused my neck to tighten.

"Hey, I've missed you. Hope your day wasn't as crazy as ours."

"Uh, just the usual. Tell me what you found out. Were you able to track down the whereabouts of Lamont Rooney?"

"Oh, we tracked him down, all right. Located his apartment and everything. Only one glitch. The guy doesn't exist. At least not in flesh and blood."

"Huh? How's that possible?"

"Everything was done online, including his lease and payment via an electronic bank transfer. Had to be a cash deal. Similar to a cashier's check only electronic. We were able to meet with the landlord and scope out the apartment, but we might as well have been looking at the residential suites at the Marriott. The place came completely furnished and there was no sign of anyone living there. The landlord thought he might have been in the process of moving in but hadn't done that yet. Frankly, Nate and I aren't so sure."

"Now what?"

"We'll ask around and work with Rolo on the money-trail end of things. At this rate, Nate and I will be buying burner phones in bulk. Tell me about your day."

"Are you familiar with *The Lion, the Witch, and the Wardrobe*? Because it's sort of like that."

CHAPTER 39

"I'm afraid to ask so you might as well clue me in," Marshall said. "It was a long, tangled chase to seek out information from an entirely different source. Only it involved Paul and you can only imagine how that turned out."

"More freshly caught fish in all the wrong places?"

"Not quite, but bad enough. It started with an innocent conversation I had with Augusta regarding widening my net."

"Your net? You *have* been hanging around Paul too long. And as for Augusta . . . well, go on."

"I've been so focused on finding out who that maintenance man was in the photo Lyndy took that I hadn't considered the other possibility regarding Buster's murder. Paul mentioned something about the concession stand and some sticky business going on. Then, serendipitously, he told me the owner had a poker game tonight and needed people to cover for him. I couldn't pass on the opportunity to pry around."

"Let me guess. You talked Paul into working the refreshments with you."

"Bingo. And he talked Karl into letting us. For minimum wage, mind you."

Marshall roared with laughter when I mentioned the exploding hot dogs and subsequent reaction from the hungry fans who wanted something to eat. "At least you picked a very public spot with a more-than-conspicuous accomplice for your snooping. Any luck?"

"That's what I'm working on now. I figured out Karl's computer password and photo'd the account spreadsheets he had. Not only that but I located a desk key and found a little black book. Copied that, too."

"Rolo would be proud."

"Forget Rolo. What about you?"

"Nervous as hell. I'll be glad when we can get out of here but we've got a few leads to follow and we can't quit now. Lamont, whoever he really is, is quite the clever mastermind. Either he faked his own death already and is waiting for his accomplice to come through with the beneficiary monies or he's about to fake his death. Not to mention he garnered quite a bit of money with that other insurance scam that resulted in the Gilbert standoff. From what Nate and I figure, this Lamont guy has got to be in pretty good physical shape to have gotten out of the Gilbert location so fast. Aargh. Talk about a double play. The guy's quick on his feet as well as his brains. Actually, make it a triple play."

"What do you mean?"

"He's got to have certain style, or wit about him. He'd need it to convince others to do his bidding."

"Either that or he could simply be one of those old-fashioned gangster types. You know what I mean—menacing."

"You may be right. Hey, before I forget, we got a text from Bowman but you probably knew this already. Augusta's pretty quick on the draw with that fax machine. The lab found ball field dirt on Shirley's Swiffer. No doubt about it. Whoever was in her house was also on the ball field."

"Yep. That narrows it down to what? Eleven or more teams if you count Sun City?"

"There's more. They also found— Sorry, hon, I've got to go. A call's coming in on one of our burners. Must be Rolo. Nate's down the hall getting ice. Looks like we may have a fun night ahead. I'll text you tomorrow and call at night. Love you."

"Love you, too. Be careful."

"Always."

If my brain wasn't swimming in circles before Marshall's call, it was in a virtual vortex when I hung up. It was a few minutes past eleven and I decided to peruse the month of February on Karl's spreadsheets before turning in for the night. Funny, but that sort of thing usually relaxes me. Unfortunately, that wasn't the case this time.

February was almost the spitting image of January when it came to cost regarding hot dog and hamburger buns. So much for getting to bed. I moved rapidly through March, April, May, and June, concentrating only on the line for those darn buns. And again, the same thing, only less money expended. If something fishy was going on, I wondered why Karl would have been so honest about it on his spreadsheets. Then two thoughts crossed my mind. His tax returns for federal and state would only indicate the totals, not the itemized products, unless he was audited. Or, there was a "doctored" spreadsheet lurking around that I hadn't opened.

By now, it was impossible to drift off to sleep. I closed that program and opened the only other file on there, the one marked "Misc. Documents." Sure enough, it was a duplicate of the spreadsheet I'd been reviewing but not in Excel. Some sort of homemade job. It didn't matter. It showed me what I expected. Instead of bargain-basement prices for the hot dog and hamburger buns, this one had amounts more akin to what I had in mind. No doubt, this was the spreadsheet Karl used for his taxes and the other was what he was finagling on the side.

Since I focused only on that column, I quickly scanned all of the months until I reached the current one—September. Then I did the same with the first spreadsheet. Same deal. Same difference for each month. And when I totaled the difference between the actual cost as opposed to "the deal of the century," it was in the low thousands. I did the math again and again I was right. That made me wonder—were there any other anomalies I hadn't noticed? After all, this was only a cursory look as far as I was concerned.

I'd passed the Cinderella witching hour and couldn't hang on much longer. My probing would have to wait until break time tomorrow. I put the thumb drive in my bag so as not to forget it, shut down the computer, and called it a night.

I fell asleep within minutes of getting into bed, but a three fifty-five a.m. bathroom call left me wide awake. Maybe it was the unfinished business I had with Karl's spreadsheets or the nagging feeling I had overlooked something obvious, but I chose to forgo some Zzz's in exchange for delving further into Karl's business.

That little black book, or in this case the photos I took of the pages, were itching to be read. I grabbed my phone and painstakingly emailed them to my personal address so I could pull up a larger version on the computer. The process seemed slower than usual and I attributed it to my being anxious and antsy. Finally, all the pages were on my desktop and ready for my prying eyes.

Snippets of information coupled with short commentary dotted the pages along with what appeared to be monetary payoffs. No dates, no rhyme or reason, only random comments. The only thing working in my favor was the fact that most people write in notebooks in sequential order, so at least I knew where to begin. And once I got started, it was like a Danielle Steel novel. I couldn't put it down. But I did manage to isolate the vital parts Karl had written. And mumble to myself every step of the way.

"Paid the rat-faced snake five bills to keep his trap shut. Need to figure out who tipped him off." *Who's the snake? Buster? I wouldn't put it past him. Tipped him off about what?*

"The SOB upped the amount. Told him I wasn't going to play his game."

"Told him I needed to put a stop to this. Got a pretty nice deal going on. SOB's costing us." *What's the deal? Who's the "him"? The silent partner?*

Then, five or so pages later—"Payback time for the snake. I know his dirty secret. Who's gonna pay Daddy now?" *What secret? If it's Buster, is that what got him killed?*

It was a little past five and all the melatonin in the world wouldn't get me back to sleep. I made myself an early toast and jam breakfast and washed it down with two cups of coffee. Then, I took a wake-up shower to get my brain in gear and headed to the office with one quick stop on the way—Dunkin'. I figured I'd need a sugar fix before ten and Augusta never turned down a donut.

The entire time in the car, I asked myself over and over again—"What could Shirley possibly have to do with any of this?" She wasn't privy to Karl's little scheme, so that connection made absolutely no sense.

Nate had once told me that when everything seems impossible to draw together, that's when a tiny piece of information seemingly comes out of nowhere and *voilà*! Case solved! Too bad no little morsels of the kind were anywhere near the convoluted mess I had in my lap. The worst part of all of this was Lyndy. She really liked Lyman and didn't believe for a minute he had anything to do with Buster's murder. "I don't know what to do or say," she confided in me when we last spoke. "It's not as if we have a relationship and I'd feel funny visiting him at the Fourth Avenue Jail."

At the time I told her to let things play out. Now, I was doing exactly that with Karl, the new player who'd surfaced. Not to mention his possible entourage consisting of the silent partner and the person giving him the "pretty nice deal."

The office was locked and dark when I arrived. Usually, it's Augusta who gets there with the roosters and boots everything up. I let myself in, locked the door behind me, and turned on her computer and mine, along with the copy machine and the Keurig. A quick glance at the fax machine told me nothing had arrived.

Since I had spent such an inordinate amount of time playing amateur detective, I used the early morning hour to focus on the real work at my desk—a pile of invoices. It was amazing how much I could accomplish with no interruptions and only the hum of office machinery.

I sat upright the moment I heard the key in the door. It was immediately followed by Augusta's voice. "Are those donuts I see on the counter? The early morning news didn't mention anything about a melee at the concession stand last night so I figured everything was honky-dory. What'd you find out? And why are you in so early? Did Marshall call you? Is there something I need to do?"

"Yeah, grab a donut and catch your breath. I'll tell you."

"Thanks for starting up my computer. I could swear that thing gets slower and slower each day."

Augusta pulled up a chair near my desk and took a bite of the sprinkled strawberry frosted donut. "Well? Don't keep me in suspense."

"In a nutshell, I'm in early because I stayed up most of the night going over what I found in Karl's office at the concession stand. And no, Marshall didn't call this morning, but Paul came dangerously close to burning the place down last night. He may be a good fisherman but his cooking skills leave a lot to be desired."

"Forget the cooking skills. What dirt did you dig up?"

CHAPTER 40

I gave Augusta the complete rundown about the prior evening and the in-depth review of Karl's spreadsheets and little black book. When I was done, all she could do was shake her head and make little tsk-tsk noises. "Yep, I'd say the guy was being blackmailed about something but then it turned upside down. Karl found out some nasty little secret about his blackmailer. Maybe nasty enough to cancel out the original arrangement and send the snake packing. Only one problem the way I see it."

"What's that?"

"You need to find out who the silent partner is. Oh, and it wouldn't hurt to find out what the nasty little secret is while you're at it."

"If I could do all of that, I'd have Buster's murder solved by now and Lyman out of jail. Aargh. Too bad Nate and Marshall are stuck in Laughlin chasing after someone who's got more disappearing acts than David Copperfield."

"It's a doozy, all right."

"Oh, and there's more. I almost forgot about Shirley. She called to tell me that out of the blue, she heard from her friend Geraldine in Nevada. Seems Geraldine caught a seat on the rumor train and learned about Buster's demise. Wanted to know if it was true. Geraldine's the one who borrowed money from Buster in exchange for setting up a shared bank account with him."

"Is that all she set up?"

"As far as I know. Geraldine is in her eighties."

"Honey, age doesn't matter when it comes to sins of the flesh."

"Ew! Augusta! Bad enough Marshall and Lyndy thought the same thing when I told them a while ago. Anyway, I should be getting back to this pile of invoices. If you get an epiphany about how I can find out who the silent partner is, let me know. I'll be right here, tethered to my desk."

"At least you found out something—Lyman wasn't the only one with a motive to murder Buster. Sounds like Karl had a place in line, too. *If*, of course, Buster was the rat-faced snake you mentioned."

"Lots of 'ifs' if you ask me."

Augusta chuckled and walked back to her desk while I spent the next two and a half hours doing what I was paid to do—accounting and bookkeeping.

At precisely ten fifteen, when I chose to take my break and have my third cup of coffee for the morning, my mother called. No greeting, just a go-for-the-jugular howdy-do. "Please don't tell me you're going to be like your aunt Ina and tell me you can't handle anything impromptu."

It was the tiger behind the door dilemma. No matter my choice, it wouldn't end well. "Impromptu? What are you talking about?"

"Myrna just called. The Homey Hut is featuring its summer send-off salad, soup, and sandwich specials tonight. Also includes free pie. The book club ladies are meeting there at six thirty. Herb, too. And maybe Kenny. Or was it Kevin? Anyway, all of us are going, except of course for your aunt. I thought you'd like to join us. Especially since Marshall is out of town on some other case."

"Like to join you or like to get badgered by everyone about Buster's killer?"

"No one will badger you. They may prod a little but that's about it."

"Oh, brother."

"So you'll come?"

"I suppose."

"Good. Six thirty."

At first, the thought of being grilled by the book club ladies gave my stomach a twist, but then I realized something—I could use the time to grill them. Maybe in the weeks since Buster's unfortunate passing, one of them picked up a piece of scuttlebutt that could be useful in the investigation. As far as I was concerned, this evening's meal at the Homey Hut would be a two-way street.

The remainder of the day was about as uneventful as they come. Augusta and I sent out for sandwiches and worked straight up until the official office hours ended.

"I've got to exercise the boys tonight," she announced as she locked the front door.

"What boys? Are you babysitting someone's dogs? If so, I'm handing Streetman off to you."

"Fat chance. The boys are my guns and I'm meeting a few friends at Shooters World of Peoria. They stay open until seven so that'll give me a good hour to get in a few rounds."

"That actually sounds better than my evening. It's the Homey Hut with the book club ladies." *And the shooting off of mouths, not guns.*

"Stuff your face as much as you can so you can dodge their questions."

"*That*, or dodge back."

I told Augusta I'd keep her posted if I heard from Nate or Marshall and she agreed to do the same. Then, it was off to Sun City West and the Homey Hut's summer send-off.

• • •

The Homey Hut was Arizona's answer to Midwest farm dining. With its cutesy checkered tablecloths that matched the curtains and its tableware with chicken, cow, and pig motifs, it was hard to escape the down-on-the-farm theme. Shirley and Lucinda were already seated at a large table near the rear windows and beckoned me over as soon as they spotted me.

"We're early," Shirley said. "We were at Big Lots looking for bargains and it didn't pay to drive all the way back home and then out again. Besides, I didn't want our comings and goings to upset Thor. I left him with a solid rawhide bone and the TV on so he should be fine. Goodness, how I'm going to miss him."

I took a seat and picked up the paper menu in front of me. "Do you know when Gloria's getting back?"

"Late Sunday night. She called and said she'd pick up Thor Monday morning. That's only four days from now, if you count today. Don't say anything to anyone, but I'm terrified that if they don't catch Buster's killer by then and find out who's after me, I'll go out of my mind."

Lucinda looked directly at me. "I told Shirley she should insist the sheriff's office bring back their night patrol in front of her house."

"Uh, not a bad idea."

At that moment, Cecilia, Myrna, and Louise made a beeline for the table. Like flies on a honey-cake, they were all over us and it was impossible to answer the questions that were hurled our way.

"Did we miss anything?"

"Any word on your stalker, Shirley?"

"Where's Harriet? She's usually here before us."

"I ran into Herb at the post office. Kevin and Kenny are coming, too."

Just as the ladies got settled, the men arrived, with Herb insisting on the captain's chair at the end of the table so he could stretch out his legs. Something about needing to have them in prime shape for Saturday's Cactus Slow-Pitch game.

"All of you need to get there by one fifteen the latest," he announced. "The good seats will be taken after that. And don't mumble about hair and nail appointments because those shops are open all the time. This game is a one-only."

"Yeah," Kenny chimed in. "The one chance I get for a bird's-eye view of those Sun City pom-pom chicks." Then a loud "Hey" as Myrna kicked him under the table.

Before he could respond, my mother did. "What's going on? What did I miss? Why's Kenny bending down and grabbing his knee?"

I fanned the menu in front of my face with one hand and motioned to the seat next to me with the other. "You didn't miss anything. The waitress hasn't been around to take our orders yet. The summer send-off specials are all on the menu."

"Don't need to see the menu," Herb said. "I'm getting the hot roast beef sandwich with gravy and mashed potatoes."

Cecilia looked up from her menu. "I thought you had to lose weight according to your cardiologist."

"Don't worry. I'll lose plenty of it running around those bases on Saturday and fielding balls on third. Maybe I'll even beat Buster's record. Rest in peace."

Suddenly Shirley clapped her hands together and we jumped. "Goodness. I almost forgot to mention this. Geraldine called me this morning at a little past nine. She needed the address for the Arizona Department of Health Services so she could order a copy of Buster's death certificate."

"Why did she need their address? Doesn't she have a computer or smart phone?" Myrna asked.

"Forget why she needed the address," my mother replied. "Why does she need a copy of his death certificate?"

CHAPTER 41

Shirley steepled her fingers and leaned her head against her hands. Her new yellowy nail polish sparkled against her ebony skin, making me self-conscious about the haphazard state my nails were in.

"One thing at a time," she said. "Geraldine told me she wouldn't be able to get a good night's sleep until she actually had an official notice from the state that Buster was dead. And as for needing the health department's address, she only owns a flip phone and uses her son's computer to play solitaire."

"No email? No Amazon?" Louise's voice got more and more high-pitched with each word. "You mean to tell me she just draws breath in and out?"

Shirley shrugged. "She still sews."

None of us said a word and, in fact, everyone immersed themselves in the menus. A few minutes later the waitress arrived to take our orders and was immediately greeted with, "Put these on separate checks," from Lucinda.

Herb babbled on and on about the softball game while the women offered up their ideas as to who could have murdered Buster. Sadly, the consensus was that Lyman might have done it, after all. If nothing else, I was glad I didn't invite Lyndy to join me for the summer send-off special. It would have sent her off, all right—crying in the ladies' room.

My hopes of picking up any pertinent hearsay diminished by the time dessert was served. Then, the death certificate conversation resumed and I all but choked on my strawberry shortcake.

"Honestly," Shirley said, "Geraldine had to be walked through everything. She even asked me if she should submit her request for Buster's death certificate under Millard LaRoo or Millard L. LaRoo. I told her middle initials are better since they narrow the search, but if she knew his full middle name, it would be best. Then she said she had his full name on the shared bank account and spewed it off—Millard Lamont LaRoo. I told her to go with that."

"Lamont?" I had to grab my iced water and swallow it quickly because a strawberry stuck to my throat. *Geraldine doesn't want that death certificate to make sure he's dead. She wants it to make sure she gets the insurance money!*

Shirley nodded. "That's right. Lamont. It's a common enough name."

Common, but not that common.

"Excuse me a moment," I said to no one in particular. "I'll be right back. I think I left my phone in the car." *And it better not ring right now.*

With that, I raced out the door and went directly to where I'd parked. Then, I plunked myself in the driver's seat and speed dialed Marshall. Unfortunately, it went to voicemail. I took a deep breath and spoke as clearly and succinctly as I could.

"Buster LaRoo's full name is Millard Lamont LaRoo. Lamont! I think he's your ghost. For real. Lamont Rooney is most likely Buster. That unlived-in apartment was his next move. Most likely he planned to fake his death and settle in Laughlin. Only he didn't have to fake it. Call me. Love you!"

Granted, it was a hunch, but I've played around with anagrams and near-anagrams for a long time. I'd also read somewhere that people who take on other identities tend to choose similar names as their own. Same deal with similar passwords. Makes life easier for the hackers. In this case, I hoped it would solve a case for Nate and Marshall.

Back once again at our table in the Homey Hut, Herb was still rambling on and on about his softball game. At one point, Myrna threatened to stuff the ball in his mouth if he didn't shut up.

"Find your phone?" my mother asked.

"Huh? Oh, yeah. Fine."

"Those things have become little encyclopedias," Louise said. "I'd be lost without mine. I don't even use one of those small phone books anymore. Remember when the welcoming committees gave us those? Now, all the names are in my contacts list. That's why I can't imagine why Geraldine lives in the Dark Ages."

The minute Louise mentioned "all the names," it was as if the proverbial lightbulb went off in my head. If Buster was Lamont, then maybe he had some deal with one of those three maintenance men who checked out a golf cart the morning Shirley saw the body. Maybe the pieces would fall into place, after all.

I'd written the names on yet another obscure business card and fished it out of my bag while Louise went on and on about having to adapt to changes in technology.

"What are you doing, Phee?" my mother asked. "Did you forget something else?"

"Don't tell me you're getting as bad as the rest of us old coots," Kevin said. "Why do you think the TV plasters us with all those commercials for memory supplements?"

"Uh, no. In fact, I just remembered something. Give me a second." I looked at the names on the business cards and mulled them over: Bruce Finlay, John Chu, and Jaime Dahl. "I don't suppose any of these names mean anything to any of you, do they? Here goes: Bruce Finlay, John Chu, or Jaime Dahl?"

"They sound like the same names your mother read us a few days ago," Cecilia said. "I wrote them down and Lucinda and I checked with our church roster but none of them are on it."

"They're not on the bocce list," Myrna added.

"Don't look at me," Louise said. "I can't even remember who's in the Sunshine Animal Club."

Just then, the waitress who stood behind Kenny with a stack of individual checks spoke up. "I know Jaime Dahl. Only he should spell it D-o-l-l. The guy's a hunk. He lives in Surprise and comes in here with his father all the time. Or gets dragged in, I should say. The dad's a real trip. I think he may have something to do with the food industry because not too long ago he spoke with someone about steam cleaning an industrial freezer. His name's Raymond R. Dahl, if that means anything to anyone. And the only reason I know is because I had to look at his credit card."

Raymond R. Dahl. That has to be the silent partner. How many people talk about steam cleaning industrial freezers?

"Wait," I said. "Before you distribute those checks, *because that could take this table a century to peruse*, do you mind looking at a photo I have? It may be Jaime Dahl."

I whipped out my cell phone, tapped the screen, and held it in front of her.

"Yeah, that's him, all right. Quite the hunk for an older guy. I've seen the man he's with too, but I don't know his name. Why are those guys on your radar? Have they done anything I should be worried about?"

Only if murder is a concern . . .

"No. They're maintenance workers in my mother's community. We thought one of them might have seen something on a golf course. That's all. No big deal."

"I think I have your check, Myrna," Cecilia said. "I ordered the BLT, not the loaded grilled cheese."

As the waitress went to straighten the checks out, I stopped her and whispered, "Let them sort it out. Much more fun." Then I handed her my tip with an extra five dollars. "Thanks for your help with those names."

"No problem. Thank *you*."

When she was out of sight, I motioned for the crew to lean into the table. "Jaime Dahl may turn out to be the man who drove that maintenance golf cart away from where Shirley first saw Buster's body. I need to let those deputies know. And Nate and Marshall, of course. Meanwhile, everyone's lips need to be sealed. Not a word of this."

"We're not a bunch of busybodies," Kevin said. Then he looked at Herb. "Well, not all of us."

As a few of us stood and pushed our chairs into the table, Herb said,

"Don't forget. Get to the game by one fifteen on Saturday for the good seats. It's not every day you get to see me round the bases."

I did a mental eye roll and refrained from saying anything. But that was not the case with my mother. "I'll be tickled pink if you can move from one base to the next. But don't you worry, Streetman and I will be cheering for you."

"You're bringing your dog?" Myrna asked.

"If Shirley's taking Thor, I can bring Streetman. Besides, I'll have him in the stroller."

I escaped from the Homey Hut before my mother and Myrna could continue their discussion. Then, as soon as I got in the car, I saw a text from Marshall.

Got your tip about Lamont and I let Rolo know. Nate's ecstatic. FYI, you're amazing. Will call tonight. Miss U like crazy.

I smiled at the *U*. At least he was getting a bit better with text messaging, which was more than I could say for myself. Texting was still another language as far as I was concerned. Rather than second-guess myself, I left him another voicemail. "I may have tracked down the man who drove that maintenance golf cart the morning Shirley found Buster's body. And I have a bizarre and somewhat unsettling idea about where he hid it. Call me as soon as you can. Love you."

CHAPTER 42

I saw the landline's answering machine blinking the moment I got in the door and read the caller ID—Lyndy. "Hang on," I called out to the phone. "I'm putting on comfy pj's first."

Seconds later, I returned the call, wishing I had some good news to give her.

Lyndy's words rushed out at me before I could say hello. "Are you making any headway? Is anyone making any headway? I can't believe Lyman's still in jail. They won't let him out on bail since he's charged with murder. I was able to speak with him for a few minutes on the phone. He's got a good criminal lawyer but he's beside himself. Said he would never, in a million years, kill anyone. And I believe him, Phee. I really do."

"I know," I said. "And I don't believe he murdered Buster either. Listen, I may have a lead on the man in the maintenance vehicle. He might not have murdered Buster but he very well could have transported him to the golf course entryway."

"But the body was gone. Are you saying he dumped a corpse, then had second thoughts and put him back in the golf cart?"

"Uh-huh. Only he couldn't have done it alone. He had to have had someone sitting next to him. Two people could lift the dead weight but I doubt one person could. Listen, I really need to have that conversation with Bowman and Ranston since Nate and Marshall are in Laughlin. Only those deputies aren't the most receptive when it comes to considering theories that aren't theirs."

"Then make them think it's theirs. I do that all the time with my supervisor."

"Lyndy, I think the fraud case Nate and Marshall are tackling may have something to do with Buster."

"Is there anything I can do to help?"

"Actually, yes. Join me Saturday at Liberty Field for Herb's Cactus Slow-Pitch game. According to Herb, this is a real big deal and all the usual fans will be there. If I'm not mistaken, maybe we can flush out a killer. I just need some time to figure out how. I've got a plan but it needs work."

"My looney aunt mentioned that slow-pitch game but said she'd made plans with her bunco group to eat out in Scottsdale. Good news—you'll get my help without her tagging along. What do you say we commiserate over pizza tomorrow night and polish up that scheme of yours? I'll get delivery and we can do it at my place. Seven thirty?"

"On the nose."

I had a rough plan brewing in my head but Lyndy was right. It needed

175

to be refined. Refined, hell. Who was I kidding? It needed to be organized, articulated, and executed. One mistake and Lyman would be whisked away from the Fourth Avenue Jail and into the state prison in Florence. My options were running out.

Rather than mindlessly channel surf or, worse yet, wait for Marshall to call, I took out my murder notebook and looked for connections. As I was about to jot them down, the landline rang and I nearly knocked over everything on the counter to get to it.

"Hello. Marshall?"

"Boy, it's good to hear your voice. If I sound exhausted, it's because I am. Nate and I have been all over the place. We could write a tourist guide for Nevada. Listen, you were right about Buster LaRoo. He is, or I should say *was*, Lamont Rooney. But that's not all. He was also Monty Dill and Dillard Romont. The guy had quite the scheme going. Too bad we had to traipse to Henderson and Pahrump."

"Par ump?"

"It's a little-known golf haven that borders California. Great views and gambling. I'd say Buster did his homework. Rolo followed some insurance trails that dated back a decade. Buster kept faking his own death and had a partner who claimed the beneficiary monies for him."

"Geraldine Kremler. I figured as much after listening to Shirley and finding out Geraldine's in Laughlin. I take it you paid her a visit or plan to do that in the morning?"

"Uh, no. That's not the name that appeared as the beneficiary for the two policies we checked—Monty Dill and Dillard Romont. The person listed on those policies lives in Nevada and has an ironclad alibi for Buster's murder. We tracked him down and verified his story. He was in the Caribbean on a cruise at the time. Seemed Buster gave him five percent of the beneficiary monies."

"Gee, big spender."

"With Nate and me breathing down the man's neck, he contacted his lawyer and will turn himself in to the local sheriff's office in Henderson. Meanwhile, we've got another possible alias we need to check out while we're here. Could turn out to be a wild-goose chase, but as long as we're here we might as well pursue it. Nate and I figured we'd hit the road early Saturday morning and be back in town by afternoon."

"Are you sure Geraldine's name didn't come up on Rolo's radar?"

"Not yet. I thought she was the woman who borrowed money from Buster to get a new air-conditioning compressor and the loan came with a caveat. She would be forgiven for the money if she was willing to do something for him."

"Uh-huh. She had to set up a shared bank account for all of his little gambling payoffs, but I think that was only part of the deal. Shirley thought something else was going on, too, but Geraldine wouldn't say."

"You're thinking insurance fraud? And she was a named beneficiary for a bogus death?"

I gulped. "Not intentionally. I think she was sucked into it. I believe the real reason Buster let her off the hook was if she'd agree to be listed as the beneficiary and file the death certificate with the state. Then, when the money came through, she'd claim it and give it to him. No tax penalty for insurance monies. Look, I'm positive I'm right. Can you at least check on it? She lives in a residential community off of Needles Highway. It's near the elementary school. Wish I had the exact address."

"Not a problem. We'll find her."

"Um, I hate to ask, but if it turns out Geraldine was in cahoots with Buster, will she be arrested?"

"She's not named on the other policies, and even if she's named on this one, there's nothing wrong since Buster really did die. Of course, the fact that it was murder may slow the speed in which the insurance company will pay on the policy."

"If I understand correctly, Buster was in the process of getting his Lamont Rooney identity up and running. So, he would fake his death in Sun City West somehow and hightail it to Laughlin. Then he'd have to start all over with a new life insurance policy for Lamont. Yeesh. I hate to say it, but if he didn't wind up dead, Geraldine would have been in a heap of trouble for insurance fraud if she was named on Buster's Millard Lamont LaRoo policy and he wasn't pushing up daisies."

"Yep. Correct on all accounts. Boy, does this case keep getting trickier and trickier. If something else crops up, I'll text or call."

"Augusta is chomping at the bit to find out what's going on. Want me to tell her tomorrow?"

"Knock yourself out. I'm sure she'll have a few choice theories of her own."

We ended our call like we always do when we're apart. Lots of sweet words and the usual "Love you." I didn't bother to mention the Saturday Cactus Slow-Pitch game because I knew Marshall would be inundated the minute he returned to the office. The fraud case was ongoing and new cases needed some attention.

I had to put my loosely woven plan in action for Saturday because the softball game's venue was the only place where I knew my murder notebook suspects would convene. It was a high-profile event, and if all went well, I'd be able to target the real culprit responsible for killing Buster and terrorizing Shirley. I spent the next hour brainstorming and jotting notes to review with Lyndy tomorrow night.

For the first time that day, the tension that had built up in my neck subsided. I made myself an old-fashioned egg cream with chocolate syrup, milk, and seltzer. Then, I settled in to catch the evening news before pulling the covers back and creeping into bed.

• • •

I wasn't wrong when I told Marshall that Augusta would be itching to know what they uncovered. What I didn't expect were the gales of laughter when I mentioned Geraldine's name the next morning when I got to work.

"What a hoot! First a shared bank account and now a beneficiary. Sounds like Shirley's friend may be cagier than we think."

"Come on, Augusta, the poor woman was roped into it. According to Marshall, since Buster really did die, there's no fraud going on. Not with the other beneficiary who's lurking somewhere in Nevada. That person is named on two other policies."

"No surprise Buster wound up dead. I can spell motive with a capital *M*. Now they need to ferret out the culprit."

"Funny you should mention that. Lyndy and I plan to do the very thing tomorrow at that slow-pitch game. We're working on a plan tonight."

Augusta rubbed her chin. "You and Lyndy, huh? Not the book club ladies?"

"Uh-huh. Only Lyndy and me."

"Good. Less people for me to bail out."

"Don't you want to know what I have in mind?"

"Nope. Otherwise I'll be an accessory to, well, whatever it is you get charged with. But keep my number on speed dial, will you? I'm a fast driver."

I smiled and walked to my office. It was Augusta's way of saying she approved. The only trouble was, I still had no idea what Lyndy and I were going to do.

CHAPTER 43

That night, between bites of pizza and gulps of Coke, Lyndy and I dissected the information I had as if we were in a tenth-grade biology class. I held my breath that she would concur with my theory.

"It makes sense, Phee," she said. "Given that information you found in Karl's office, it's pretty obvious the snake had to be Buster. He must have found out about Karl's little deal for all the free bread products and blackmailed him."

"Yeah, I took it one step further and figured it had to be that bread delivery guy who was seated behind us at the softball game. He must have given Karl all that free stuff. Or the 'family and friends discount,' to be more precise. Trouble is, it would have shown up somewhere on the accounting records for the companies the guy serviced."

Lyndy adjusted one of her dangling earrings. "Not if the products were expired. Expired products are tossed. And face it, expired bread products can be used a day or two after the date before they get moldy. Trust me, I know this from experience."

I laughed. "Yeesh. Me, too."

"What about the 'dirty little secret' deal Karl mentioned?" She held her glass of Coke an inch from her lips and waited for me to respond.

"Oh, I think Karl found out about Buster's insurance fraud scam and wanted a piece of the action. That would make sense considering his reputation for being greedy."

A quick swallow and Lyndy smiled. "It could be a double blackmail. Not the kind that results in a revenge killing or it would have been Karl's body behind the ball field, but something else entirely."

"I'm listening."

"Suppose Karl confronted Buster and used his knowledge as leverage. You know, Buster keeps his mouth shut and so does Karl. Only Karl doesn't trust Buster so he—"

"Poisons him." I reached for another slice of pizza. "And gets the bread guy to do the dirty deed by blackmailing *him*. Of course, that's kind of a stretch."

"It may not be such a stretch," Lyndy said. "First off, you told me how meticulous Karl was. To chop up dried dieffenbachia and put it in someone's tobacco tin takes a methodical thinker and a good planner. And as far as the bread guy goes, we know he was friends with Jaime Dahl, the man who works for the maintenance department. That's the very one who checked out a utility golf cart the morning Shirley first saw Buster's body. And it would have taken two people to move that body . . ."

"Um, before we fly with this one, there may be another explanation for Buster's demise. And I won't know until Nate and Marshall check the beneficiary for his policy. If it's not Geraldine Kremler, then that beneficiary may have killed him." I closed my eyes and rubbed my temples. "I hate to muddy the waters but there's one thing we didn't consider."

Lyndy widened her eyes. "Only one?"

"The silent partner. Karl's silent partner. I'm thinking it's Jaime Dahl's father, Raymond R. Dahl. The waitress at the Homey Hut overheard him talking about industrial freezers."

"I talk about SpaceX. Doesn't mean I plan to buy a ticket and fly."

"Aargh. You're sounding more and more like Augusta."

The grin on Lyndy's face made the Cheshire cat's look like a frown. "I always knew I liked that woman."

We polished off the pizza and plotted out a plan. The words *wing* and *prayer* immediately sprang to mind, but when I left her house, I was ever the optimist. Too bad the word *cockeyed* didn't spring to mind at the time.

• • •

The combination wall and chain-link fence around Liberty Field was fully decorated in patriotic American flag buntings with a few Arizona flags hanging from the poles that circled the diamond. Lyndy and I had taken our own cars rather than share a ride since I worked at the office that morning and drove straight from there. I needed all the extra time to get caught up with billing, something that gave Augusta great pleasure since she didn't relish eating lunch alone.

"Remember," she said when I headed out, "I'm on speed dial in case things go south."

Terrific. Augusta on speed dial and her "boys" at the ready.

When I pulled into the parking lot, I was sorry I didn't leave sooner. It was jam-packed and I wound up crossing to the other side of the street and using the lot shared by the posse station and the Sun City West Foundation.

Lyndy stood to the right of the ballpark entrance and waved. Unlike professional ball games, this was strictly small-time leagues and that meant no admission charge. However, Karl's concession stand, along with two food trucks, were about to do a booming business.

My mother had called me first thing in the morning to let me know she and the book club ladies would be seated behind home plate along with my aunt Ina. Something about a panoramic view. I figured Herb's pinochle guys would be there as well. Somehow, those two klatches seemed to be joined at the hip at times like these.

"Is that your aunt Ina over there?" Lyndy pointed across the diamond as we made our way through the crowd. The national anthem had just ended and the crowd shoved its way to the seats.

"Yikes. I'm afraid so. I've never seen a larger sombrero and I've been to lots of mariachi events. Look at those colors! The thing is blinding. Gee, you'd think I'd be used to my aunt's wardrobe choices by now."

We both laughed and made our way to where the women were seated. It was a good enough spot but Lyndy and I didn't intend to stay there. We needed to mill about and locate Jaime Dahl and the bread delivery guy. But the real prize was Jaime's father. I was convinced Raymond R. Dahl orchestrated Buster's sudden death with the help of his son. As for motive, I assumed Raymond was the beneficiary on that insurance policy.

The tip-off was when the waitress at the Homey Hut said Raymond was concerned about steam cleaning an industrial freezer. And I knew exactly which one. No wonder Karl kept it under lock and key. I was certain that's where he stored Buster's body when the guys in that maintenance golf cart thought Shirley had seen them. Yep, it was a foursome, all right, only they weren't playing cards. They were getting even with Buster for any number of grievances.

True, I wasn't exactly sure of the sequence of events but it would have been pretty easy for Karl to swap out Buster's wintergreen chewing tobacco with a tainted dieffenbachia blend.

I figured Jaime and company dumped the body by the golf course entryway but then moved it ASAP once Shirley spied it and rushed off to my mother's house. It was serendipitous that the bread guy had some deal going with Karl, enabling him use of that giant freezer in the concession stand building. However, they had to keep up the ruse to make Shirley think she lost her mind. That meant Marshall's gaslighting theory was spot-on.

I also knew why that freezer was locked. In order to remove trace DNA, only certain solvents could be used. Therefore, a simple wipe down with Clorox wouldn't suffice. Securing a company to perform a task like that can take days or weeks. I was positive I had it right. Now all I had to do was get Raymond to confess.

Like a New York City subway at rush hour, the entire book club and pinochle entourages were crammed next to each other with Thor in his own seat next to Shirley and Streetman in his carrier wedged in between my mother and the person in front of her.

"Myrna, scootch over," my mother shouted. "Phee and Lyndy can squeeze in."

"Um, no, we can't," I said. "We've got seats elsewhere. We just stopped by to say hello to everyone."

"Okay, okay," Kevin said. "Step back. You're obstructing the view. The pom-poms are about to start. Look! Here they come!"

"Honestly," Louise said to the men, "you're worse than adolescent boys."

To the tune of "Take Me Out to the Ball Game," the dancers moved to the center of the baseball diamond and began their routine. I told my mother we'd catch up with her later and then proceeded to put the "seek and find" portion of my plan in place.

It was simple, really. Lyndy and I would walk along the space that separated the bottom row of seats from the field while perusing the crowd to spot our culprits. Then, once sighted, we would make our way near them and proceed to have a conversation that would compel Raymond to race to the concession stand to confront Karl.

It was junior high all over again but the plan had a good track record. What we didn't count on, however, was that the concession stand and the two food trucks weren't the only places doing business that afternoon. No sooner did the pom-pom women finish their routine when servers carrying hot dogs made their way through the crowd. It was an open invitation for Thor and he took it just as the visiting team came up to bat.

CHAPTER 44

"That announcer's voice sounds familiar," Lyndy said as we started to circle the stands. "Oh, no! It's not who I think it is, is it?"

"Good grief, yes! It's Paul. My mother and Myrna must be seething that they weren't asked to do the honors."

Just then we heard a loud yell and turned to see hot dogs and rolls flying in the air as someone shouted, "He better not bite."

Next thing we knew, some of the hot dogs landed on the ball field and Thor was all over them. The poor batter never got in a single swing. Shirley rushed to the field shouting, "Stop that, Thor!" but apparently Thor's hearing was selective.

I grabbed Lyndy's elbow. "We can't get tangled up in this mess. Not when we're so close to catching a killer. Come on, act like nothing's happening and check out the stands for our suspects."

"I don't think that's possible."

She was right. As soon as the word *suspects* left my mouth, throngs of spectators rushed to the ball field in an attempt to remove Thor. I rolled my eyes, turned away, and tried to stay calm. "This is a disaster. An absolute disaster. Only thing worse would be if Streetman got out. He's chewed through the meshing of that stroller on at least two occasions."

"Then don't turn around."

"Oh, hell, no!"

Sure enough, I spied Streetman crawling under an open spot in the chain-link fence. In a nanosecond he was on the ball field along with Thor. I gulped. The game was on and it wasn't softball. But that didn't stop the crowd from hooting and hollering.

"Will someone get those mutts out of here before I call animal control?"

"Stop chasing them. They think it's a game!"

"Did that dog do what I think he did?"

"Blow a whistle or something!"

Lyndy took my arm. "Maybe we should get some more hot dogs from the concession stand and lure them away. Shirley's not having much luck and from the looks of things, neither is your mother."

Terrific. My one chance to ferret out a murderer and what happens? That neurotic chiweenie and his friend ruin it.

"I suppose you're right. Let's go."

Shouts, screams, and gales of laughter filled the air as Lyndy and I rushed to the concession stand. As we approached, I saw Blaine working behind the counter and spied Karl in the kitchen area, hands on his hips, talking to someone. I surmised it was a not-so-pleasant conversation with the other party but I couldn't tell who it was.

At least five people were in line before us and from the way they stood their ground, they weren't about to budge on our account. Meanwhile, I tried to catch a glimpse of the person who stood in front of Karl, but no luck.

"I need to skirt around this line," I whispered to Lyndy. "Stay put or we'll lose our place."

Drat. No way for my plan to work now. The person's face is obscured. And everyone wears khakis. No matter. I can take a guess.

Suddenly, Paul's booming voice exploded. "Everyone get off the field. The Blue Team pitcher will toss a ball and when the dogs go for it, their owners will be able to catch them."

Fat chance.

Again, I rolled my eyes. Then, I had an epiphany like none other I've ever had before. I rushed back to Lyndy and yanked her sleeve. "Forget the hot dogs. We're back to plan A. Sort of."

As I charged toward the announcer's booth at the top of the stands behind home plate, I paused for a brief second to let Lyndy know what I had in mind. "You know how Paul, Myrna, and my mother wind up broadcasting over the air during their radio program when they think the sound is turned off? Well, I think we can use that tactic to our advantage."

"What do you mean?"

"No time to explain. Follow my lead."

Paul drummed his fingers against the table that held the sound equipment as he watched the melee on the field, oblivious to our entry into the booth.

"Psst, Paul," I whispered. "Is the sound off?"

He turned. "For now. Got quite the circus going but at least it's only the dogs chasing softballs."

"Look, we've got to hurry. I think I know who killed Buster, and if I'm right, he and his buddy will try to duck out of here as soon as I call them out."

"Like that? You're going to get on the air and announce it?"

"Not exactly. We need you to make some general announcement or commentary and then Lyndy and I will have a conversation that gets carried into the ballpark. The players and spectators will think the sound was left on by mistake. We'll let it slip that Lyman was released from jail since the deputies zeroed in on the real killer, who's at this game. We'll say the place is surrounded and that the only exit is the path behind the baseball diamond. The killer should know where that is since it was the spot where he or his cohort pretended to be a dead body in order to confuse Shirley."

"You mean bop her over the head with a softball."

"I don't think they intended to hit her. Anyway, is it a go?"

Paul scratched his head and nodded. "Got nothing else going on. The dogs are still at it."

"Great. Turn the sound on and say something."

Paul sat up straight and cleared his throat. "Ladies and gentlemen, the situation on the ball field will be resolved shortly. Meanwhile, grab a hot dog if you can beat the dogs to it, get a drink, and enjoy this wonderful weather. I'll be back on the air in a jiff."

I nudged Paul and took one of the two empty seats next to him, motioning for Lyndy to grab the other. Then, I leaned into the mic. "That's right, Paul. I thought you'd want to know. The sheriff's office released Lyman when they discovered the real evidence in the concession stand after you and I left that night. Trace DNA. Not just Buster LaRoo's body but the killers' who stuck him in there so he wouldn't thaw."

"Folks will be spitting out their hot dogs if they knew where they were stored."

I winced and kept talking. "Got a call a few minutes ago from a friend of mine who works for the sheriff's office. That's how I know. Look, mum's the word. Wouldn't want anyone to find out they've got deputies posted at all the exits and sidewalks."

"Oh, crap! Mic's been on all this time!"

Paul clicked if off and I gave him a thumbs-up. "Our guys will quickly ascertain the only way out would be on that dirt path behind the ball field and the only way to get there would be to skirt the perimeter of that field."

"Now what?" Lyndy asked.

"Put on your track shoes and follow me."

Before Lyndy or Paul could utter a word, I was down the bleachers and directly in front of the ball field. The game was still on hold but we were down to one dog—Thor. Streetman was safely nestled under my mother's arm and on his way back to the stands. Meanwhile, Thor pranced around the field ignoring Shirley's calls to "stop it" and "get over here." Then, the pitcher gently lobbed the softball out of the ballpark and over the fence. Thor took the bait, and next thing I knew the visitor team was called up at bat.

I don't remember feeling as energized in my entire life. "If we run fast, we'll catch up to Buster's killer. Look! Two guys are making a run for it behind the fence. My money's on the freezer-cleaning guy. That's our murderer."

Thank goodness the only gambler in our family was my uncle Louis because once again I'd gotten it wrong.

CHAPTER 45

E nergized, my foot! I was out of breath by the time Lyndy and I got to the path behind the ball field. We could see the two men ahead of us with one in the lead and the other tailing behind. All of a sudden, a fly ball passed us overhead and next thing we knew, Thor had made a break from Shirley and moved faster than a greyhound to get to that ball.

The dog passed us as if we weren't even there, and all Lyndy and I could do was watch the gruesome scene that unfolded in front of us. Had this been a recorded movie, I would have pushed the fast-forward button. The fly ball pinged the slower-moving man, hitting him in the shoulder and causing him to totter to the ground.

Thor then pinned him in place. From where I stood, I expected the dog to chew off the man's nose.

"Help! Get him off me. He's going to kill me!"

By now, the other man was only a yard or so away, but he didn't move any closer. Instead, he climbed over the chain-link fence and made a quick getaway behind a row of houses.

"I'm bleeding!" The fallen man's screams were deafening. "I can feel the blood dripping down my face. Help!"

"I can't look, Lyndy. This is horrific."

"Horrific? It's hysterical! Thor's licking that man's face. Must be the guy just finished eating one of those hot dogs."

"What?"

Sure enough, Thor was frantically licking the man, but that didn't prevent the guy from yelling, "Get him off me! Get him off me!"

I nudged Lyndy. "Can you see who the man is?"

"Not really."

"We'll know soon enough."

I tromped over to where Thor stood sentry on top of the guy. He was still licking him and I had no intention of making him stop. I prayed the body on the ground belonged to Raymond Dahl, but the second I peered at his face I knew I was wrong. The man on the ground appeared to be much younger. And not a single gray hair.

Using my most authoritarian voice, I said, "I'll get the dog off of you if you come clean about Buster LaRoo's murder. Otherwise, one little command and you'll want the names of the best plastic surgeons in the valley."

Thor must have understood my intent because he nuzzled the man's neck and continued licking. This time with even more gusto.

"I don't know what you're talking about."

"Thor!" I shouted. "Show teethees!"

In a flash, the dog bared his teeth, not budging from the inch between his face and the man's.

"All right! All right! Just get him off me."

"Stay put on the ground and I will. One move and I'll give him the command to do more than show his pretty whites. And tell me your name while you're at it. Your real name."

I couldn't believe those words actually came out of my mouth. They sounded like the dialogue from an old forties gangster movie. Even Lyndy's face registered surprise.

When Thor backed up, I got a good look at the man. It was the clean-shaven bread delivery guy. He inhaled and let out a slow breath. "Arnold. Arnold Dahl."

Boy, talk about keeping it in the family. I motioned him to continue.

"You have to understand what Buster was going to do to us," Arnold gasped. "Do you have any idea what the penalties are for selling expired food products? Hell. In 2018, Walgreens got sued for over two million. It was a big-deal baby formula case."

"So you thought murdering him was a better option?"

"Well, yeah. I suppose. Not like we had a choice. Look, it wasn't only the food scam Karl and I had going. Karl would have lost the business and he owed money to my, um, er . . . to his partner. Lots of money from gambling debts. Then Karl found out about Buster's identity fraud and tried to turn the tables, so to speak, but Buster had one up on him."

"Go on."

"He told Karl he named him as the beneficiary for a life insurance policy in Nevada, so if Karl were to turn him in, Buster would claim they were in cahoots."

I turned to Lyndy. "Are you getting all of this? I'm already confused."

Just then, a thunderous voice came out of nowhere, and when I turned to see who it was, Deputy Bowman was fast approaching. "We've got this, Miss Kimball . . . er . . . Mrs. Gregory. Get ahold of that dog and stand back."

I took Thor by the collar and we stepped away as Deputies Bowman and Ranston got the bread delivery guy up from the ground and in handcuffs.

"He's not alone," I said. "He's got a partner who climbed the fence over there."

It was the first time I'd heard Bowman laugh. "Oh, yeah. He climbed the fence, all right, and landed in the neighbor's pyracantha bushes. Also known as firethorn. Those bushes have nasty thorns that dig deep into the skin, and to add insult to injury, their leaves are serrated. Talk about a double whammy. The homeowner called the posse to have the man removed for trespassing but we were already on to those two thanks to your boss and your husband."

"What? They knew? And they called you?"

"About a half hour ago. They should be here any minute."

I pulled my cell phone from my pocket, and sure enough there was a text message from Marshall. In all the madness, I never heard the phone and didn't read the message carefully because everyone talked at once. Had I read it, I would have realized it said, *You were right about Geraldine and she withheld lots of info. Don't do anything. Alerted Bowman and Ranston. Love you.*

Lyndy elbowed me as soon as I took my eyes off the screen. "Was that from Marshall? Does he know who those men are?"

"I'll save you the trouble," the bread guy announced. "It's my cousin Jaime."

"Then who's the silent partner?" I asked.

"Not now, Miss Kimball," Deputy Bowman said. "I need to read this man his rights and question him back at the posse station."

"Tell me one thing," I started to say, but I never got to finish. Amid huffs, puffs and all sorts of breaths in between, Shirley made her way to where we stood and shouted to Arnold, "Are you the murderous hooligan who tried to kill me with a softball? And tried to make me think I lost my mind with disappearing bodies?"

Deputy Ranston held out his arm, preventing Shirley from getting any closer, but that didn't stop her from spouting off at Arnold. "What did I ever do to you? And going after a senior citizen! There are laws against that." She turned and faced the deputies. "Charge him with elder abuse while you're at it. No, wait! Charge him for bugging my house. There are morality laws against that sort of thing."

"Um, I think that's Canada, not the United States," I said. "But rest assured, they'll charge him with everything he deserves. Come on, let's take Thor back to the stands and watch the rest of the game." Then I stopped in my tracks. "You and Lyndy go back. I have to make a quick phone call."

As the ladies and Thor walked toward the ball field, I phoned Augusta. "We nailed them! Dead to rights! Wanted to be the first one to tell you."

"Take a number and stand in line. You're number two. Mr. Williams just called me. About fifteen seconds ago. He got a text from Deputy Ranston and wanted me to know."

"Unbelievable. Anyway, your 'boys' can stay safe and sound at home with you. See you on Monday."

"I'll want all the details. Mr. Williams and Mr. Gregory always give me the abbreviated version."

"No problem." *Once I figure it out.*

CHAPTER 46

A pparently, the melee behind the ball field fence didn't interrupt the game. Herb's team was up at bat and one man was already on first. Lyndy and I escorted Shirley to where my mother and her friends were seated and watched as she and Thor scootched into their row.

"What was all that ruckus about?" my mother asked. "All I could see were two men running away from you and Lyndy while poor Shirley went after Thor. Please don't tell me you chased a killer. I heard you and Paul on those announcements. And by the way, Myrna and I should have been asked to MC this event."

And here it comes . . . my mother's broadcasting ego at work.

"Um, we sort of lured them out but it was Thor who was the real hero. He held the one guy at bay until the deputies got there. The other guy was caught in a neighbor's yard."

"Oh, no!" my mother said.

"What do you mean 'oh, no'? That was a good thing."

"Not that. Herb! I was so busy talking to you I missed watching Herb hit the ball. He must have hit it because, look! He's on his way to first base. Didn't even know he could move that fast. And what's Paul doing up there in the broadcast booth? He should have announced it."

Sure enough, Herb got to first base unscathed and the next batter was up. "I won't know the full story until later but the best I can figure was that Karl from the concession stand, along with the bread delivery guy and heaven knows how many other accomplices, were responsible for murdering Buster and trying to gaslight Shirley."

"Why? Do you know why?"

"Blackmail over expired food products."

"Food poisoning? I ate one of those hot dogs." My mother clutched her stomach.

"Not the meat. And no one's been poisoned. Oh my gosh—Herb's headed to second base."

"And how! Look at him go. Maybe Paul will wake up and announce it. Myrna and I would have done a better job."

"Uh-huh. Listen, Lyndy and I need to—"

I never finished my sentence because Paul was back on the air with the following announcement: "Ladies and gentlemen, due to unforeseen circumstances the concession stand is now closed. I repeat, the concession stand is now closed."

Comments could be heard everywhere and some of them should have been censored.

"Now what are we supposed to do? I come here for the food, not the lousy game."

"Did that dog get into the building and eat the rest of the hot dogs?"

"Better get to those food trucks before they close down."

"No hot dogs at the food trucks. Only tacos."

"Who's selling hamburgers?"

"No one. Buy a $%*# taco!"

I leaned over and spoke softly. "I think the deputies must have closed down the concession stand because they're checking for DNA evidence related to Buster's murder."

My mother wasn't so quiet. Or discreet, for that matter. "What evidence? You said expired food products. Are you saying Buster was killed in the concession stand building?"

"Shh! Not killed. Stored."

"Oh, my gosh! They refrigerated a dead man where they store the hot dogs!"

Thankfully, only Lyndy, Myrna, and Kevin heard my mother's comment. That's because Paul was back on the air announcing another hit, only this time a home run by someone on Herb's team. That meant Herb scored a run as well.

"We'll never hear the end of it," Louise called out from the far end of her row. "Herb will be reliving that run for the next two months."

"Try two years," Kenny added.

I bent down and looked directly at my mother. "Please, not another word about dead bodies in refrigerators. Or the arrest that apparently only you saw. We'll talk later. I promise. I need to get going. Marshall is on his way over here. In fact, he and Nate may be with the deputies now."

"Call me the minute you get a chance."

Lyndy and I waved goodbye to everyone and darted out of there as fast as we could. When we were a few feet from the park's entrance, I slowed down and took out my phone. "I'm texting Marshall," I said. "He and Nate should be here by now."

"Don't bother. Isn't that him talking with those deputies by the concession stand? Geez, I didn't think the county had that many deputies to spare."

I widened my eyes and watched the scene in front of me. Not only was it far more exciting than the Cactus Slow-Pitch game, but it moved a whole lot faster. A team of four deputies systematically wove yellow crime tape around the concession stand building while another deputy led Karl and the person wearing khakis out of the building and into an official sheriff's vehicle. My jaw nearly dropped when I watched a baseball cap come off her head, revealing a lock of platinum and blue hair.

"Lyndy, that's the woman from the house next to where Shirley first found Buster. Good grief! I saw dieffenbachia plants in the windowsill. Who the heck is she?"

Two men exited a newer vehicle with lettering that read *MSCO Forensics Lab* and went directly into the building. Meanwhile, Blaine sat on the ground a few feet from the door frantically typing something into his phone. Either that, or he had discovered a new video game.

The second Marshall looked up, he spotted Lyndy and me and rushed over. "Nate and I got here a few minutes ago. Ranston texted us the details except your current location. That's why I was chatting with those deputies over there." Then, without saying another word, he gave me the biggest, softest bear hug I'd ever had. "Don't scare me like that again. Chasing a killer."

"For the record, it was *two*, but one got away temporarily. Hmm, better make it four if you count Karl and the streaky-haired woman in the concession building. Gee, maybe even five if the maintenance man's father is who I think he is."

Marshall released me from the bear hug but held on to my arm. "Quite the show, huh? Geraldine's tell-all was like a dam breaking. If it wasn't for her, we'd be spinning in circles. Which begs the question—How did you know Karl got his niece to prepare the poison? Turns out that streaky-haired woman, as you put it, was Geraldine's part-time caregiver. From what Geraldine told us, she was really into herbal cures. Ha! That's a new word for it."

"Huh? What? His niece? I didn't. And I didn't even know he had a niece. Must be Blaine's sister."

"That's what Bowman told us. She's a certified nursing assistant. And get this—she was the one who suggested dumping the body by the golf course entryway. The elderly man she took care of had no idea about any of this. I'll bet he didn't even know it was his plant that did Buster in."

"Holy cow. Talk about a convoluted mess. As far as Lyndy and I were concerned, we had a darned good idea of the perpetrators but we needed a setup to see if we were right. Guess we had lots of loopholes for sure. All I can say is thank goodness Paul Schmidt was the one doing the announcements for the game."

Lyndy stepped toward Marshall. "Does this mean they'll release Lyman from jail?"

"I think it's in the cards but the deputies will need a full confession before they can go any further."

"How about a recorded one?" I pulled out my cell phone and tapped it. My voice was clear and succinct and so was Arnold's.

"So you thought murdering him was a better option?"

"Well, yeah. I suppose. Not like we had a choice."

Marshall grinned. "Amazing job. Now the fun part is sorting out the players."

"I was convinced I had the whole thing figured out, but when I saw Arnold on the ground and not Raymond Dahl, I knew I goofed. Plus, I didn't think Raymond could climb a chain-link fence in record time."

"No, that acrobat was his son, Jaime. He got into this murder scheme in order to make sure Karl would repay his father, Raymond. According to the info those deputies had, Raymond was Karl's silent partner."

"That would explain why he wanted to find a cleaning service to take care of the DNA evidence in the freezer."

"No. Not at all. The sheriff's office sent someone to Raymond's place to question him earlier in the day. That's why he wasn't at the game."

"Then why the cleaning service?"

"Raymond R. Dahl owns a compounding pharmacy lab in Phoenix and their regular cleaning service went out of business. He was looking for another one."

"Oh, boy. When I get something wrong, I really get it wrong. You mean to tell me he had nothing to do with his nephew's dirty deed?"

"None whatsoever."

"Then what about Jaime? How did he fit in?"

"Good question. Once he's Mirandized, he may open up. Then again, he may stay tight-lipped while he waits for a lawyer."

"I can't believe those deputies knew all of this and didn't do anything."

"You didn't give them a chance, hon, but that's what I love about you."

Just then Lyndy cleared her throat. "Before the two of you get all mushy, turn around and see who's coming down RH Johnson Boulevard."

My jaw dropped. "Good grief! It's a regular news parade only the vans aren't decorated."

"Hmm, this time it's FOX 10 in the lead followed by KPHO and channels 12 and 15."

I looked at Marshall and bit my lower lip. "You know what this means, don't you? The Buster LaRoo murder will be back on the air. Only this time it will include blackmail, concealing a corpse, and insurance fraud."

"I heard that," Nate announced from a few feet away. I was so engrossed in my conversation with Marshall that I didn't see him approach. "Maybe the news media will be able to untangle this mess, but from the looks of it Lyman Neal will be handed his get out of jail free card this evening. Deputy Bowman got the official word from MCSO a few minutes ago."

Lyndy was one step away from doing a full cartwheel. "Oh my gosh! Oh my gosh! This is fantastic! I'll see if I can leave a message for him at the jail. I want to tell him I'll drive down there and pick him up. I can't hang around here. I've got to go home and do my hair. And look for a decent outfit. Oh my gosh!" With that, she took off faster than Thor did on the ball field.

"I don't want to hang around here either. Between the ball game and the media circus by the concession stand, I'll be lucky if I don't get hives," I said. Then I thought of something. "My mother and that wacky crew of hers will be clamoring for details and we won't get a minute of peace. I never thought I'd be the one to say this, but maybe I should call her and tell her to set up brunch tomorrow at Bagels 'n More."

"I think I'll be filling out paperwork," Nate mumbled, "but you folks have fun."

CHAPTER 47

F un wasn't exactly the word I would have used to describe the gathering at Bagels 'n More the next morning, but at least it allowed Shirley to get the closure she needed to feel safe in her house again. Especially since Thor was going back to his own home the next day. At least for a while. According to Shirley, she would have the dog for three full weeks in December since Gloria was finally able to book the European vacation she and her daughter always wanted.

The waitstaff at Bagels 'n More had to add an additional large table to the one my mother had reserved. Everyone in the Booked 4 Murder book club was there along with Herb and his pinochle crew, my aunt and uncle, and Paul. This time without a bucket of his recent catch.

"I can't believe it," Myrna said the minute she polished off her poppyseed bagel. "We had our own crime syndicate right under our noses in Sun City West."

I flinched. "I wouldn't exactly call it a crime syndicate, but it was certainly well-orchestrated. Raymond Dahl and Karl were partners in that concession stand business but Karl gambled away much of Raymond's investment. Karl had to keep the place afloat. So when Buster threatened to blackmail him over the expired bread products, Karl had to get him out of the picture but needed a way to do it discreetly. He asked his niece, who was in debt up to her elbows, to make the poisonous concoction for him. Naturally, he paid her quite well for her culinary talents. She was the one who chopped up leaves from a dried dieffenbachia plant and mixed them with wintergreen chewing tobacco so Karl could switch tins with Buster on the Saturday night before Shirley found the body. When Buster choked to death from the poison, Karl got Arnold to help him put the body in the freezer until the following day. Remember, Karl was one step away from turning Arnold in for deliberate violation of the public trust regarding expiration dates."

"It gets better," Marshall said. "According to Bowman, Arnold had to convince his buddy, Jaime, who just so happened to be Raymond's son, to help him move the body to a spot where the general public would find it."

Cecilia brushed off some crumbs from her black cardigan and looked directly at Marshall. "Why would Jaime agree?"

"Because Arnold threatened to tell the authorities that Raymond was part of the scheme if Jaime didn't agree."

"I've seen soap operas with fewer threads," Lucinda said.

"I still don't understand why my house and car were bugged and why someone felt they just had to lob a softball at my head." Shirley wadded up her napkin and gripped it in her hand.

Marshall rubbed his chin. "Unfortunately, it was all a matter of timing, nothing personal."

My mother nearly jumped out of her seat. "Timing? No one's baking a cake. What do you mean by timing?"

"Jaime drove the golf cart with Buster's body stashed in the bin. He and Arnold had just finished dumping the corpse by the golf course when Shirley drove up and spotted it. They were positive she had seen them pull across the road and into the other section of the golf course. They had to make sure she didn't identify them so they put the body back in the golf cart to be disposed of later, along with the tainted tobacco tin, only when they went to retrieve it, they only had a half. Still, they set up Lyman by putting that piece of evidence under the driver's seat of his car. Meanwhile, it set up the ruse that Shirley imagined things."

"I get it," Kenny said. "And pass me the garlic smear. In order to keep that ruse going, they had to set up another instance of a disappearing body. In order to do that, they had to track Shirley's moves. Real easy to break into her house and plant that device. Even easier with the car. They tailed her in order to figure out what to do next."

"Kenny's right," I said. "Arnold pretended to be dead when Shirley was on that path behind the ball field. The deal was for Jaime to lob her with the ball and when she fell, Arnold would take off. Jaime never meant to hit her in the head. Believe it or not, he aimed for her shoulder. At least that's what Bowman and Ranston told us. Hmm, now that I think of it, maybe that's why Lyman replaced him with Buster in the first place."

"Should have put him on the Green Team with Herb," Kevin said and laughed.

"Not funny." Herb puffed out his chest and made no attempt to suck in his stomach. "For your information, we almost won yesterday."

"Lordy, this is a regular can of worms, isn't it?" Shirley tossed the napkin on the table and reached for her coffee. Then she looked at Paul. "And don't you dare start talking about worms. I've had enough horrible images going through my mind. What I'd like to know is what Geraldine Kremler had to do with any of this?"

Marshall leaned back from the table and stretched his arms. "That could take all day but I'll give it a stab."

"Who's Geraldine Kremler?" Kenny asked.

Lucinda, Cecilia, Myrna and Louise all answered at once, "A friend of Shirley's."

"Should have known," Kenny muttered.

My mother proceeded to give him the quick rundown while Marshall used that opportunity to finish his bacon and egg sandwich and wash it down with coffee. Then, he rolled his neck and spoke. "Buster used Geraldine as a ploy for an insurance fraud scheme he had going. He named her as a beneficiary on a life insurance policy that he planned to cash after feigning his own death. It wasn't the first time. Under a series of aliases, he had gotten away with it in the past."

"Now that's what I call karma," my aunt said. "Never beguile the forces of the universe." She adjusted her pink and red bola and stabbed an olive from the little bowl on our table.

Marshall smiled and nodded. "Geraldine knew a lot more than what she professed. She was able to lead us to the beneficiary of a few Buster LaRoo policies. Good news for the Nevada Sheriff's Office and the insurance company whose fraud case we took on."

"So it's over?" my mother asked.

I smiled. "Looks that way."

"Wait a minute," Herb said. "What about that email from Buster saying he was in Baltimore?"

Marshall chucked. "Nothing like a good old cyber scam. Karl admitted to setting up a fake email address in Buster's name. Real easy to send a message to Lyman."

Just then, my aunt leaned forward and motioned for us to be still. "This is far too compelling a mystery to simply let it pass by us."

"What are you suggesting?" I held my breath in absolute fear.

"I believe I shall embark on a new venture. I shall write my first murder mystery based on this case. I'll title it, *The Dieffenbachia Death*."

Oh, yeah. That's a winner for sure.

Cecilia looked at my aunt. "Have you ever written anything before, Ina?"

"Only her grocery list," my uncle replied.

The entire table broke out laughing but I seriously wondered if my aunt would indeed write her first novel.

"Well," my mother said, "now that everything is settled, I've got to get to work on those clay creations for the fall craft show. I'm thinking of introducing stemware with Streetman and Essie's faces on the glasses."

"How will you fit in their whiskers?" Louise asked.

I turned to Marshall, grabbed his wrist, and whispered, "If we hurry, we can avoid this entire conversation."

Seconds later, we made excuses about work piling up and slipped out of Bagels 'n More.

"Please don't tell me your aunt is serious," Marshall said.

"Only time will tell. But at least she'll be writing about murders, not solving them."

ABOUT THE AUTHOR

Ann I. Goldfarb

New York native Ann I. Goldfarb spent most of her life in education, first as a classroom teacher and later as a middle school principal and professional staff developer. Writing as J. C. Eaton, along with her husband, James Clapp, she has authored the Sophie Kimball Mysteries, the Wine Trail Mysteries, the Charcuterie Shop Mysteries, and the Marcie Rayner Mysteries. In addition, Ann has nine published YA time travel mysteries under her own name. Visit the websites at: www.jceatonmysteries.com and www.timetravelmysteries.com

James E. Clapp

When James E. Clapp retired as the tasting room manager for a large upstate New York winery, he never imagined he'd be coauthoring cozy mysteries with his wife, Ann I. Goldfarb. His first novel, *Booked 4 Murder*, was released in June 2017, followed by nine other books in the series and three other series. Nonfiction in the form of informational brochures and workshop materials treating the winery industry were his forte, along with an extensive background and experience in construction that started with his service in the U.S. Navy and included vocational school classroom teaching. Visit the website at www.jceatonmysteries.com

Made in the USA
Middletown, DE
07 January 2024